Praise for *IOU L*
by Dr. J

M000202124

"*IOU Life Leadership* is a treasure trove of tools and strategies to help anyone perform at peak levels and get the most out of life. Dr. Joe's work inspires you to transform passion and potential into vision and results. This book is a must read for anyone who wants take control of their life and make it great!"

—**JON GORDON**, #1 *Wall Street Journal* best-selling author of *The Garden*, also best-selling author of *The Carpenter* and *The Power of Positive Leadership*

"Weaving stories and lessons gleaned from a great American sailor, Dr. Joe Famularo immediately catches the reader's interest and makes complex concepts accessible to all. I was particularly impacted by Dr. Joe's detailed process for decision-making, the Life Map Cycle, which involves carefully considering the information available before formulating and implementing a solution. *IOU Life Leadership* takes you on a journey of self-discovery, demonstrating how to create life by your unique, intentional design leading to a dynamic positive culture for yourself, your family, team and/or organization."

—**CHARLES CAMARDA**, NASA Astronaut, inventor, author, internationally recognized speaker, Founder/CEO of The Epic Education Foundation, Sr. Advisor - NASA Langley Research Center

"Anyone looking to develop and sustain peak performance for themselves, their families, their teams, and their organizations will find a useful, practical, transformational guide in Dr. Joe Famularo's *IOU Life Leadership*. Dr. Joe will inspire you to develop your purpose and passion by reflecting inwardly on your life maps and paradigms. *IOU Life Leadership* demonstrates that powerful culture change is possible and sustainable. Do yourself a favor. Be the leader you are meant to be and reap the benefits of greater *Peacefulness, Happiness, Healthiness, and Excellence.*"

— **JOHN J.** MURPHY, Award-winning author of *Beyond Doubt: Four Steps to Inner Peace* and *The Miracle Minded Manager*

"*IOU Life Leadership* will help activate your ability to create and sustain positive change. Dr. Joe Famularo broadcasts an optimistic message demonstrating how to take charge of our own Life Journey as well as propel others to shift their perspectives and achieve measurable results. Readers will benefit from *IOU Life Leadership's* practical approach to creating and sustaining Dynamic Positive Cultures for themselves and their families, teams and organizations."

— **MICHELLE GIELAN,** Best-selling author of *Broadcasting Happiness: The Science of Igniting and Sustaining Positive Change*

"*IOU Life Leadership* will ignite your soul by helping you find your identity, passion, purpose and direction. Dr. Joe Famularo lays out a clear path to increase your upward living of peacefulness, happiness, healthiness and excellence."

— **KARY OBERBRUNNER,** CEO at Igniting Souls, author of *Unhackable, Day Job to Dream Job,* and *Elixir Project*

"I celebrate Dr Joe...for this progressive work on organizational results starting with Self Awareness and Self-Regulation. Combining the dynamic ways leaders show up in this world— Inward work and aligning it with how we show up to others— Outward work leading to the results in our organizations and how both of these fuel the Upward work—expansion and scaling excellence in our Self, Families, Teams, Organizations and Communities. Brilliant for our times."

—**SUSAN LEGER FERRARO,** Founder/CEO G3

"I have known Dr. Joe Famularo as an inspirational, principle-based leader for over 15 years and have always been impressed by the way he lives his vision and mission. His book, *IOU Life Leadership* is a must read and will inspire you to take charge and live life by your design filled with purpose and fueled by your passions. Using down-to-earth examples, Dr. Joe demonstrates how to develop your personal brand or SelfCulture and focus on the important and essential principles to anchor your life and give it direction. Dr. Joe's wisdom will lead to immediate, short-term improvements and, more importantly, will profoundly inspire you to make long-term lasting change to benefit both yourself and those you lead - in your family, teams, and organizations."

—**GARY McGUEY,** National Speaker, Executive Coach, author of *The Inspirational Teacher* and *The Mentor: Leadership Trumps Bullying*

"At a critical turning point in our nation's history when leaders are challenged to navigate the murky waters of crises, *IOU Life Leadership* provides a great resource to steer us toward a destination where obstacles are overcome and positive, dynamic growing cultures are established. Through the use of timeless life principles, nautical themes, and personal stories, Dr. Joe Famularo invites the reader to become more reflective and intentional in achieving their highest potential. These practical strategies are timely gifts to achieving the life imagined."

—**LORNA LEWIS, Ed.D.**, Educational Leader, Past President of the NYS Council of School Superintendents, Board of Directors SCOPE, NCCSS, NYSCOSS, and Erase Racism

"Dr. Joe Famularo has developed a framework which those in leadership positions may reference as they strive to develop a positive culture within their organization. Focusing on the *IOU Life Leadership Principles* of Inward Living, Outward Living and Upward Living will assist all constituents within the organization in the achievement of a more positive and productive culture resulting in greater satisfaction, productivity and happiness. Dr. Joe Famularo provides us with the tools to take control and responsibility for 'navigating your Life Journey,' resulting in '*Upward Life Gifts of Peacefulness, Happiness, Healthiness and Excellence.*'"

—**GEORGE DUFFY III,** Executive Director/ CEO, SCOPE Educational Services

"As a coach, my focus is always centered around the fundamentals. I highly recommend Dr. Joe Famularo's *IOU Life Leadership* because it provides a systematic approach to the fundamentals of Life Living. Dr. Joe's insights are extremely helpful, practical and relevant. *The 12 Essential Life Anchors* presented in the book are life principles that will coach you to live and perform in a way for you to reach your highest potential."

—**COACH MIKE JARVIS,** Former NCAA Basketball Coach, author of *The Seven C's of Leadership, Skills for Life,* and *Everybody Needs a Head Coach*

"Dr. Joe Famularo's *IOU Life Leadership* is a must-read for anyone who is seeking a positive and effective life for themselves and those they lead. Inspired by stories from a US Navy sailor and filled with practical and actionable tools, *IOU Life Leadership* presents 12 Essential Life Anchors which will transform your leadership by teaching you to focus on your inward thoughts and outward actions. Becoming an effective leader begins—and ends—with people, and leaders are most effective when they keep relationships - with themselves, their families, teams, and/or organizations – at the center of everything they do. I highly recommend *IOU Life Leadership* for its new and valuable insights which can propel leaders, and their families, teams, and organizations to greater effectiveness and results."

—**JON S. RENNIE,** Business Leader, author of *I Have the Watch: Becoming a Leader Worth Following,* speaker, and former US Nuclear Submarine Naval Officer

"Dr Joe Famularo taps into a deep self-understanding of your personal intent. You will become very astute to the skills you need to develop true self-empowerment. You will step Inward to your soul, Outward to those you love and work with, and Upward to your next adventure towards happiness and success! You owe IOU to yourself so you can empower everyone around you!"

—**DOM FAMULARO,** Drumming's Global Ambassador, motivational speaker, author of *The Cycle of Self Empowerment*

"Dr. Joe's book presents a very doable exploration of the *12 Essential Life Anchors* or virtuous harbors that effective managers of their own lives must know deeply and must practice engendering trust and confidence in everyone who shares the same voyage. If you want to spend time sailing through the reflective process, enjoying what the outward world offers for discovery and finding the peaceful perspective one hopes to be the course of one's life, this book will give you a clear view into that expansive journey."

—**ROBERT J. MANLEY, Ph.D.,** Editor in Chief of *The Journal for Leadership and Instruction*, author, Dean of Education and Educational Leader

"Securing and sustaining success in an environment where demands continue to escalate depends heavily on effectively carrying out roles and responsibilities while building positive cultures with key stakeholders. *IOU Life Leadership* can serve as a helpful tool, not just for the C-Suite, but anyone striving to improve one's professional practice, climb career ladders, and improve overall health and wellness."

—**DAN DOMENECH,** Executive Director, AASA - American Association of School Administrators

"I highly recommend Dr. Joe Famularo's *IOU Life Leadership* as an inspirational blueprint that will develop and enhance your ability to be both personal and authentic by focusing on your Inward (thinking and reflecting) and Outward (relationship with others) dimensions. Dr. Joe's book will transform your thinking about leadership concepts and enable you to intentionally design and grow a dynamic and positive personal, school, and/or classroom culture. *IOU Life Leadership* clearly demonstrates how to inwardly and outwardly focus on controlling the controllables, especially in the midst of adversity. Just as importantly, it gives you practical tools to model this mindset to others. This is an incredible resource for you to grow both personally and professionally."

—**THOMAS C. MURRAY,** Director of Innovation, Future Ready Schools, best-selling author of *Personal & Authentic: Designing Learning Experiences that Impact a Lifetime*

"A must read for leaders but also for anyone who is striving to achieve a balanced, fulfilling life at work and at home. *IOU Life Leadership* is a lesson about what you owe yourself and how to attain it. Not only will you be better prepared to lead an organization, but you will feel better doing it. The three principles of *IOU Life Leadership* will help you reflect on who you are, create positive interactions with others, and change the way you look at life and the world around you. You will truly find yourself doing better in your career and with your relationships because you have finally called in that *IOU* that you have owed yourself for so long."

—CHARLES S. DEDRICK, Ed. D.,
Educational Leader, Executive Director—
New York State Council of School Superintendents

IOU LIFE LEADERSHIP

I O U
LIFE LEADERSHIP

Foreword by
STEPHEN M.R. COVEY

DR. JOE FAMULARO

Published by Author Academy Elite
P.O. Box 43, Powell, Ohio 43035

For information on discounted bulk purchases for corporations, institutions, educational settings, and other organizations, contact us at www.iouliving.com

Library of Congress Control Number: 2020918186

ISBN 978-1-64746-527-8 (paperback)
ISBN 978-1-64746-528-5 (hardcover)
ISBN 978-1-64746-529-2 (e-book)

Printed in the United States of America

Dedicated to My Children

Amanda Rose ~ Emma Ann ~ Eric Bartolo

Table of Contents

PART III
Executing IOU Life Leadership
Launch Your Life Ship
& Navigate Your Life Journey

The 12 ESSENTIAL LIFE ANCHORS

Foreword
Stephen M.R. Covey

For many years now, I have been asserting that trust is the critical leadership competency of our global economy. In a very real sense, trust has become our new currency. Organizations become and remain successful to the extent that their leaders create, extend, and restore trust among all stakeholders. The positive results that emerge are what I call "high-trust dividends."

I have made it my mission to attempt to be a co-catalyst, along with many others, to help bring about a global renaissance of trust—to increase trust in our world, particularly in these turbulent and disruptive times.

I feel I have found a fellow co-catalyst in Dr. Joe Famularo. When Joe first introduced me to *IOU Life Leadership*, the title immediately grabbed my attention. The concept of owing something to ourselves resonates with me and aligns with my belief that development is best achieved from the inside out, that is, we must grow ourselves inwardly before we can professionally develop outwardly. We first assess who we are, what we stand for, and solidify our values and beliefs as well as challenge ourselves to improve continuously—what I call Self Trust.

One of the bigger deficiencies of our times is not solely insufficient resources *per se*, but also our inability to access the most valuable resources at our disposal. Today, when so many of us do not have the luxury of adding or transferring resources to tackle significant challenges, we must find the capabilities within ourselves. *IOU Life Leadership* can help us channel and multiply the resources and intelligence to which we already have access to change outcomes and increase our quality of life, both personally and professionally.

Joe's book is both timely and timeless—timely given the uncertain and volatile world we are living in, and timeless as its insights transcend recent events. *IOU Life Leadership* provides a useful map of living from the inside out, with the ultimate goal of Upward Living and receiving the great gifts of life that we all desire: *Peacefulness, Happiness, Healthiness, and Excellence.*

IOU Life Leadership discusses three universal, enduring principles that can be applied in any context. Understanding and then putting the *Inward, Outward,* and *Upward Principles* into action will help you develop your leadership skills and improve your personal, family, team, and organizational cultures.

What I especially like about what Joe has done in this book is that he has made *IOU Living* into a learnable skill, within reach of everyone open to new ways of thinking and living. The positive outcomes of *IOU Leadership* for families, teams, and organizations are numerous and real. It leads to increases in the Upward Life Gifts of *Peacefulness, Happiness, Healthiness, and Excellence*, which Joe has termed as *PH2E*. Additionally, qualitative benefits include the development and blossoming of relationships. You will find new energy, creativity, and inspiration in your relationships by putting the *IOU Life Leadership* principles into action.

While *IOU Life Leadership* is foundational, inspirational, and aspirational, its ultimate usage is that it's immensely practical. It's filled with relatable examples, clarifying diagrams, and actionable tools. Joe delineates *12 Essential Life Anchors* as the foundational framework for *IOU Living*. He takes you on a journey—*Inward*, *Outward*, and then ultimately *Upward*. He will lead you to focus first on your Inward SelfCulture, which I would relate to as your integrity and intent. Then, you will focus on your Outward actions, or your behaviors toward others and the outside world. He will show you the importance of not only *what* you do but *how* you do it. Results flow from your Inward Thinking and Outward Actions—they will be the byproducts of your productive and principle-centered living.

In today's world, the need to collaborate, innovate and engage others are all vital skills critical to success and they flow from the inside out. *IOU Life Leadership* will guide you on a journey to develop and nurture these skills first in yourself and then in others. This is one journey I predict you'll want to take—and that will be worth it. You owe it to yourself and others!

Stephen M. R. Covey
The New York Times* and #1 *Wall Street Journal* bestselling author of *The Speed of Trust

Introduction

You are the captain of your own ship; don't let anyone else take the wheel.

—Michael Josephson

We all have a great gift—a life! Are you living yours by your design or by the design of others? Who is sailing your ship? It's your life voyage, and you are the only person who can understand and design your purpose and *Life Vision*.

IOU Life Leadership is a foundational framework for *positive and effective* intentional living and *Life Leadership*. Living by the *IOU Life Leadership Principle* is key to navigating toward a *Dynamic Positive Culture* for *self, family, team, and organization*. *IOU*, which stands for *Inward-Outward-Upward*, is based on timeless, universal principles evident in all societies. When we hear the term "*IOU*," we typically think of owing someone something. However, in the context of *IOU Living*, we owe *ourselves, our families, our teams, and our organizations* a *Dynamic Positive Culture* that provides and cultivates *Peacefulness, Happiness, Healthiness, and Excellence*—which I call your "*PH2E*." Take control of your life, and start living the *IOU Life Leadership* principles and becoming an *IOU Life Leader*!

This book offers lessons from Vincenzo, a great *Life Leader* and US Navy sailor who served in both the First and Second World Wars. He immigrated alone from Italy at 13 years old, carrying only a black trunk and $30 in his pocket in search of a better life for himself and his family. In 1918, while serving in the US Navy during WWI, he became very ill at the height of the Spanish flu crisis. He was admitted to a US Naval Hospital in Paris and fought his way to recovery. Through his modeling the lessons of *Life Leadership* along with my many years of research, this book will provide a systematic approach to help you live your life by design in a *positive and effective* intentional manner using *The 12 Essential Life Anchors*. It's for anyone seeking deeper insight into themselves, looking to live according to a plan, and wanting to become an *IOU Life Leader*!

The three principles that make up the *IOU Life Leadership Principle* are:

- *Inward Living*—the principle of thinking and self-reflection
- *Outward Living*—the principle of interacting with others and the world
- *Upward Living*—the principle of receiving the *Life Gifts* of *Peacefulness, Happiness, Healthiness, and Excellence*, which I call your "*PH2E*."

As an *IOU Life Leader*, you will have the skills, strategy, and tools to lead yourself through life, as well as to guide your *family, your team, and your organization.*

From kindergarten through receiving my doctorate, I was never offered a class about *Inward Life Living*: how to think, question who I am, and discover my purpose in life—my *"I."* I was never offered a class about *Outward Life Living*: my actions with others and the world—my *"O."* No class was offered about *Upward Life Living* and its gifts of *Peacefulness, Happiness, Healthiness, and Excellence*—my *"PH2E."*

At any given point in the day, we live in one of two modes: *Inward Living* or *Outward Living*. Based on how we are *Inwardly* and *Outwardly Living*, we receive a feeling or byproduct that comes to us, which can be positive or negative. We all want a positive feeling, which I call *Upward Living*, where we receive the *Upward Life Gifts*. Those gifts come from living *Inwardly* and *Outwardly* in a *positive and effective* intentional manner.

The *IOU Principle* is a natural timeless principle that will begin to shift *yourself, your family, your team, and/or your organization* toward a *Dynamic Positive Culture* when understood and practiced positively.

Whether it's *you, your family, your team, or your organization*, the relationships within will define the culture. The culture around us can quickly shift from positive to neutral or even negative due to varying life circumstances. The goal is to keep pushing back toward a *Dynamic Positive Culture*, which will give you the ability to lead all members effectively to a shared purpose and to make meaningful contributions, which will help you feel valued and supported. The culture you foster can raise everyone to the highest level of success and happiness possible—until the next day, when new highs will be reached.

There are *12 Essential Life Anchors* that make up our *Inward* and *Outward Living*. These *12 Essential Life Anchors* are the foundational framework for *positive and effective* intentional *Life Living*. *Life Anchors* are solid, immovable, timeless, and universal *Life Principles* found in all effective life plans for *positive and effective* intentional living. There are *6 Essential Life Anchors* for *Inward Life Living,* and *6 Essential Life Anchors* for *Outward Life Living*. Chapters 11 and 12 will describe each *Essential Life Anchor* in detail and provide you with practical strategies to apply them in your life immediately. When you practice and apply *The 12 Essential Life Anchors* in your daily living, you will begin to move to a higher level of *Upward Life Living*. You will receive *Peacefulness, Happiness, Healthiness, and Excellence* (*PH2E*) and, in turn, move toward a *Dynamic Positive Culture* for *yourself, your family, your team, and/or your organization.*

This book, inspired by Vincenzo, uses a nautical theme based on the analogy that you are the captain of your ship, navigating through life with beauty and obstacles along the way. Each chapter begins by telling a story about Vincenzo, a great American US Navy sailor. He literally and figuratively sailed the seas of life and provided essential *Life Leadership* lessons for everyone around him.

You owe it to yourself and others to learn and practice *IOU Living* and become an *IOU Life Leader*!

Overview

Life Leadership
Living the IOU Principle

Life is a voyage, but who is sailing your ship? Is it you or someone else? Is your *Life Ship* on course, drifting, or even sinking? If you're off-course or struggling to stay afloat, how will *you, your family, team, or organization* meet their *Life Vision* and *Life Goals*? There's a way to get back on course! *IOU Life Leadership* is a foundational framework for *positive and effective* intentional living based on timeless, universal life principles that will provide you a *Life Map* to *IOU Living* to help you become an *IOU Life Leader*.

The captain is the ship's leader who steers the vessel through both the calm and storms. The captain studies the *Outward* environment, makes crucial decisions by turning the wheel, and sets the course based on *Inward* decisions. The *Upward Reward* of great satisfaction is received along the journey as the captain stays on course to the destination.

We all need to become *Life Leaders* and receive the benefits of *IOU Life Leadership*. When we have *Life Leadership*, we receive the *Upward Living Life Gifts of PH2E—Peacefulness, Happiness,*

Healthiness, and Excellence. Living the *IOU Principle* will lead to *Life Leadership.* Everyone needs to be a *Life Leader* to lead themselves through the obstacles faced in life.

Let's examine the *IOU Principle.* First is the *Inward Principle,* which I refer to as *Inward Life Living.* When you are *Inward Life Living,* you are thinking. You are *not* interacting with another person or the world in any form, such as speaking, texting, or emailing. You are focused on your thoughts and pondering who you are, your purpose, your paradigms or *Life Maps,* and your passions. Your *Inward* intelligence is more than just a mindset and more than your opinions—it's your total *Inward Being.* You are already *Inward Living* most of the day, but the question is, are you doing it in a *positive and effective* intentional manner?

Outward Living is when you are interacting with the world. You are *Outward Living* as soon as you speak to someone, send an email, or perform any action that can affect a person or the world. If you are in a room with others but not speaking or interacting, you are still *Outward Living* because of the need to be aware of the others and your effect on them since even your body language can affect others.

Upward Living refers to receiving the *Life Gifts of PH2E* based on living *Inwardly* and *Outwardly* in a *positive and effective* intentional manner. These *Life Gifts* are universal and sought by all. When you examine and continuously improve your *Inward* and *Outward Living,* you move closer to the highest forms of *PH2E.* As your *PH2E* increases, your inner "*SelfCulture*" becomes more *Dynamic* and *Positive.* Once you learn and apply the *IOU Principle* to yourself, you can teach and apply it to your *family, team, or organization.* You will witness those cultures shift to a *Dynamic Positive* environment for all.

An anchor represents stability, steadfastness, and security, even in the roughest seas. What anchors or *Life Anchors* are steadfastly and securely guiding your journey through life? While there are many *Life Anchors* that make up both your *Inward and Outward Living*, this book will discuss *The 12 Essential Life Anchors* that will lead to the *Upward Living Life Gifts*, and provide you with a *Life Map* for *IOU Living*. When you are in tune with the *IOU Principle* and continuously improve upon your *12 Essential Life Anchors*, you become a *Life Leader* and receive all the benefits of *IOU Life Leadership*.

You are the captain of your life so let's begin navigating your *Life Journey*!

PART I

Why IOU Life Leadership?

Begin Building Your Life Ship

Chapter 1

What Is Life Leadership?

*This is your life. Chart your course, take the helm
and begin the voyage!*

—Dr. Joe Famularo

In 1908, Vincenzo, a 13-year-old boy, crossed the Atlantic
Ocean alone on a steamship to America. It was a weeklong journey
in search of a better life for his parents, brothers, and sisters.
Three years earlier, on a small volcanic island named Stromboli
in the Tyrrhenian Sea just off the mainland of Italy, he had lived
a wonderful life enjoying the fruits of the land as part of a family

of seven. Dominick, his father, owned a shipping company transporting goods between their small island and France. The two-ship company was thriving, and demand was high for the service Dominick and his family provided.

Meanwhile, the country was experiencing challenges. They were celebrating the 50th anniversary of Italian unification, but the country was divided over the government's attempt to nationalize the railroads, which led to a railroad strike. At the same time, a 7.2 magnitude earthquake rocked the southern regions, leading to many fatalities. Vincenzo and his family knew they had to stay close, support each other, and work hard on the family business during those tough times. Vincenzo was an important member of the crew, and his father boasted how Vincenzo never slacked off or got distracted from the task at hand.

Many years later, Vincenzo recounted, "I remember that cold misty morning. We knew there was a massive storm coming from the north." As they had lived through and survived past storms, they needed to go into action quickly. Dominick gave the order to tie a rowboat to the 165-foot sailboat and anchor it just offshore where the vessel would have the best chance to survive, bobbing up and down freely as the rain and the high winds of the storm passed. Vincenzo said, "When I was rowing back to shore after anchoring the first ship, I could feel in the air that this storm was different and was going to be a big one."

The family team repeated the task with their second 165-foot vessel. The storm violently approached. Vincenzo understood that the family's lifeline was in jeopardy as the boats rocked ferociously from side to side, and then he saw both vessels capsize and sink before his eyes. It was the end of the family shipping company. There was an immediate need to find a solution. Vincenzo was a thinker (*Inward Living*) and advocated that he should move to America to find and create a new life for his family (*Outward Living*). As you will read in this book, he made the journey across the Atlantic Ocean alone and found a new life and prosperity for his family and generations to come (*Upward Living*).

Like Vincenzo, when faced with adversity, you have two choices. You can succumb to the event, complain, and let it define you. Alternately, you can think *Inwardly* and consider all the options, begin to design a new *Life Map*, chart your course with specific goals, and then execute it *Outwardly* into the world. You will then receive the reward of the *Upward Living Life Gifts*.

Life Leadership is the *Upward* byproduct of how a person *Inwardly* defines themselves and their *Outward Actions* and interactions. It's about leading yourself, leading alongside others, and leading others. You can't grab *Life Leadership*. It comes to you based on your *Inward*

At any given time, you are either living in an *Inward Mode* or an *Outward Mode.*

Positive Thoughts, planning, and *Outward Positive Actions*. In other words, it is based on how you develop and mix your *Inward Thinking* with your *Outward Actions*. The results are the *Upward Living Rewards of Life Leadership*. You can't govern *Upward Living* directly. You can only indirectly influence its levels through *positive and effective Inward* and *Outward Living*. Therefore, *Life Leadership* comes to principle-centered people living the *IOU*

Principle. At any given time, you are either living in an *Inward Mode* or an *Outward Mode*. When you practice *Inward Positive Thinking* and then *Outward Positive Actions*, you will receive the *Upward Living Life Gifts of PH2E*. Throughout this book, I will interchange using the letter "*I*" for *Inward*, "*O*" for *Outward*, and "*U*" for *Upward*.

The question is, are you living your life by design, purpose, and intention or by disorder, luck, and chance? We all have received a great gift—a gift of life, and we only get one shot at it. Have you defined your *Inward* guiding *Life Principles*? Unfortunately, many people go through life and have never taken the time to think about their "*I*" or *Inward Living*. We think about our possessions more than our *Inward Life*, which is your life's most important possession. So, the question is, "What are your *I*'s?" Many anchors make up your *I*, such as your *I Vision*, your *I Mission*, your *I Values*, your *I Relationships*, your *I To Do's*, etc. Your *I* or your *Inward Living* is who you are, your purpose in life, your *Life Plan*. Your *Inward Life Principles* are your core and what you believe. They are the ideas that guide your thoughts, actions, and decisions. Your guiding principles are reflected in your actions, which, in turn, define your *Life Leadership*.

We are all living in what I refer to as the "*Life Leadership Age*," a world where we must all be leaders.

Living *IOU Life Leadership* brings you the most precious *Upward Living Life Gifts*. They come to you by living a *positive and effective Inward* and *Outward Life* of high character and competence.

You can't reach out and grab the *Upward Living Life Gifts*, such as your *PH2E*. Those gifts only come to you through hard work, reflective thinking, and positive relationships. As you move to higher levels of your *PH2E*, you will feel your *SelfCulture* turn *Dynamic* and *Positive*. As you live the *IOU Principle* with your *family, team, or organization*, the *Upward Life Gifts* will be felt by all stakeholders, navigating toward a *Dynamic Positive Culture of PH2E*.

Life Leadership Age

IOU LIVING

Self - Family - Team - Organization

Twenty years from now, you will be more disappointed by the things that you didn't do than by the ones you did do. So, throw off the bowlines. Sail away from the safe harbor. Catch the trade winds in your sails. Explore! Dream! Discover!

—Mark Twain

We are all living in what I refer to as the *"Life Leadership Age,"* a world where we must all be leaders. Let me explain. A person can have many leadership roles—a son or daughter, friend, parent, spouse, coach, teacher, administrator, executive, CEO, etc. However, if you ask the average person to define a leader, the answers usually include the following:

- the person in charge of a group of people
- the head of a company or organization
- the person calling the shots

Those answers demonstrate that leadership is typically defined by a position rather than through actions and behaviors. However, the people holding those positions may or may not be leaders in a *Life Leadership Age*. Understanding and living the *IOU Principle* will guide your leadership in every role you live in life. We must first be a leader of ourselves. You and you alone are calling the

8

shots for your life. *Life Leadership* is not a position but rather a principle by which to live.

A report published by the World Economic Forum states that the world is at a turning point, referred to as the Fourth Industrial Revolution, with major shifts underway in technology, geopolitics, environment, and society. The authors suggest that the new top skills needed are creativity, critical thinking, and complex problem-solving. These skills are not developed or learned from the typical college course of study; instead, these are leadership skills. As we move into this *Life Leadership Age*, everyone will need tools to be leaders of themselves and others and to lead with others.

Another aspect of *Life Leadership* is to be a leader of your family. In a family, you may be leading alone or with a partner. Additionally, you may be a team leader, whether it's a team in a company or a sports team. You may also be a leader in a school or organization. Everyone is a leader in a school—the teachers, students, parents, staff, and administrators. In an organization, you are a leader alongside all your associates and department heads. The *IOU Principle* is for everyone and every role in your life. Everyone in your *family, team, or organization* needs to learn and practice the *IOU Principle*. This experience will raise the level of each person's *SelfCulture*, which will ultimately produce better results aligned to your vision and mission.

The *IOU Principle* has already happened in your life. When you experience impressive results and receive a positive feeling from your planning and implementation of a task, you are living the *IOU Principle*. The wonderful relationships in your life are due to *IOU Living* in a positive manner. The success at work or with your team is due to living the *IOU Principle*. Did that happen by chance, or are you aware of the specific principles that led to your successes? This book will explain the *IOU Principle* in great detail so you can replicate it, make it an intentional practice, and continuously receive the highest levels of your *PH2E!*

> *The highest reward for a person's toil is not what they get for it, but what they become by it.*
>
> —John Ruskin

Be Your Own Life Coach

What if there were a life coach who would be available for you 24/7 for an entire year to help you reach your goals with a positive attitude? Michael Serwa is one such life coach who claims to be the highest-paid personal life coach in the United Kingdom.

The 12 Essential Life Anchors **are a systematic approach to aligning your innate internal wisdom to your purpose and passions and then moving *Outwardly* toward fulfilling your goals and dreams.**

He works with top executives for an annual fee to help them feel peaceful and happy. Several of Serwa's clients said they felt balance in their lives and better understood themselves and what was important to them after working with him. Many coaches will work with you one-on-one to find balance in your life, build positive relationships, and improve your outlook on life. As I reviewed many of these

10

coaches' goals, I noticed one common theme: success is measured by their clients' happiness and fulfillment. Serwa states that general happiness is almost always the average of all the other areas addressed in his consultations. So, what's the secret to happiness? It's quite simple—it's the average of everything going on in your life. It's common sense that there is no way you will be happy if your relationships are toxic or your career is failing. We need to ask what areas provide the most growth opportunities and concentrate on them to grow our happiness.

The ultimate goal is to increase your happiness level. By studying your *Inward Intelligence*, you will begin to understand yourself and then create a plan to improve your *Outward Actions,* ultimately leading to the *Upward Living Gifts of your PH2E. The 12 Essential Life Anchors* are a systematic approach to aligning your innate internal wisdom to your purpose and passions and then moving *Outwardly* toward fulfilling your goals and dreams.

It doesn't cost anything to live the *IOU Principle*, but you must start and be persistent. You need to choose to begin walking the path to take control of your life, which will start with understanding your thinking and your *Inward* purpose and passions to gain more clarity, confidence, and an *Outward* action plan to move forward and build upon them.

It's your own fault if you're living by default.

—Richie Norton

Are You Aware of Your Default Setting?

What's your default setting? Did you ever notice that many times when you make a change and try something new,

The key to lasting change is to examine and correct the principles that guide you.

it doesn't last, and you go back to your default setting, which is what you did before you tried to initiate the change? The key to lasting change is to examine and correct the principles that guide you. Stephen Covey said, "If you want small changes in your life, work on your attitude. But if you want big and primary changes, work on your paradigm."

We often think we've changed our fundamental thinking; however, we are just behaving differently, and inevitably, we will go back to our default setting. We must first examine our principles by reflecting *Inwardly*, which will lead to different *Outward Actions*, and those will then result in positive *Upward* changes or consequences to our lives. We can control our *Inward Thinking* and our *Outward Actions*, but we cannot control the consequences of our *I* and *O*. Those consequences are based on universal natural laws. If our *I* and *O Living* is *positive and effective*, the natural result is to receive *Upward Living* and the great gifts of *PH2E*. *Upward Living* can only come to you.

12

Conversely, living *Inwardly and Outwardly* in a *negative and ineffective* manner will lead to *Downward Living* or, as we will explain later, *Wayward Living*.

In Chapters 11 and 12, we will examine *The 12 Essential Life Anchors* of the *IOU Principle* that will begin the process of positive change in your life. Remember, you need to be persistent; otherwise, you will revert to the same default behaviors you have always used with no permanent change.

The pessimist complains about the wind;
the optimist expects it to change; the realist adjusts the sails.

—William Arthur Ward

What's Within Your Control?

How does it make you feel when you eat something delicious? Where does that feeling originate? Can you recreate that same feeling without eating? Of course not. That *Upward* good feeling from eating the delicious meal arises from the action of eating. *Life Leadership* is the action you take to provide you with the *Upward Living Life Gifts of PH2E*. Just as you cannot simply create the feeling of that delicious meal, we also cannot produce on demand the feelings of *Peacefulness, Happiness, Healthiness, and Excellence*. Only *positive and effective Inward Thinking* and *Outward Actions* will lead to the *Upward Living Life Gifts* we all desire.

Do you have a victim mentality about the many life challenges you face? Think about this: when an adverse event happens in our lives, the event itself does not cause our response; instead, we allow ourselves to choose our reaction to the event. Viktor Frankl was a renowned neurologist and psychiatrist who was also a Holocaust survivor. He explained how he suffered unspeakable horrors in concentration camps during the Second World War. Nearly everything was taken away from him, but the Nazis failed to take his freedom because he remained in control—he had the power to choose his response to their atrocities. Frankl famously wrote, "Between stimulus and response there is a space. In that space is our power to choose our response. In our response lies our growth and our freedom."

We have total control over how we react to an event. That does not mean we are never sad. It just means we allow ourselves to be sad based on the event. Sometimes being sad is the most appropriate response to an event. You are in complete control. This understanding will help us greatly when the event is minor, and we typically react by complaining, being angry, or stressed. This is where we need to think about our response and change the script from being a victim to a victor. We need to believe we will overcome the adversity and take care of what we have control over and let go of what we cannot control.

> ⚓
>
> Only *positive and effective Inward Thinking* and *Outward Actions* will lead to the *Upward Living Life Gifts* we all desire.

When a negative thought comes into your head, think of something for which you are grateful. The better you understand your *Inward Living*, the easier it will be to have a positive response.

I will discuss your *Inward Living*, such as your *Inward* or *I Triggers*, in Chapters 7 and 8. *I Triggers* are events that happen and result in you changing from being calm to extremely aggravated. When we understand our *I Triggers*, we will be better positioned to act *Outwardly* using a different script.

You were born with all the skills and tools to live a life receiving the *Upward Living Life Gifts of your PH2E*. The secret is to focus on what we have control over and make positive changes with those things. We should just accept that certain factors cannot be controlled. However, so many individuals spend their whole day worrying about those uncontrollable items. Control the things in your control, and leave the things you cannot control.

We need to live an "I can" life, and that begins with items we have full control over - our *Inward Thinking* and *Inward Living*. In *Outward Living*, when we interact with others and the world, we only have influence because we cannot control what others say and do. We can control only our actions, which may or may not influence others. The byproduct of our relationships is either *Upward Living*, which is positive, *Wayward Living*, which is neither negative nor positive, but rather mediocre, or *Downward Living*, which is a *Downward Life Drain*. We have no direct control over these byproducts because they come to us due to our *Inward* and *Outward Living*. Our control lies in our *Inward Thinking* and our *Outward Actions* with the goal of receiving *Upward Living and the Upward Life Gifts of PH2E*.

Remember, you are not a victim; you are a victor. You have complete control of your *Inward Living* and thoughts. You have no control over the *Outward World* but can influence it. In other words, it's important to remind yourself you only influence what others may say and do. You do not have any actual control over their words and their actions, so focus on what's in your control!

I believe in not trying to control things that are out of my control or none of my business.

—Tobe Hanson

What's Not Within Your Control?

Identifying and accepting what's not in our control can be exceedingly difficult, especially when it involves dealing with a loved one. Emotions will take over if we are not aware of what we cannot control. There are numerous facets of life we have no control over, yet we spend so much time focusing on them. When a loved one is in need, we should be present and provide the support that may result in a slight *Upward* positive feeling for them instead of a *Downward* negative feeling. Here's a story to illustrate what I mean.

My 15-year-old son was playing in a competitive soccer game and made a brilliant defensive play, slide-tackling the opponent player on a break-away. He prevented the goal but unfortunately didn't get up when he hit the ground. I could feel his pain from the sideline and instantly knew this was different from other falls. The fractured collarbone was obvious as the bone pressed outward from his skin. Collarbone breaks are treated one of two ways: with a sling if the bones are close enough and aligned or surgery. As the doctor explained each option, I knew I had no control over the two possibilities. I did have control over bringing my son to the doctor and being part of the decision process moving forward. Unfortunately, no matter which decision was made, the first week of recovery would be excruciating. Nowadays, narcotics are not routinely given for pain control, which is understandable given the number of addictions that have resulted from attempts at pain management. Ibuprofen and Tylenol are the preferred course of action to manage pain. My son was in a tremendous amount of pain; he sat in a chair, trying not to move since any slight motion caused an additional sharp bolt of pain. Not only did I have no control to make him feel better, I had no control to get anyone to help him since the doctor said nothing could be done until surgery. Emotions were high, and I was in *IOD Living* (*Inward-Outward-Downward*, which will be explained further in Chapter 6), which is not productive for anyone. It brings you and others around you closer to the lower levels of the *PH2E Life Gifts*; it's a negative *Downward Life Drain* causing high stress and anxiety.

I had to turn the situation around. I had to stop complaining, thinking negatively, and asking all the "why" questions. Why did this happen? Why is he in this pain? Why him? Why now? Why? Why? Why? After asking those questions, my son was not in a better place, and I was way off-course from my goal of helping him. In fact, he might have been in a worse position because the time spent on things I couldn't control, took me away from the things I could.

By understanding and living the *IOU Principle* in this situation, I began to move in the right direction. With even the smallest aspects I could control, I began to move closer to comforting him. *IOU Living* kept me focused on what I could control instead of focusing on the things I could not control, which prevented me from helping him.

When a loved one is in need, it is the most challenging time to sort out what you can and cannot control because of the high emotions involved. It is, therefore, the most difficult time to put this in practice. Instead, to begin your voyage toward *IOU Living*, think of times in your life that aren't emotionally charged situations, and try putting *IOU Living* into practice then. Become conscious of what you can control and what you cannot. Build up your *Inward* and *Outward Living* and practice to the fullest, so when difficult situations arise, you will be better prepared to focus on what you can control and be aware of what you can't, which will yield a positive outcome for you and your loved ones.

Captain's Log for Chapter 1

What is Life Leadership?

Captain's Log:

Point 1   Becoming a *Life Leader* will help you lead yourself, lead others, and lead with others.

Point 2   At any given moment in a day for the rest of your life, you are either living *Inwardly* or *Outwardly*.

Point 3   *Upward Living* and the *Upward Life Gifts* are byproducts of your *Inward* and *Outward Living*.

Point 4   *Upward Living Life Gifts* are *PH2E—Peacefulness, Happiness, Healthiness, and Excellence.*

Point 5   Living the *IOU Principle,* you will move toward developing a *Dynamic Positive SelfCulture, Family Culture, Team Culture, and/or Organization Culture.*

Point 6   You have 100% control over your *Inward Living*, and no control of others and the *Outward World.* You have no governance over your *Upward Living.* The *Upward Living Life Gifts* are the byproduct of *positive and effective* living *Inwardly* and *Outwardly*.

Point 7   Be aware of what you have control over and what you do not.

Point 8   Be your own life coach and live your life by design, not by default.

Teach to Learn

The best way to deepen your understanding and, at the same time, share and stimulate new conversations with others is to teach. At the end of each chapter, share what you have learned with a friend, family member, coworker, or anyone else who will listen. Teaching is, by far, the best way to deepen one's understanding of new insights and concepts. Consider any of the Points from the Captain's Log or throughout this chapter for thought-provoking discussions.

New Daily Voyage:

Activity:

Being aware of when you are *Inward and Outward Living*—

Throughout a 24-hour period, notice when you are *Inward Living and Outward Living*. Think to yourself, *I'm in I Mode or O Mode at this moment*. When you are completely alone and thinking, you are *Inward Living* or in *I Mode*. When you interact with another person or the world, you are *Outward Living* or in *O Mode*.

Ask yourself:

How do my *I* and *O Modes* differ?

Estimate what percentage of each day you are living *Inwardly* and *Outwardly*.

Chapter 2

Living and Leading by Design

Don't be a victim of circumstances and let life design you.
Take an active role and be the one who designs your life.

—Anonymous

It's 1908, and a focused, brave 13-year-old boy with a clear *Life Vision* is determined to find a better life for himself and his family in America. Vincenzo, traveling alone with $30 and his small black trunk, boards the SS *San Giorgio* in Messina, Italy, along with 920 other passengers headed for America. Over the years, Vincenzo shared many stories about his 3,000-mile journey crossing the Atlantic Ocean on the 307-foot steamship. He remembered every detail about the ship, even though he began his voyage 75 years earlier in his life. He boasted, "This was some ship. It had a 50-foot beam, two funnels, two masts, and a single screw propeller; it would sail 11 knots." The journey to America lasted seven days with both calm and rough seas, although Vincenzo was accustomed to these conditions and shared, "It didn't bother me at all," as he referred to himself as a "seadog" his whole life.

He remembers hearing cheers as the passengers began to see land. "America! America!" they shouted, as the SS *San Giorgio* maneuvered the waterways. The ship docked just off the coast of Staten Island before entering New York Harbor, where the passengers disembarked at Ellis Island. At this quarantine checkpoint, doctors checked each passenger for dangerous, contagious diseases. The doctor was concerned about the redness in Vincenzo's eyes but cleared the boy to proceed to Ellis Island. Vincenzo remembers the long lines and being excited as the inspector reviewed the manifest document. The document supplied his name, age, and destination, his cousin Domenico's house. Domenico lived on 8th Avenue in Brooklyn and had arrived in America six years earlier. Although the Immigration Act of 1907 declared unaccompanied children under 16 were not permitted to enter America, thousands came over. They were allowed to enter if a destination and the child's relationship was recorded on the manifesto. The journey to America was remarkable for a 13-year-old boy with a clear vision to find a better life and a focused *Daily Mission* to work hard and create opportunities for success.

When Vincenzo arrived at his cousin's small apartment, there was a great celebration. There was no room for him to sleep, so

Vincenzo slept on the floor. He spent time *Inwardly* reflecting and immediately planned his next days. After asking many questions, Vincenzo designed a plan to sell fruit and vegetables on a street corner in Brooklyn. He often said, "If you get up early and don't waste your time, you can get more done before everyone even gets up!" He put his plan into action, getting up at 3:30 a.m., walking several miles to a farm, and bringing back fresh fruit and vegetables. He carried the black trunk he had brought with him from Italy, situated himself on a busy corner in Brooklyn, put the fruits and vegetables on it, and sold them. He sold the fresh produce cheaper than local stores and sold out every item making three times his cost. He continued every day and, in a short time, was making enough money to get an apartment at the YMCA. After a few months,

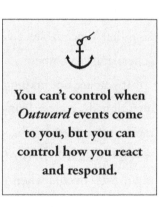

You can't control when *Outward* events come to you, but you can control how you react and respond.

Vincenzo sent money so his brother Sam could come to America. A few months later, Sam came over from Italy and stayed with Vincenzo at the YMCA apartment. They worked together and began selling their fresh fruit and vegetables on two corners. They hustled, worked hard, and were successful, always selling out of their stock. Their profits were high, and they felt positive about the success they experienced. Vincenzo said you didn't stop selling until everything was gone because anything not sold would be thrown out. Vincenzo had a *Life Plan* he enacted with discipline and confidence each day.

You can craft your life any way you want. You can't control when *Outward* events come to you, but you can control how you react and respond. You cannot control things that come onto you, but what you make out of it is 100% within your control. Do you want to live by design or by default? Vincenzo lived his life by designing and planning (*Inward Living*) and then executing his plan (*Outwardly Living*) in the world in a *positive and effective* intentional manner. When a storm destroyed his family shipping business, he didn't let that control him but instead devised a plan to save his family. The *Upward Living Life Gifts* that Vincenzo received not only helped him but also helped generations to come.

If you are not taking the time to examine the *IOU Principle* intentionally, you are living by default or on autopilot and thereby, most likely receiving disorganized results. The opposite of *IOU* is *IOD,* which is *Inward, Outward, Downward Living.* Living in an *IOD* occurs when you do not spend time *Inwardly,* have negative *Inward* thoughts, or live reactively or randomly with no plan. This will result in a *Downward Life Drain* and being filled with stress and concern.

> *It's more comfortable to let life happen to you than making it happen. But if your autopilot is always on, you are just existing, not living.*
>
> —Gustavo Razzetti

According to Dr. Mark Williamson, living on autopilot is a growing problem. Increasingly, it's becoming a default mode of operation. It is estimated that an adult makes about 35,000 conscious decisions each day, and many are centered around various technology platforms that surround us. Our environment is continually putting us into an autopilot mode with less *Inward Thinking* and less *Outward* interactions with others. Think about it: does spending 10, 20, 30, or more minutes interacting with social media contribute to your *PH2E*? Social media certainly has a place in our lives; however, our use of it should be controlled and acted on by design.

Social media certainly has a place in our lives, however, our use of it should be controlled and acted on by design.

When we delve deeply into the *Inward Living Anchors* in Chapter 11, you will understand that you have full control of this mode. You will be living in the moment and avoiding the "wandering mind." Many people spend much of their time thinking about what is not currently around them. They think about the past or future—anything but living in the moment. In a survey of 3,000 participants, 96% responded that they are living on autopilot. This is concerning because remaining on autopilot impacts the decision-making process. It prevents people from using all available data and results in an autopilot decision, which often produces negative results. When this happens, the byproduct is a *Downward Life Drain* leading to your *Life Ship Sinking*. Dr. Mark Williamson said, "Autopilot has gone from being an evolutionary protection mechanism that stopped our brains overloading, to our default mode of operating whereby we sleepwalk into our choices." Does anyone truly want to sleepwalk through life?

Noelle Bloom discussed 10 signs of living life on autopilot. Do any of the following describe you?

- You dread the day ahead
- Your daily routine is predictable
- You do things without thinking
- You can't seem to put your phone down
- You stay deep in thought about things other than the task at hand
- You have a difficult time remembering
- You can't seem to let go
- You're not making meaningful progress
- You say "yes" more than you say "no"
- You know there's a better life to be lived

None of these signs will move you closer to receiving higher levels of your *PH2E Upward Life Gifts*. The good news is that you have the power and control to live by design. Living the *IOU Principle* will guide you to live intentionally with a clear vision and mission and giving you joy and purpose as a *Life Leader*.

You can't use an old map to explore a new world.

—Albert Einstein

Design Your Life Map

Before you start to create a new *Life Map*, you need to examine your current ones. Your *Life Maps* result from all the experiences and thoughts you have had since you were born. You have made sense of the world, formed opinions, and arrived at judgments about many things. You certainly believe they are correct. The question is, were your *Life Maps* created intentionally, or were your

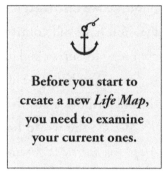

Before you start to create a new *Life Map*, you need to examine your current ones.

thoughts and opinions based on random experiences and people you have interacted with during your life? Your thoughts and views were most likely not all intentionally created, but the good news is you can change.

We have the tools to examine our *Inward Life Maps*, test them, and adjust them to be more accurate. We have an amazing ability to evolve in our thinking. The brain is estimated to have 100 billion neurons communicating via chemicals called neurotransmitters. Our brains are like computers with amazing capabilities; however, we may have the wrong software installed or, even worse, have a virus. When we have a virus on our home computer, we run an antivirus program to fix it. It is similar with us. Our "hardware" is unaffected; what we need to do is run our antivirus program or update our *Inward* software. As you go through *The 12 Essential Life Anchors* of the *IOU Principle*, you will feel your software renewed and updated to meet life challenges.

You have been programmed by many people in your life. Maybe someone said you don't have what it takes, or you'll never be able to do something you are trying to accomplish. It's time to run the antivirus and remove those negative scripts from your mind. As we discussed in Chapter 1, you are in control of your life. You have full control of your *Inward Living*, and you can choose to feel upset and distressed, or you can choose a different response. You have one life, and starting today, decide to change the old script to a positive design. Change your *Life Map*.

We see the world based on our *Life Maps*. We have *Life Maps* for *ourselves, families, teams, and organizations.* Are they correct? I enjoy boating in the Great South Bay on Long Island, NY. A challenge in navigating those waters is knowing where the sandbars are located. During low tide, a captain needs to be aware of the many obstacles below the water's surface. From the point of view on the boat, the water seems to be the same in all areas of the bay, but this is not accurate.

Ask yourself if your *Life Maps* match reality. Your *Life Maps* may indicate that you can easily navigate wherever you want to go; however, that is certainly not the case, especially during low tide. There are sand bars, rocks, and underwater structures that may be right in front of you, but invisible below the water. Your internal map of the area is inaccurate because what you see on the surface tells you something different from reality. You see an obstacle-free path, while, in fact, there are many complications you can stumble over. We must continually examine our internal *Life Maps* and adjust toward better accuracy. We have no control over the *Outward* territory, but we do have control over our reactions to it. So, therefore, our *Outward Actions* need to be based on reality. Even though we control our *Outward Actions*, if we base our actions on inaccurate assumptions, it will be difficult to achieve the success we want. Examining our *Life Maps* is a lifelong process to continuously improve our *Inward Beliefs* and *Life Maps* toward the reality of the *Outward World*.

You have 0% control of the (O) Outward World's actions pressing on your (I) Inward Living, but you have 100% control over your reactions to them.

—Dr. Joe Famularo

OI ACTIONS

You have no control over what the *Outward World* brings to you on any given day. For example, you could get an email from someone asking you to do them a favor, you might be driving to work and suddenly realize you have a flat tire, or you may get a call from a friend who asks if you want to go out. These demands come from the *Outward World* to your *Inward World* and are *OI Actions*. You can't control *Outward Actions* that come to you, but you have 100% control of your *Inward Reactions* to them. Once you realize that, you will feel an inner peace—the inner peace that you can choose your response to all *OI Actions* pressing on you.

You can't control *Outward Actions* that come to you, but you have 100% control of your *Inward Reactions* to them.

When someone asks you for a favor, you have the choice of whether to say yes or no. If it's something you want to do to build your relationship with the other person, then you may say yes. However, if you feel it's not connected to your *Life Journey* and is not important to you, the answer should be no. When you feel the thumping of a flat tire as you are driving to work, you should immediately recognize that you have no control over it happening, but you have control over how you react. You either pull your car over and call for service or fix the flat yourself. You have control over your reaction, and complaining or getting upset does nothing but give you stress and puts you in a *negative and ineffective* mindset, pulling you downward, moving you away from your *PH2E*. Everyone in the world gets flat tires, and there is never a good time to get one. It will happen again, so prepare now for your response. We have more control over our lives than we realize. In fact, we have 100% control of all our *Inward Thinking* and our *Outward Actions*. By recognizing and beginning to pay attention to this remarkable fact, you will feel propelled to a higher level of your *PH2E*.

> *Things which matter most must never be at the mercy of things which matter least.*
>
> —Johann Wolfgang von Goethe

The LIFE LEADERSHIP MATRIX

The *Life Leadership Matrix* is an important planning and decision-making tool based on the principles of urgency and importance. It helps you prioritize your time and life tasks to keep you on course for your *Life Journey*. President Dwight D. Eisenhower first developed the Eisenhower Matrix and has been quoted as saying, "I have two kinds of problems, the urgent and the important. The urgent are not important, and the important are never urgent." This tool was also used as a time management tool by Stephen Covey, who called it the Time Matrix. I have further developed it using *Inward* and *Outward Living Environments* and a nautical theme.

The *Life Leadership Matrix* has four categories, each represented by a captain and a ship in four distinct *Environments*.

The 4 Life Living Environments

Environment 1 (E1): Important and Urgent; Ship Sinking

You are the captain, and your ship is taking on water. You must bail the water immediately. It is your top priority, and if not addressed, your ship will sink.

Environment 2 (E2): Important and Not Urgent; Ship on Course

Your ship is on course. As the captain, you have provided proper maintenance for your ship over time. You have planned your journey and have taken the time to chart your course and to be prepared for possible future obstacles, including *Outward* weather.

Environment 3 (E3): Not Important and Urgent; Ship Stuck at Port

You want to leave port with your ship, but other people are holding you back with their important and urgent matters. Their issues are not aligned with your life plan and do not support your journey. Therefore, their *OI Action* issues are pressing onto you because they are urgent to others, but they are not important to you.

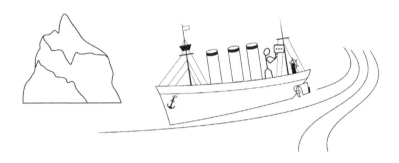

Environment 4 (E4): Not Important and Not Urgent; Ship Drifting

You are distracted, off-course, and spending excessive time on such activities as social media, watching TV, web surfing, gaming, and escape/avoidance activities.

The *4 Life Living Environments* are placed on a 2x2 Matrix. On one side are the *Environments* that are *Important* and *Not Important.* The other side depicts *Environments* that are *Urgent* and *Not Urgent.* (see the following illustration)

LIFE LEADERSHIP MATRIX

	Urgent	Not Urgent
Important	Environment 1 - E1 Ship Sinking	Environment 2 - E2 Ship on Course
Not Important	Environment 3 - E3 Ship Stuck at Port	Environment 4 - E4 Ship Drifting

Life Leadership Matrix Descriptions

Below are descriptions of the *4 Life Living Environments*:

	Urgent	Not Urgent
Important	**Environment 1 - E1** - Crises - Pressing Problems - Deadline Driven **Ship Sinking**	**Environment 2 - E2** - Planning - Preparations - Inward Reflections - Relationship Building - True Recreation/Relaxing - Health/Nutrition **Ship on Course**
Not Important	**Environment 3 - E3** - Interruptions - Other People's Priorities - Some Notifications **Ship Stuck at Port**	**Environment 4 - E4** Excessive: - Social Media - Television - Web Surfing - Escape/Avoidance Activities **Ship Drifting**

Life Leadership Matrix Action Plan

The goal is always to be above the midline of the *Matrix* and in *Environments* that are important to you, preferably in *E2*. *E1* items will always occur, but the more time we spend in *E2*, the less our ship will be sinking because we will be prepared for those occasions.

	Urgent	Not Urgent
Important	Environment 1 - E1 **Must Do Now** Ship Sinking	Environment 2 - E2 **Plan-Schedule** Ship on Course
Not Important	Environment 3 - E3 **Say No - Delegate** or **Do in E2** Ship Stuck at Port	Environment 4 - E4 **Eliminate** or **Do in E2** Ship Drifting

E1. Your Ship is Sinking, characterized as *Must Do Now.*

Your problem must be acted on now, or you will sink. When you are in *E1*, you are in crisis. You are dealing with a pressing problem, or you have a deadline with little time to complete the task.

E2. Your Ship is on Course, characterized as *Plan and Schedule.*

We must intentionally go to this *Environment.* Because the tasks are *Not Urgent*, they will not come to us. We have to take the initiative to make time for planning, preparation, and renewal.

E3. Your Ship is Stuck at Port, characterized by, *Say No, Delegate, or Do it in E2* as an *Important* and *Not Urgent* item.

When you are asked to work on someone else's pressing issue, you have a choice. If you feel you want to help, consider it a relationship-building item and move it to *E2*. You decide to make it important—not because of the task but because of your relationship with the person. However, be aware that if you are constantly being asked to help others with their pressing issues, you will never be on your own *Life Journey* and will always be off-course. At times you simply need to say no, or if possible, delegate the task to someone else to complete. This is a tricky environment to be in, but you must get out of it by saying no, delegating, or moving the task to *E2*. All these options take you above the midline of the *Life Leadership Matrix.* Leo Babauta nicely sums up *E3,* "By saying 'yes' to every request from others, you allow all your time to be taken up by tasks that are important to others, not necessarily to you."

E4. Your Ship is Drifting, Characterized as *Eliminate or Do in E2.* This quadrant is the *Environment* of waste and must be eliminated. You may be thinking you need your downtime, and of course, we all need time to refresh and recharge. The keyword for *E4* is excessive. Excessiveness occurs when you escape from the world to the point that you actually feel bad when you stop doing the activity. You are not relaxed, and you realize you wasted too much time and neglected items that may now be in *E1* (*Important and Urgent*) and must be addressed immediately. A better way to engage in activities that refresh and recharge yourself, is to do it as a planned *E2* event. In *E2*, these activities are not excessive because you stop at the appropriate time and feel better afterward. You will not be stressed in *E1* with a sinking ship, but will be on course and renewed to continue with *Important and Not Urgent* items.

Both goal setting and understanding your *Life Plan* are particularly important when using the *Life Leadership Matrix* because, without them, it may be challenging to determine what's important and what's not. The *Life Leadership Matrix* is a simple tool that will help you to create an action plan to live *Inwardly* and *Outwardly* in a more positive, productive, and effective manner.

The goal is to spend more time in *E2* (*Important and Not Urgent*), which will move you to a higher level of *PH2E*. You must commit to spending as much time as possible in *E2,* which will reduce the amount of time spent in the other *Environments* and keep you on course for what's most important in your *Life Journey*.

Starve your distractions, feed your focus.

—Anonymous

Life Leadership Matrix Exercise

Try this.

Watch a television commercial, and right before the person is going to say the main point about the product, quickly turn to another channel. How does that make you feel? If you do this a few times, you'll see you won't miss anything of importance. What does this teach you? At the moment before you switched channels, it felt urgent. You needed to hear and see the next moment of the commercial. How could you possibly miss it? It felt urgent, but it wasn't important. This is *Life Environment 3 (E3)*.

We spend a large part of our day in *E3*, which unfortunately keeps us off-course of our *Life Journey. Environment 3* is *Urgent and Not Important*, thereby keeping us away from our *On Course, Life Environment 2, Important and Not Urgent. Environment 3* comes to us all day, every day, and is filled with *Outward Inward (OI)* events that come from the *Outward World* pressing on our *Inward World (Inward Being)*.

Right now, I'm typing on my tablet with my phone next to me, and it just lit up with a notification: "Special sale at Bed Bath & Beyond for a limited time today!" The message screamed, 'urgent, look at me,' but it was not important at all. I don't need anything from Bed Bath & Beyond, and I don't know why I received this notification because I always refuse them. Companies are finding more ways to send these unsolicited "*Not Important*" but "*Urgent*" messages to distract and entice people to buy their goods and services.

In an instant, with the momentary buzz of my phone, the *E3 OI Event* distracted me from writing this book, a goal that keeps me on course for my current *Life Journey*. When you start to notice and count all the *E3* events coming to you in a day, you begin to realize why it's hard to stay on track and achieve your *Life Goals*.

OI events are unavoidable, but our reaction to them is based on our *Inward Thinking*. We have control over our *Inward Thinking* and our *Outward Actions*; therefore, we control how we react to *OI Events*. When an *OI Event* presents itself, you have two choices. One is to say no, and the second is to find a reason in *E2* to engage with the event. If I happened to need a new frying pan and received the Bed Bath & Beyond notification, I might have put that information in *E2* and taken a ride to the store

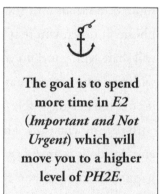

The goal is to spend more time in *E2* (*Important and Not Urgent*) which will move you to a higher level of *PH2E*.

later to purchase that frying pan. However, that is rarely the case. For example, how important is a frying pan to my *Life Journey*?

Stop and think of a loved one you want to call or send an email. That's an important but not urgent task that will propel your *PH2E*. It is directly related to your *Life Journey* and your goal to foster deep, fulfilling relationships. In contrast, the television commercial will keep you either drifting and *Wayward Living* or draining and *Downward Living*. The examples discussed regarding commercials and notifications are *Urgent and Not Important E3 Environment* events. We are wired to respond to the urgent continually. However, we need to differentiate between the *Important and Urgent* and the *Not Important and Urgent* before acting. We need to look out for these *E3 OI Events* intentionally. When you identify an *E3 Event*, you must either say no or find a reason to move it to *E2*, where it will keep you on course toward meeting your *Life Goals*.

Think of all the times you are focused on something important aligned to your *Life Vision*, but then the phone rings. Of course, you glance at it and probably take the call. However, more often than not, the call is an *E3 Event*. If you notice the phone number, you may even know what the person wants or will share with you, and you must decide if you want to continue with your project and stay in *E2*. If you don't answer the phone, it's ok; the person will leave a message or might send you a text with the information. Then you can respond at a later time. If you decide it is an *E2 OI Action*, answer. These *E3 OI Actions* happen more than you realize throughout the day. Don't you wonder why you often question where all the time went? Over the next 10 hours, try to place each *OI Action* into one of the *4 Life Living Environments*. As you practice, you will begin to respond naturally in a way that will keep you longer in *E2* and on course for your *Life Journey*.

Have you ever run out of gas? I'm embarrassed to say I have. Liverpool Victoria, one of the United Kingdom's largest insurers, issued a report indicating over 800,000 people run out of gas daily. Does anyone want to run out of gas? There are millions of drivers in the world, and no one *wants* to run out of gas. Every new car has some sort of warning indicating the need to refuel. When it happened to me, I saw the warning light, but knew I wouldn't run out of gas immediately and kept driving. Of course, I got distracted and drove home without refueling. The next day I woke up excited and thought about all the things I needed to do. I drove to work and, in a matter of minutes, felt the car's acceleration slow down. That's when I noticed the warning light and suddenly ran out of gas.

On reflection, I was busy thinking about many different projects while on my daily commute along a beautiful road parallel to the beach. It's peaceful, and I spend quality time *Inwardly Thinking*. However, the lesson I learned is that I should immediately proceed to a gas station and fill the tank whenever the low fuel warning light appears. What are the excuses of the other 800,000 drivers who ran out of gas? Most people probably see the warning light and think they can go several more miles. Maybe some are like me and completely forget about it. Why don't the car companies make an audible alarm that sounds when you only have a few miles left of gas? Would anyone ignore it and think they could somehow overcome the empty tank and stay on their journey?

Keeping the gas tank full is an excellent example of the need to live in *Environment 2 (E2)*, where life doesn't come to you, but instead, you have to go to it. It takes effort to live in *E2*. If we think we don't have time to stop for gas, we'll eventually end up in *Environment 1 (E1)*, *Urgent and Important*, where we will be forced to stop. It will undoubtedly occur when we're not expecting to stop and need to be somewhere else. How many other things arise that we don't stop and take care of? How many other important things must we make an effort to go to? Think of those life events. If we ignore them, they will eventually come to us in an *Urgent and Important* form as an *E1* event that we must deal with—or else sink.

Another example is health. If we don't exercise and eat correctly, we will eventually end up in *Environment 1* and need to take medication or go to the doctor or the hospital. Significant relationships are another example. You must make the effort in *E2* to build and nurture those important relationships with your family, friends, or colleagues. If these relationships are ignored, they will eventually become strained. You will then feel stress and pressure to repair the relationship by going above and beyond to build the trust back. However, if you spent the necessary time in *E2* communicating and supporting those special relationships, then you and the other people will continue to build on the trust and understanding you already have established. The goal is for us to live in *Environment 2* as much as possible. However, we need to seek out *E2*. It does not come to us—and if it does, it's too late, and we are in *Environment 1,* where we must tend to the issue immediately, or our *Life Ship* will sink.

Smile, breathe, and go slowly.
—Thich Nhat Hanh

Cognitive Shifting - Mindful Breathing

Taking charge of your *Inward Living* means taking control of your *Inward Thoughts.* You need to turn your attention in a positive direction, which will create more productive results for *yourself, your family, and your team or organization.* If you are stuck in a negative thought pattern, you need to shift your thoughts, as a captain on a ship would change course due to turbulent waters. Hannam and

Taking charge of your *Inward Living* means taking charge of your *Inward Thoughts.*

Selby suggest "cognitive shifting" is a mind management tool you can use when you are in a less-than-optimum mood, your mental clarity is low, or you feel distracted. Cognitive shifting helps when you are off-course and in rough seas and need something specific to get you back on course. It's a technique to help you take charge of your *Inward Thoughts* to feel in control of your *Outward Actions.*

There is a science behind cognitive shifting. At any given moment, your brain can have only one conscious thought. It can have multiple, simultaneous, low-level thoughts when performing automatic tasks, such as walking, running, or eating. However, during conscious thought, although you may think you are focusing on two things simultaneously, your brain is switching back and forth between the two. Therefore, the way to change your negative thoughts is to push them out with positive ones. That may not be easy, but it is attainable. Here is a technique I have used for years to help me.

Practice mindful breathing and focus your attention on the rise and fall of your chest and the air flowing in and out of your nose. Negative thoughts may creep in but keep pushing them out and stay the course. Don't try to push them down, but rather, picture them pushing away and leaving you. At some point, think of your *Life Vision*—your big picture life purpose, which I will discuss in Chapter 11. Your *Inward Positive Living* will kick in, and your negative thoughts will melt away. Focusing on your breath will provide you with an immediate physical sensation of air flowing in and out of your nose, which will instantly shift your awareness away from the negative emotion to a feeling of being present in the now. You must practice mindful breathing regularly, so it feels automatic. Then, during stressful times you can effortlessly move into the practice. The art of cognitive shifting involves learning how to move your thinking rapidly from a negative state to a positive one.

Whenever you are *IOD* (*Inward-Outward-Downward*) *Living* and feeling *Downward Negative Drains*, you must remember that you have complete control to focus on your positive *Inward Living* and reconnect with your *Life Vision, Life Principles, Life Values,* and *Life Goals*, which will reconnect you and put you back on the unique course you designed.

Don't let the world tell you who you are.
You get up, and you tell the world who you are.

—A.D. Posey

Design means Design

Living by design is not a quick thought; it's understanding your *Inward* intelligence and moving forward in a clear, well-planned, and goal-directed life. If you are living even slightly on autopilot, it can alter your life destination. For example, if a ship is off-course by only three degrees, it can significantly affect the destination. You probably think it will arrive close enough to the target destination. Still, as the illustration depicts, a three-degree deviation over 100 miles will take you to a completely different destination, five miles from where you intended to go! We must revisit our *Life Vision, Daily Mission,* and *Life Goals* constantly to make sure we are on our desired course.

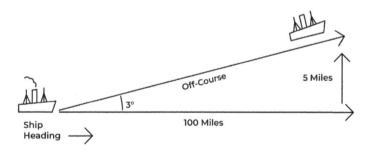

Drifting a few degrees off-course without immediate correction can change the navigation line to your desired destination. For the first 50 miles, you might not even realize you are off-course. It takes constant and persistent internal *Inward* checks early in your journey with minor adjustments to get back on course. If you ignore your course and fail to adjust, it will be too late to act, and the byproduct will ultimately be *IOD Living* and a *Downward Drain*.

Message Design

Dr. Albert Mehrabian documents the importance of verbal and nonverbal messages. He asserts that when individuals communicate their feelings and attitudes, the receiver of the information gains the most meaning from nonverbal body language cues and not from spoken words. In fact, spoken words account for 7% of the meaning and tone of voice accounts for 38%, while body language accounts for 55%. Therefore, for effective *Outward* communication, those three components need to be aligned. When the message conveys different signals in words, tone, and body language, the receiver might be confused or irritated by the mixed message. They will discount the verbal words and instead give weight to the tone and body language.

If we aim for highly effective communication, we need to be aware of and align our *Outward* words, tone, and body language to the message we want to communicate.

Our body language holds great weight in our *Outward* messaging. If we aim for highly effective communication, we need to be aware of and align our *Outward* words, tone, and body language to the message we want to communicate. If not, our body language will be the dominant factor in interpreting our message—even if our words and tone are giving a different message. If "I'm not mad at you" is spoken while acting agitated and with your body turned away from the listener, your message will probably be interpreted based on your non-verbal cues (93%) rather than your words, which only account for 7% of the message. Therefore, the listener will most likely believe that you are, in fact, angry at them.

Language by Design or Default?

Observe your *Inward* and *Outward* language. Are your words the language you would hear from a coach or a critic? As you design your life based on your *Life Vision* and *Daily Mission*, your language sets your *SelfCulture*. Often, we repeat the language we hear from the relationships around us and the social media we interact with all day long. When we simply repeat things and do so without checking to see if it is aligned to our *Inward Being*, we are living by default.

We all know somebody who always shares something they recently heard and shares it as if it has been their opinion for years. Nobody takes that person seriously. You don't want to be that person and must consistently examine the way you speak. There is great *Inward* satisfaction discovering an area that needs improvement, making an adjustment, and taking *Outward Action* that produces a happier, more peaceful culture. Whether it's

We all have an internal "Life Gauge."

between you, a friend, a family member, or a colleague, make the small adjustment like the ship that is only off-course by three degrees. Using more positive language will produce *Upward Life Gifts* that you and the people in your *Outward* relationships will feel. Remember, we are always looking for positive *Outward Actions* to act on so we can receive *Upward Living Life Gifts* into our *PH2E*.

Recently, I realized that every time I spoke with a particular colleague, I felt a *Downward Negative Drain* immediately afterward. We all have people with whom we must communicate, but it is not a positive relationship. What are our options? We control our language and actions, and we have no control over the other person's. We all know this, but continually think the next time we speak will be the time they will change. That rarely happens. Simply by not expecting our colleague's language to change, but beginning to change our language to be succinct and positive, the previous *Downward Negative Drains* will move to *Upward Positive Gifts*.

The next time you are in *Outward Mode* with someone, ask yourself how you feel as soon as the conversation ends. We all have an internal "Life Gauge." Did you receive an *Upward Positive Gift*, a *Downward Negative Drain,* or was it neutral? What does that tell you?

> *The most important thing in communication is hearing what isn't said.*
>
> —Peter F. Drucker

The Hidden Outward Living Dimension

Is Yours by Design or by Default?

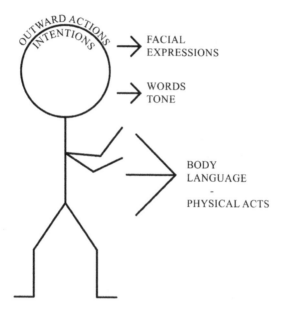

Your *Hidden Outward Living Dimension* is your nonverbal communication, which can produce a positive or negative environment in your interactions with others. You continually send out clues to what you might be thinking or feeling. Burgoon, Guerrero, and Kory suggest that most meaning is generated from *Outward* nonverbal communication. The question is whether it is by design or default. If you are not thinking about your body language, you may be giving unintended signals. Your physical movements and actions are comfortable to you; however, take notice of what occurs during your next face-to-face conversation.

By definition, body language is an *Outward Action*. As soon as you are in a room with another person, you are in the *Outward Mode*. Your nonverbal clues affect everyone in proximity to you.

Your *Hidden Outward Living Dimension* is your nonverbal communication, which can produce a positive or negative environment in your interactions with others.

For example, bad posture—slouching, leaning over, slumping, and hunched shoulders—is associated with a lack of confidence, weakness, and low self-esteem. As an adult, it is unlikely someone will tell you that you have poor posture. Therefore, you have to self-assess. Think of keeping your spine straight, shoulders back, and head tall. If you do this right now, you will feel better, and it will be easier to focus.

The full range of feelings is shared through facial expressions. Psychology professor Paul Ekman is considered a world-famous face reader. He pioneered the study of emotions related to facial expressions and specifically studied the six most common emotions associated with facial expressions—happiness, surprise, fear, anger, disgust, and sadness. Interestingly, four of those are negative emotions. The six universal emotions are expressed by using the 43 muscles in your face. Ekman and his colleagues found that these six emotions are universally found in all cultures. We are pre-wired to move our faces unconsciously and effortlessly to represent any of the six core emotions.

Your *Inward Feeling* at any given time should match the *Outward Actions* of your facial expression. However, at times you may try to hide your feelings with a smirk or try to mask your fear or anger. If you feel you are trying to change or force an expression, it will be obvious to other people that your feelings are not matching your expression. Similarly, suppose you notice that your family member, friend, or colleague's facial expression doesn't match their spoken emotions. In that case, you could ask questions to foster honest and open communication, which will ultimately build your relationship and ultimately lead to the *Upward Living Life Gifts of PH2E*.

When it comes to smiling, is it your default? When you meet someone new, do you smile, or do you maintain a stern expression? Think about what a smile says to another person: "I'm not threatening," "I'm not going to hurt you," or "I'm not aggressive." Smiling reportedly uses 17 muscles in your face, while frowning uses all 43 facial muscles. Smiles are contagious. According to Hatfield, Rapson, and Le, when you smile at someone, they often smile back. That is because people often mimic the facial expressions of others.

Additionally, smiling can lift one's mood and the mood of others. A study completed at London University College found that people who are happy and smiling are 35% more likely to live longer. It is believed that smiling lowers the heart rate and can reduce blood pressure while relaxing the body.

A genuine smile is one of the most powerful body language tools. As several studies have shown, a smile can help your *Inward Being* and *Outward* relationships feel happier and more comfortable. There are also moments when you may need to offer a social smile even though you are not *Inwardly* feeling it. Your smile may be needed to comfort someone or express a sense of welcome and interest when you are being introduced in a business setting. You don't want your smile to come off as phony or forced. There is an easy fix! Practice smiling in the mirror. First, try to think of something that would make you smile and notice how you look. Notice three things—your eyes, your cheeks, and your mouth. Exaggerate your smile, and then relax it to a comfortable level. Practice it often until you can get right to the smile with no effort or thought. We all have a social smile that we put on every day. Why wouldn't we intentionally improve it to give us more confidence? You will also receive the *Upward* benefits of smiling, feeling happier and more peaceful.

What about a neutral facial expression? Right now, as you are reading, you probably have a neutral facial expression. Be aware of this when you are interacting with others because if you are not giving any signals, you are leaving it to that other person to interpret your feelings. Perhaps when the other person makes a point or offers an opinion about something, you may consciously choose not to tip off your emotions or thoughts by design. However, if you do want to show a reaction, you need to be sure your expression is intentional and not by default. Your expression should match and support the point you are trying to make.

In terms of eye contact, looking into another person's eyes when speaking shows confidence and trustworthiness. You can intentionally do this and improve every day. If you usually begin a sentence with good eye contact but find yourself looking down to gather your thoughts, then looking back up to finish your thoughts, you may be acting by default. You can intentionally improve this, and it is an area we can take control of and live by design starting today! Begin slowly, and observe your *Inward Thoughts* as you maintain eye contact during conversations. You will feel an *Upward* lift of confidence as you improve your relationships. The more you are conscious and practice, the more comfortable you will become. You will see and feel the positive response from others.

What you do speaks so loud that I cannot hear what you say.

—Ralph Waldo Emerson

Additional Outward Living Hidden Actions

Body position. Make sure your body is not turned away from the person you are speaking to—this is known as sideways talk and projects uneasiness and lack of trust.

Sitting position. As cited in an Ohio State University study, sitting up straight gives you more confidence. Researchers found that people sitting straight up while speaking were more likely to be believed than those who slouched. Also, the person sitting up straight felt more confident in their thoughts. The study suggests that people's thoughts are dramatically influenced by their posture.

Social Space. Not only do your environment, body language, and gestures affect your *Outward* communication, but also, the space or distance you place between you and the other person plays an important role in how we communicate. Proxemics is the study of the amount of distance or space people feel necessary to set between themselves when interacting. The term proxemics was coined by Edward Hall, who discussed how differences in space between two people could make them feel more relaxed or anxious. There are some cultural differences on acceptable distances; however, Dr. Hall shared the following distance zones that seem to be universally agreed upon.

- **Intimate distance** involves direct contact, such as in loving relationships, comforting, protecting, some sports.
- **Personal Distance** is from one to four feet, which is about an arm's length distance where physical contact—such as holding hands—can happen, or some negative contact could happen—like getting punched in the nose.
- **Social Distance** is between four and 12 feet, which is the distance for most social and formal business interactions.
- **Public Distance** is between 12 and 25 feet. This distance is observed when you are in public, such as in malls, parks, airports, or walking on the street. There is no physical contact and minimal eye contact.

In addition to Dr. Hall's distance zones, I would like to add:

- **Social Distance During a Global Health Crisis** –The Department of Health will provide guidance on what is considered the appropriate distance to be from another person. During the worldwide health crisis of 2020, social distancing was recommended to be six feet or more.

Hand Motions. The most nerve connections are between the hands and the brain; therefore, the gestures and positions of the hands can be an insight into our emotional state. Hand gestures can help emphasize your words and are an added source of communication.

Voice. Paralanguage, a word coined by George Trager in the 1960s, is the nonverbal part of your speech. Every day you speak a paralanguage. It's not the words, but rather the vocal quality, pitch, rate, and verbal fillers. The saying, "It's not what we say but how we say it" relates to paralanguage as it is the study of "how" you say words. Are you monitoring how you say words—especially when there may be high emotion? Does your paralanguage match your message intent?

Be aware of other body language you may be using as your default without realizing it. Next time you are speaking to someone, assess yourself. We need to analyze our *Outward Actions* to make sure our *Inward Intentions* are being interpreted correctly.

Captain's Log for Chapter 2

Living and Leading by Design

Captain's Log:

Point 1   *Life Leaders* live their lives by design and not by default. They use their *Inward Thinking* to plan and then adjust their *Life Journey*, never living on autopilot.

Point 2   Examine your *Life Maps* to see if they match reality. That is an important first step for your growth. Are your assumptions about the world (e.g., *yourself, family, teams, or organizations*) correct or distorted?

Point 3   *OI Actions* occur when the world makes demands on us. You have no control over the world, but you have 100% control over your reaction.

Point 4   The *Life Leadership* Matrix helps you prioritize your tasks to keep you on course. *Environment 1 (E1)* contains tasks that are *Important and Urgent, Environment 2 (E2)* contains tasks that are *Important and Not Urgent, Environment 3 (E3)* contains tasks that are *Not Important and Urgent,* and *Environment 4 (E4)* contains tasks that are *Not Important and Not Urgent.*

Point 5   Have a *Life Leadership* action plan. Stay in *Life Leadership Matrix* environments which are important. While *Urgent and Important* events will always occur, we can minimize them by attending to our *Environment 2* activities.

Point 6   Practice cognitive shifting by pushing out your negative thoughts with positive ones. Remember, your brain can only have one conscious thought at a time.

Point 7   Take care to design your verbal and non-verbal messages proactively so your intent is accurately conveyed. Be aware of what your verbalizations, tone, facial expressions, and body language are communicating.

Point 8   Be aware of the *Hidden Outward Living Dimension* created by your verbal and non-verbal communications. Design your communications to convey the intent you desire. Don't leave it to default or unintended consequences may result.

Teach to Learn

The best way to deepen your understanding and, at the same time, share and stimulate new conversations with others is to teach. Share what you have learned with a friend, family member, coworker, or anyone else who will listen. Teaching is, by far, the best way to deepen your understanding of new insights and concepts. Take any of the Points in the Captain's Log or this chapter for thought-provoking discussions.

New Daily Voyage:

Activity:

Take some time to think about the *4 Life Living Environments*. How often are you in *Environment 1, 2, 3*, and *4*? Plan to increase time in *Environment 2*.

Ask yourself:

Do my non-verbal communications match my words?

Chapter 3

The *Life Map* Cycle

The map is not the territory.

—Alfred Korzybski

After several months selling fruits and vegetables on the streets of Brooklyn, Vincenzo was ready to use his profits to take his business to another level. He bought a horse, which he named Charlie, and cart so he could cover more territory. "I always kept thinking and finding ways to be better," he said. Vincenzo and his brother Sam were extremely successful in selling fruits and vegetables, traveling up and down the streets in several Brooklyn neighborhoods. Vincenzo explained that he learned and changed his thinking constantly based on daily experiences. He used the analogy of sailing the seas and how the waves, tides, and winds are always shifting and changing. "A good seaman is always adjusting to the conditions," he explained. It was clear that Vincenzo understood the need to be flexible and was unafraid to take risks and change his thinking— his mental *Life Map*—based on relationships he developed with his customers. He learned quickly that circumstances are always changing, and you need to adapt to the changes and not get stuck in your old ways.

Vincenzo interacted with hundreds of people every day, listening and making changes based on what his customers wanted. At first, he thought he knew which fruits and vegetables would sell based solely on his *Inward Thoughts*, but he later learned that reality was different from his original ideas. He changed his *Life Maps* based on new data he received from interactions with the people he served. Our thinking is never entirely correct based on what we see or believe. There is always room for improvement in our opinions and conclusions on every aspect of life, and we need to leave space and be open-minded at all times. With clear *Inward Thinking* and receiving new information from the *Outward World*, we can improve our thinking and get closer to life's realities.

The *Outward World* is always changing, and we must always reflect on our opinions, views, and conclusions and then make adjustments to move us closer to reality.

The philosopher and scientist Alfred Korzybski said, "The map is not the territory." We think our *Inward Life Maps* represent the correct reality of the world, but they do not. Our maps or paradigms need constant revisions to align better with the actual territory. The *Outward World* is always changing, and we must always reflect on our opinions, views, and conclusions and then make adjustments to move us closer to reality. Just as the menu is not the meal, our mental maps are not the reality but only our *Inward* interpretation of the real world. Our life experiences from birth onward provide us with a reference point, and we compare ourselves to others based on this *Inward* reference point.

We all have psychological biases. Tversky and Kahneman showed how our biases create a tendency to make decisions or act in an illogical manner, which leads to the development of inaccurate *Life Maps*. How can we move closer to reality when psychological biases are at work? We must be aware of our biases and learn how to overcome them to make better decisions and conclusions and create more accurate *Inward Life Maps*.

Psychological Biases Overview:

- **Confirmation Bias** - You use only the data that support your belief, and you ignore or reject data in opposition to your belief.
- **First Impression Bias** - You make a quick initial determination of the situation, and it's hard for you to adjust and see other options.
- **Overconfidence Bias** - You place too much weight on your knowledge and opinions.

- **Gambler's Fallacy** - You use past results to influence your current decision. You believe the results will change based on the notion that all things change. For example, if you are playing roulette and red came up several times in a row, you might assume there is a higher chance that it will be black on the next roll because it hasn't happened in a while. In fact, the odds are always 50/50.

- **Fundamental Attribution Error** - You blame others for the failure of a situation based on stereotypes or perceived personality flaws.

Psychological biases are not often noticed because they operate subconsciously in our thinking. However, based on these fallacies, we reach conclusions and form opinions about the *Outward World* and believe them to be the reality. Since that is a common process for everyone, what are we doing to move continuously toward more accurate opinions and *Life Maps*? The *Life Map Cycle* is a tool to aid in moving our *Inward Opinions* and mental *Life Maps* closer to reality.

The *Life Map Cycle* is a tool to aid in moving our *Inward Opinions* and mental *Life Maps* closer to reality.

The world as we have created it is a process of our thinking.
It cannot be changed without changing our thinking.

—Albert Einstein

The LIFE MAP CYCLE

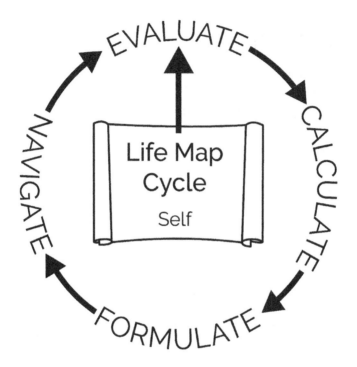

There is reality in life, and there are our perceptions of reality. Are our perceptions accurate? Another way to think of perception is as our opinions or our *Life Maps*. We have opinions on every *Outward* item around us, including the environment, politics, our neighbors, our in-laws, our friends—on everything. We should always ask if our perceptions, opinions, or *Life Maps* are accurate. Do our mental *Life Maps* represent the territory, the principle, and the *Outward World* around us?

The *Life Map Cycle* is a systems thinking tool, which will help you get one step closer to the true territory or principle; in other words, what really exists and not your opinion of it.

The *Life Map Cycle* is a systems-thinking tool, which will help you get one step closer to the true territory or principle; in other words, what actually exists and not your opinion of it. It's a tool that will help you organize your thoughts, develop a plan, and execute it. When used, you will feel your *SelfCulture* rise to a higher level due to your responsible *Inward* planning and *Outward Living*.

Life Map Cycle Stages:

- **Evaluate** - Take in the raw data that we observe.
- **Calculate** - Organize the data, so it makes sense.
- **Formulate** - Confirm, modify, or change your opinion and plan based on the data.
- **Navigate** - Take action and implement the plan.

As a systems tool, the *Life Map Cycle* will help us think things through to get closer to the reality or the *Life Principle* of the *Outward World*. It lets us examine our opinions and understandings of events, situations, and others. Our *Inward Being* holds all of our *Life Maps*. We have an *Inward Life Map* or opinion of everything in our world. If we understand that our *Life Maps* do not accurately portray the actual territory, we should always be open-minded and examine our thinking patterns.

The *Life Map Cycle* for *Self* is a continuous process of four stages.

1. **Evaluate** - When we experience something, the data is right in front of you; however, we naturally filter out some of it based on our *Inward* psychological biases. Be aware of this and try to take in complete data without judgment.

2. **Calculate** - Think about the data, sort it in your mind, and organize it. Try not to judge or make conclusions at this stage. View the data from different perspectives. This is a critical task in preparation for the next step—*Formulate*.

3. **Formulate** - Make conclusions based on your *Inward Thinking* about the data. You may already have an opinion about it. If you do, now is the time to confirm, modify, or change your opinion based on the new information you just evaluated and calculated.

4. **Navigate** - Now is the time to act on your opinion. You have completed the necessary work, and it is time to share your opinion or act out a plan based on the previous three stages of the *Life Map Cycle*.

As you take action and share your *Life Map* opinion, the cycle continues. When new data is presented, *re-Evaluate* the information, *Calculate* the data, and then again *Formulate* by confirming, modifying, or changing your opinion. This practice will get you closer to the accurate territory and guide you to spend more time *Evaluating* and *Calculating* before you rush to *Formulate* a plan and *Navigate* or act on it. This concept is reinforced by the saying commonly attributed to Einstein, "If I had an hour to solve a problem, I'd spend 55 minutes thinking about the problem and five minutes thinking about solutions." Practicing the *Life Map Cycle* will result in *Peacefulness* from knowing you are doing everything possible to be fair and accurate about all things in the *Outward World*. The alternative is to act solely based on our old opinions with no improvement to our thinking. When this happens, your *Life Map* is "short-circuited," which will be discussed in the next section.

On April 24, 1895, Captain Joshua Slocum sailed from Boston on a 36-foot-long oyster sloop he had rebuilt and named *Spray*. His goal was to become the first person to circumnavigate the globe solo. Captain Slocum *Inwardly* prepared for the journey creating a *Life Vision* and *Daily Mission* and carefully thinking through many obstacles he might face. Throughout his three-year journey, Slocum used the *Life Map Cycle* to consistently organize his thoughts, develop a plan, and then execute it. Without his *IO Evaluation, Calculation, Formulation,* and *Navigation*, it is highly likely that he would have failed to achieve his goal.

Before Captain Slocum began his journey, he *Evaluated* and *Calculated* data, starting with the type of supplies he would need on board, the route he would take, and how weather conditions would likely affect it. Based on his *Inward Thinking*, he

Formulated a plan to accomplish his goal. Slocum then successfully *Navigated*—that is, he left the coast of Massachusetts and began his quest.

Over three years, Slocum constantly engaged in the *Life Map Cycle* and reacted to new data that presented itself. He never stopped *Evaluating, Calculating, Formulating,* and *Navigating,* even—and especially—when it meant radically changing his plan. The most dramatic example of this occurred during the first part of his journey. Captain Slocum had decided to sail east around the world and successfully journeyed 417 nautical miles from Massachusetts to Nova Scotia, and then across the Atlantic Ocean. He passed the Azores and spent a few weeks in Gibraltar, where some repairs were made to his boat.

His original plan was to proceed through the Mediterranean Sea, through the Suez Canal, down the Red Sea, and then continue east. However, based on the *Evaluation* of new data –information from British officers about the presence of pirates on that route and then a frightful encounter with them, and his *Calculation* about the risk outweighing the benefits to continuing on his planned path—Captain Slocum *Formulated* a new plan. He determined that he would circumnavigate the globe in a westward direction. He then *Navigated* his boat in the opposite direction, toward the continent he had left four months prior. Slocum crossed the Atlantic Ocean for a second time, traveling 417 nautical miles again, completely reversing his direction.

According to his account of this journey, he was not disappointed or upset by this turn of events. He simply *Formulated* a new plan based on learning more about the territory. He changed and updated his *Life Maps* so he could continue toward his ultimate goal.

Captain Slocum continued to *Evaluate* the raw data, checking to see if the actual territory he encountered matched his maps and plans. Many times, he modified his course because of unforeseen weather conditions, such as squalls and storms. Slocum backtracked, stopped at different ports than he had planned, and found creative ways to finance the purchase of supplies and repairs to the *Spray*. Staying true to his original goal and being flexible enough to adapt to the conditions he encountered allowed Slocum to persevere and ultimately accomplish his goal. The *Life Map Cycle* of *Evaluate, Calculate, Formulate,* and *Navigate* allowed Captain Joshua Slocum to succeed at his mission after three years and two months, becoming the first person, sailing alone, to circumnavigate the globe.

Don't believe everything you think. Thoughts are just that—thoughts.

—Allan Lokos

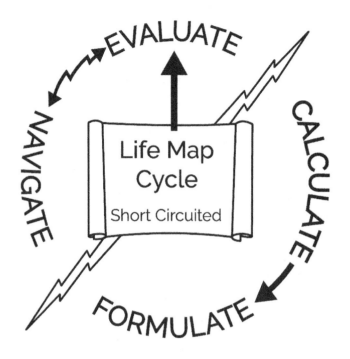

LIFE MAP SHORT CIRCUITED

As we have discussed, we have opinions about almost everything in the world, and those opinions are our *Life Maps*. Other theorists and researchers have used terms such as paradigms, mental models, and thought patterns. I think *Life Map* is a clear and understandable way to visualize this concept. *Life Maps* are how we see the world and guide our *Outward Actions,* and they are based on our experiences and life circumstances. There are two questions to ask ourselves: Are our opinions accurate, and do we examine our opinions and modify or change them often?

Commonly, the answer is no. In fact, if you think of someone you know well and your conversations with them, I'm sure you can anticipate their response to many topics most of the time because you have heard the same response several times over the years. Their response appears automatic when a keyword or topic is raised. When these automatic responses occur, what happens is their *Life Map Cycle* is "short-circuited."

When your *Life Maps* are short-circuited, you go from *Evaluate* or observation to *Navigate* and action.

The individual *Evaluates* something by observing it and goes immediately to acting on it, or the *Navigate* stage. Two important stages on the *Life Map Cycle* are omitted. The first stage omitted is *Calculate* or thinking about the data, and the second stage omitted is *Formulate*, which is to confirm, modify, or change your opinion based on data you have observed.

When your *Life Maps* are short-circuited, you go from *Evaluate* or observation to *Navigate* and action. This short-circuit happens almost every day. It creates fallacies and biases. The result is you are not living to the true principle or actual reality but are living to your flawed *Inward Life Maps*. Cognitive psychologist Peter Cathcart Wason coined the term "confirmation bias" to describe when a person processes information based on their existing beliefs and ignores all the facts. When we short-circuit our *Life Maps*, we tend to select the data according to what we believe and like to think. This keeps our opinions unchanged even when there may be evidence that contradicts our original belief. Because confirmation bias is a common default, we need to train ourselves to think through all the stages of the *Life Map Cycle*, so our *Inward* and *Outward Living* are more accurately aligned to reality.

Six hours away in Maryland, at another soccer tournament for my son, I took advantage of a lot of downtime to work on this book. Later, at a delicious team dinner in an Italian restaurant, the boys noticed a famous donut store across the street and asked to go there after dinner. The parents agreed to go to the C donut store. One parent said, "Those C donuts are famous and the best donuts!" Every parent agreed, except for one who said, "Oh no, I think D donuts are the best!" Everyone disagreed with her and argued why C donuts are the best and why she was wrong. As soon as dinner was over, the boys headed to the donut store. We paid the check and went to meet them. My son bought me an original glazed donut. My first bite confirmed that my opinion was still accurate, and C donuts were the best. I looked up and noticed the parent who advocated for D donuts had a half-eaten donut in her hand and a big smile on her face. She said, "These are amazing! They are so light, and the texture is so soft! I may have to change my opinion; these C donuts are delicious!" When I heard this, even after 15 other parents challenged her at dinner, it confirmed her ability to stay open-minded. She *Evaluated* these C donuts by trying one, and then clearly thought about the donut (data) and analyzed the texture, weight, and taste in her mind. She went through the *Formulate* stage by changing her opinion, even one she held for years, and changed it on the spot. She *Navigated* her opinion *Outwardly* by sharing her thoughts with everyone.

I know this is a simplistic example of a *Life Map* about donuts, but it is a great example to demonstrate the process of the *Life Map Cycle*. Try and go through the *Life Map Cycle* before you act out and share your opinions. Your mind is equipped to go through the stages at lightning speed. It takes little effort, and the rewards are positive. Think about how the others felt as we witnessed this parent change her mind when only 30 minutes earlier, she strongly advocated for something else. I hope her modeling helped someone in the room who resists changing their opinion or *Life Maps*. Her example may have inspired someone to examine and challenge their possibly inaccurate views and elevate their *Life Maps* to a more accurate level.

[H]e who cannot change the very fabric of his thought will never be able to change reality, and will never, therefore, make any progress.

—Anwar el-Sadat, quoted in Stephen M.R. Covey, The Speed of Trust: The One Thing that Changes Everything

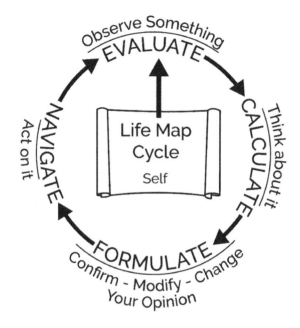

LIFE MAP CYCLE SIMPLIFIED

Life Maps can change the way we think of the world. In 1953, everyone's *Life Map* changed because of a young geologist named Marie Tharp. She worked at Columbia University and was treated poorly, underpaid, and given neither title nor a position commensurate with the important work she was doing. Despite the barriers faced as a woman in the scientific community, Marie Tharp made revolutionary discoveries about the ocean floor. Until her discoveries, scientists' *Life Maps* showed that the ocean floor was a flat mud plain. Because the top of the ocean surface was flat, it was assumed underneath was flat, too. This short-circuited thinking was evident throughout the world until Tharp, along with other geologists and cartographers, *Evaluated, Calculated,* and changed the world's current thinking.

Tharp changed everyone's *Life Maps* based on raw data she received from sonar measurements of the ocean depths. Using only pens, ink, and a ruler, Marie Tharp *Calculated* the thousands of sonar readings with longitude and latitude degrees and then drew the ocean floor in detail by hand. From her *Calculations* she *Formulated* that the ocean floor had geological features such as canyons, ridges, and mountains, similar to what is found on land.

Life Maps can change the way we think of the world.

Marie Tharp's world-changing revelation was the existence of a series of mountainous volcanoes that run north to south through the ocean. This discovery led to her theory of continental drift (an idea that all the continents were once connected as one) and plate tectonics (the idea that the Earth's crust is made up of slowly moving plates), which are both widely accepted today. In 1977, Tharp published a comprehensive map of the entire ocean called the World Ocean Floor Map. She was a brilliant woman who changed the *Life Maps* of the oceans and the minds of everyone in the world.

How many opinions do we accept as truths and continually believe that our *Life Maps* are accurate? We need to take time to absorb new data when we hear a different opinion, or when we see or experience something new. We should then put the new information in the *Calculate* stage and think about it from as many perspectives as we can without making a judgment. After we have thoroughly thought about it, only then should we *Formulate* our opinion, which may be the same as before we started or modified or even changed. When a previous *Life Map* changes based on new information, you will feel the *Upward Living Gift of Excellence.* You have evolved to a higher level while most people live their lives in the same short-circuited fashion.

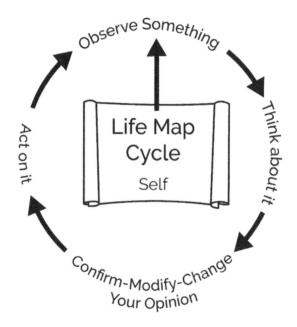

Practicing the *Life Map Cycle* stages and living by *The 12 Essential Life Anchors* (Chapters 11 & 12) will help you overcome your biases. Taking the time for *positive and effective* intentional living based on timeless, universal principles will provide you with more accurate *Life Maps* and move you closer to the reality of the territory of life.

Captain's Log for Chapter 3

Living and Leading by Design

Captain's Log:

Point 1   *Inward* perceptions and thoughts are not reality. *Life Maps* or paradigms need to be consistently revised to better align with reality. You need to make necessary adjustments to your *Life Maps* that match the reality of the *Outward World*.

Point 2   The *Life Map Cycle* is a systems-thinking tool to test your perceptions of reality and make accurate and effective decisions.

Point 3   The parts of the *Life Map Cycle* include *Evaluate*, *Calculate*, *Formulate* and *Navigate*. You take in the data, organize it so it makes sense, *Formulate* an opinion and plan, then act to implement the plan.

Point 4   When you do not take the time or make an effort to *Calculate* (organize the data) and *Formulate* (create a plan), you short-circuit the *Life Map Cycle* and move directly from taking in the data to acting on it.

Point 5   A simplified way of looking at the *Life Map Cycle* is the following: First, you *observe something*, and then you *think about it*. Next, you *confirm, modify, or change your opinion*, followed by the final step of *acting on it*.

Point 6   Practicing and living the *Life Map Cycle* will help you overcome biases and see more of *Life's Realities*.

Teach to Learn

The best way to deepen your understanding and, at the same time, share and stimulate new conversations with others is to teach. Share what you have learned with a friend, family member, coworker, or anyone else who will listen. Teaching is, by far, the best way to deepen one's understanding of new insights and concepts. Take any of the Points in the Captain's Log or this chapter for thought-provoking discussions.

New Daily Voyage:

Activity:

Think of a current situation that you can analyze in terms of the *Life Map Cycle*. Have you gone through all four steps, or have you short-circuited and neglected to *Calculate* and *Formulate* before you *Navigate*?

Ask yourself:

How can you become more aware of your biases? How will this help your actions become more intentional?

Chapter 4

Upward Life Gifts

Assessing & Propelling Your *PH2E*

I am not a product of my circumstances.
I am a product of my decisions.

—Stephen Covey

When Vincenzo was 18 years old, he returned to Italy to set the pathway for the rest of his family to eventually come to America. In 1913, he made the week-long journey back to Italy alone and told his parents, siblings, and extended family about the *Dynamic Positive SelfCulture* he created in America.

Vincenzo returned to America in March 1914 on the SS *Europa* from Napoli. For the next two and a half years, Vincenzo and his brother hustled day and night, saving their money toward their goal of opening their first brick and mortar fruit and vegetable store. In 1917, they had enough money and were ready to open a store when their plans were suddenly changed because of growing global unrest.

The Great War for Civilization was thrust upon America when the SS *Housatonic*, along with four US merchant ships, was sunk by Germany, resulting in the death of hundreds of Americans. Until that event, President Woodrow Wilson had pledged neutrality, which was the sentiment of most Americans. In fact, Wilson's 1916 reelection slogan was, "He kept us out of war." However, after the sinking of American ships, President Wilson had no choice, and on April 2, 1917, he gave his famous speech to Congress, calling for a declaration of war against Germany. The resulting congressional vote brought the United States into World War I.

The country was gearing up for war as Vincenzo and his brother Sam were running two successful fruit and vegetable routes in Brooklyn. Years later, Vincenzo recalled, "It was my duty and honor to serve for the United States of America, and I know the seas." Without any hesitation, he enlisted in the US Navy as Vincent Famularo, never again using or signing his given name Vincenzo. On April 29, 1918, he began his service, and in just five weeks, moved quickly up the ranks from Mess Attendant 3rd Class to Seaman 2nd Class, then to Seaman 1st class. Vincent stated, "They saw that I was a sailor and knew what I was talking about." An officer told him he would get a raise, but Vincent responded, "I'm not here for the money. I'm here to do my duty."

He was assigned to the ship the USS *President Grant*. This warship made 22 round trips from New York to France and England, transporting troops, supplies, and ammunition. Vincent shared many stories about sailing on the USS *President Grant* until the end of the war in 1919. During one of the trips from the US to France, Vincent became very ill. When the ship arrived, Vincent was sent to a US Naval Hospital in Paris to treat his illness. It was the fall of 1918 when the second wave of the Spanish Flu appeared with a vengeance throughout the world. This invisible enemy was a frightening illness, infecting about one-third of the world's population and killing 50 million people. Vincent recalled feeling very weak with a high fever and a hacking cough. He said, "The doctors were concerned that pneumonia could develop." One doctor suggested remedies that included eating cinnamon and even drinking wine. After two weeks in the hospital, he started feeling better. For years Vincent would boast that what made him recover was drinking a little sip of cognac each day! Without taking any extra days, he returned to duty. He thanked the doctors and said he had to get back to his ship; he had a job to do.

Vincent was always respectful but not afraid to speak up and do the right thing, whether to a subordinate or a higher-ranking officer. He often said, "Two things: One: you need to know the rules and laws inside and out, and Two: always do the right thing, then you always have your own peace." Vincent *Inwardly* understood and lived with integrity. He modeled it every day and received peace and happiness from his *Outward Actions* for his family and the country.

It was evident from listening and watching how Vincent lived his *Daily Mission* of always doing the right thing, even if it was not popular. If the goal is to have peace in your heart and mind, all *Outward Actions* must match that goal. Vincent was never persuaded by anyone else. He would listen, but if he thought his actions based on his *Inward* experiences and reflections were the right thing to do, then there was no changing his course. He had a spirited affect, but it was clear he was always at peace, immensely positive, loving, and happy.

We all want to have the highest state of *Peacefulness, Happiness, Healthiness, and Excellence (PH2E)*. Nobody can decide our *Inward* feeling. Only we decide our *Inward Being* and *Life Maps*. When we let *Outward* people decide our *Inward* state of mind, it's because we don't know where our *Inward* control center is. We need to understand our *Inward* controls to reach our highest possible *PH2E* levels. Once we reach those levels, we should feel the positive *SelfCulture* it provides. Then we will be prepared to reach for the next highest level. Our *PH2E* can expand limitlessly to ever new highs. Having that mindset will allow us to feel incredible peace and happiness. Our days will be filled with joy, and when a *Downward Negative Drain* occurs, we will be prepared to neutralize the negative withdrawal due to our high *PH2E* level. The *Downward Negative Drain* will be short-lived and not chronic.

*Real freedom is the ability to pause between stimulus and response,
and in that pause, choose.*

—Rollo May

There is a space between your *Inward Thinking* and *Outward Actions*. In that space lies your *PH2E*. When you pause to think *Inwardly*, consider the freedom you have toward how you want to act *Outwardly*. You have control over how you act *Outwardly* in all situations. You need to understand that if your *Inward Thinking* and *Outward Actions* are *positive and effective*, only then will you have the chance to receive deposits of the *Upward Life Gifts of the PH2E*. Remember that before you act

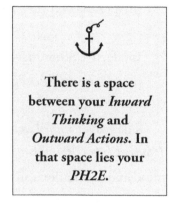

There is a space between your *Inward Thinking* and *Outward Actions*. In that space lies your *PH2E*.

Outwardly, you need to pause and think *Inwardly*. It's the pauses that give you your freedom. When you do and act *positively and effectively* based on your *Inward Life Principles* and *Life Values*, you will receive *Upward Life Gifts* into one or more of your *PH2E* reservoirs.

When you receive negative stimuli, which are *Downward Life Drains*, it's within your *Inward Being* to reverse them. Living *IOU Life Leadership* and practicing *The 12 Essential Life Anchors*, which will be discussed thoroughly in Chapters 11 & 12, will support you in those transformations. Here are suggestions for responding to specific stimuli:

Anxiety Stimulus—Pause and *Inwardly Think Peacefulness*, then *Outwardly Act Peacefully* and *Receive a Peaceful Deposit*

Sad Stimulus—Pause and *Inwardly Think Happiness*, then *Outwardly Act Happy* and *Receive a Happy Deposit*

Unhealthy Stimulus—Pause and *Inwardly Think Healthiness*, then *Outwardly Act Healthy* and *Receive a Healthy Deposit*

Ineffective Stimulus—Pause and *Inwardly Think Effectiveness*, then *Outwardly Act Effective* and *Receive an Excellence Deposit*

The goal of a *Life Leader* is to continually find ways to increase *Upward Life Gifts* and reduce *Downward Negative Drains*. The mind and meditation can be powerful tools to reverse a negative course. Exercise your freedom to choose!

> *Inward Living* **is paying attention to the inner nature of who you are and who you want to be.**

Inward Living is paying attention to the inner nature of who you are and who you want to be. It's *positive and effective* intentional living and knowing your *Inward Being*. The car you drive or the house you live in will not bring you *PH2E*—only what's inside you will. The quality of your life is determined by your *Inward Living*. Your *Inward* computer is an amazing thing. However, many of us haven't even found our life keyboard!

You don't just get, take, or grab your *PH2E*. You need to go through a process. For example, if you want to grow a flower, you need a seed, soil, water, sun, and then you have to nurture it. You need to pull out the weeds from around the plant that may be trying to choke out the stem. After a time, you will receive the flower, which is analogous to receiving your *Upward Living Life Gifts of PH2E*. You need to do the work; there are no shortcuts.

The inward journey is about finding your own fullness, something that no one else can take away.

—Deepak Chopra

PH2E

The Upward Life Gifts

Peacefulness, Happiness, Healthiness, and Excellence

Don't you wish your life was filled with *Peacefulness, Happiness, Healthiness, Excellence*, and being the best you can at whatever you enjoy?

These are *Upward Life Gifts* that come to you. You have no direct control in attaining them, but you have control over doing the things that will bring you these states of being. You cannot just choose to be any of them. However, you can choose to live a *positive and effective Inward* and *Outward* life, which will then provide you with the *Upward Living Life Gifts of all your PH2E's*.

Let's look deeper into the *Upward Living Life Gifts,* which are the byproducts when living *Inwardly* and *Outwardly* in a *positive and effective* intentional manner.

Peacefulness is the calm of life. Its opposite is anxiety. When you have a peaceful mind, you have clarity and can tap into all your background knowledge to make well-informed and decisive decisions. Some may say a peaceful life is a boring one; I disagree! If excitement and action are what you strive for and make you happy, then excitement and action are in the *Life Gift* of *Happiness*. One can have a peaceful mind and be stress-free and also enjoy excitement and action in life. It is also true that you can have peace in your life and yet not be happy, which is why we have—and also need—the next *Life Gift*: *Happiness*.

Happiness comes to us from within. You cannot go out and grab it and put it inside of yourself. Receiving it is the biggest challenge you face every day. You may think that obtaining certain things will make you happy. However, think about the things you've bought that you really wanted. How did those things make you feel when you received them? You were certainly happy, and the feeling may have lasted for a few days or a few weeks, but then what happened? You returned to your baseline, thinking about the next thing you believed would give you happiness. In psychology, this is known as the hedonic treadmill. According to the hedonic treadmill model, after receiving a rush of happiness, people return to their baseline happiness level, regardless of the event. In 1971, Brickman and Campbell first wrote about this concept and referred to it as a hedonic adaptation. In 1991, Michael Eysenck compared hedonic adaptation to a treadmill, which helped to explain the concept more clearly. Several studies have confirmed the treadmill concept. For example, a study involving interviews with lottery winners found their happiness did not permanently increase after winning. In fact, their happiness was similar to that of the control group.

Of course, everyone wants to increase true happiness and avoid the hedonic treadmill. Be a *Life Leader* by setting *Life Goals*, practicing *Inward* mindfulness, and putting more effort into your *Outward* relationships. This will help avoid the hedonic treadmill and increase true happiness.

Seneca offers a good perspective on true happiness.

> True happiness is to enjoy the present, without anxious dependence upon the future, not to amuse ourselves with either hopes or fears but to rest satisfied with what we have, which is sufficient, for he that is so wants nothing. The greatest blessings of mankind are within us and within our reach. A wise man is content with his lot, whatever it may be, without wishing for what he has not.

Healthiness is needed for us to do all the things we want to do. Our bodies are like ships on journeys. For the ship to reach its destination, all parts need to be in good working order, which takes consistent effort. Our bodies need to be the healthiest they can be to reach our goals and destination.

There are three areas we need to focus on that will significantly contribute to our *Healthiness*:

- Eating—how we nourish our body
- Exercising—how we move our body
- Sleeping—how we rest our body

Setting health goals is a necessity. Your health goals should be connected to your life purpose. What matters most to you now?

Goal setting will be discussed in Chapter 11, but don't wait. You can start now by taking small steps toward improving your health and focusing on the three areas of *Healthiness*.

Excellence in life surpasses ordinary standards. You have unique excellence within you and need to learn how to reveal it. You have *Inward* talents and skills of which you're not even aware. When I use the word *Excellence* in this book, I am referring to learning, your mind, your *Inward* knowledge, and competencies. You should continuously strive to improve on your *Excellence*. It's a process of improving, not perfecting, and a process of becoming better in all aspects of your life by your design, not by the design of others.

The key to keeping your balance is knowing when you've lost it.

—Anonymous

Balancing and Propelling your *PH2E*

Think of a four-blade boat propeller where each blade represents one of the *Upward Life Gifts*, your *PH2E*.

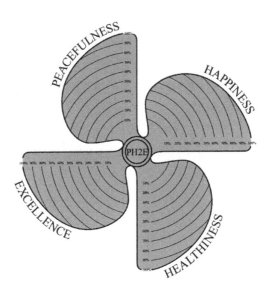

Each propeller blade is on a slight angle. When the blades turn, the propeller pushes the water away, which, in turn, creates the force that moves the boat. It may look like a simple piece of equipment; however, it has a complex design. Each blade has a precise curve, angle, special shape, and, most importantly, a calibrated balance so that it uses the least amount of energy to move the boat in the desired direction. We all have an *Inward Life Propeller* that pushes

We all have an *Inward Life Propeller* that pushes us through life, and it needs to be in good working order.

92

us through life, and it needs to be in good working order. Each blade of our *Inward Propeller* needs to be balanced and full to take us to our desired life destination.

Is your *PH2E Propeller* balanced?

When a boat propeller is balanced, the rotation makes a perfect circle, and the ability to complete a journey is optimized. On the other hand, a worn or damaged blade will create several negative issues on your journey. An unbalanced propeller can cause a steady vibration in the boat as it cuts through the water. Vibrations can then cause other parts of the boat to loosen, thereby creating several situations which lead to other problems. An unbalanced propeller also puts a strain on the engines, which must work harder to get the propeller's revolutions to the right levels. This will put more wear and tear on the motor. When a motor works harder than it is designed to do, it breaks down sooner and will need more frequent maintenance. An unbalanced propeller will also cause a boat to use much more fuel to get to the desired location.

To be *Life Leaders*, we need to strive to have our *PH2E* balanced. All of the *Upward Life Gifts of Peacefulness, Happiness, Healthiness, and Excellence* work as one and, when optimized, will begin to develop a *Dynamic Positive Culture*.

All of the *Upward Life Gifts of Peacefulness, Happiness, Healthiness, and Excellence* work as one and when optimized will create a *Dynamic Positive Culture*.

As Peter Drucker said, if you don't measure it, you can't improve it. Therefore, you need a baseline of where you currently are in your *PH2E*. Once you determine the area(s) where you need to improve, you can begin the process of propelling your *PH2E* to the highest level and enjoying your *Upward Life Gifts*. To assess your *PH2E*, think of each propeller blade as a scale. The scale ranges from 0% at the center of the blade to 100% at the outer edge. Your *PH2E* can be ranked on this scale and then shown on your *PH2E Propeller*. Notice not only what the level of each blade is but if each blade is in balance with the others. Are you more or less developed on one blade than on the others?

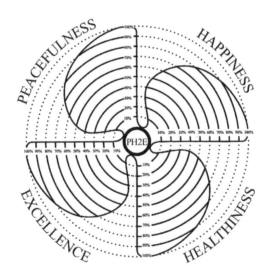

As an example of the negative impact of an unbalanced propeller, a 2019 Medscape report detailed the results of a recent survey of American doctors. A staggering 44% reported feeling burned out, while 15% reported experiencing high anxiety, feeling depressed, and having suicidal thoughts. According to the National Institute of Mental Health, that is more than double the frequency of the general US population who experience a significant episode of depression. Additionally, more than one doctor per day commits suicide, which is twice the rate of the general population and the highest rate among reported professions. The main reasons reported for depression and burn out were red tape, paperwork, feeling overworked, lack of control, and emphasis on profits over patients. Doctors reported the byproducts of those negative issues as unhappiness, anxiety, strain on relationships, and medical problems.

We all know that doctors reach the highest level of *Excellence* in their field based on many years of studying and training. In terms of their *PH2E*, surely, they would score extremely high in the area of *Excellence*. However, based on their responses, their *Peacefulness, Happiness,* and *Healthiness* would be very low. Their *PH2E Propeller* would look significantly unbalanced, as shown in the following illustration. In a boat, an unbalanced propeller will cause extreme vibrations, which will loosen screws and parts throughout the boat and put excessive strain on the motor resulting in damaged engine parts and eventually, an engine breakdown. What do you think the *PH2E Propeller* of the doctors reporting depression will do to them if not addressed? Based on the Medscape report, it appears that many doctors' *PH2E Propellers* are so damaged that even with a high *Excellence* blade, they are unable to function. Their *PH2E Propeller* may look like the following illustration:

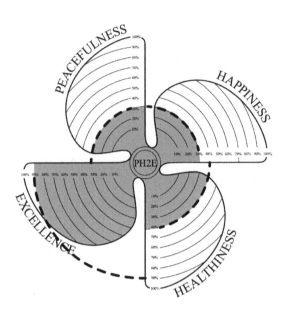

We need to maintain all of the blades on our *PH2E Propeller* to live a life of balance and fullness.

Let's discuss another example of an unbalanced propeller. If the shaded areas on your *PH2E Propeller* are unbalanced and at a low level, how well would you judge your life to be operating? This unbalanced propeller would cause serious vibrations to the boat/body and put extreme stress on the engine/life. With unbalanced *PH2E*, what damage would it do to your body, mind, and spirit? If your *PH2E Propeller* looked like the following illustration, you would need to do something about it. The first thing you should do is balance it. You shouldn't increase each blade in isolation. Instead, you should concentrate on balancing the low-level blades first, then increase and propel all the blades to its fullest level. Therefore, in this example, *Happiness* and

Excellence need to increase to balance it with *Peacefulness* and *Healthiness*. You must not neglect any of the *PH2E's*. Each of the blades has a serious impact on the others. On a boat, even a small balanced propeller will move a boat forward. However, a propeller with three full blades and one small one would damage the engine, not work correctly, and not move the boat forward at all. Balance your *PH2E* first!

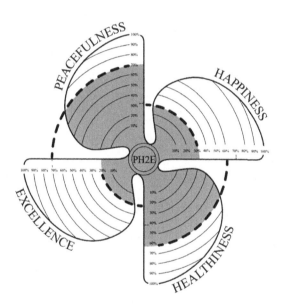

How is Your PH2E Life Propeller?

I suggest you take the *PH2E* Assessment on my website: www.PH2E.com. You will get a personalized score for *Peacefulness, Happiness, Healthiness, and Excellence* based on your perceptions. You will receive a personalized *PH2E Life Propeller,* which will show you areas for improvement.

After self-assessing your *PH2E Life Propeller*, take the lowest level blade or *Life Gift* and create a plan to increase it to the level of your other higher *Life Gifts*. Remember, we are first striving for balance. After each blade is balanced, we will work on increasing all the blades to their highest levels. By increasing your *PH2E*, you will become a *Life Leader*, leading yourself and others to begin to grow a *Dynamic Positive Culture of Peacefulness, Happiness, Healthiness, and Excellence.*

**Take the *PH2E* Assessment
at our website: www.PH2E.com
and get a personalized score for
*Peacefulness, Happiness, Healthiness,
and Excellence* based on your
own perceptions.**

Captain's Log for Chapter 4

Upward Life Gifts

Assessing & Propelling Your PH2E

Captain's Log:

Point 1   *Upward Living* comes to us based on our *Inward Living* and our *Outward Actions.* When we intentionally live and act in a *positive and effective* manner, we receive the *Upward Living Life Gifts of our PH2E.*

Point 2   *PH2E* may be thought of as a propeller with four blades, where each blade represents one of the four *Upward Living Life Gifts.* A boat propeller moves optimally when the blades are balanced. You will live most effectively when your *PH2E Propeller* is balanced.

Point 3   When your *PH2E* is optimized, you will have begun the process to develop a *Dynamic Positive Culture.*

Point 4   *Peacefulness* is the calm of life which helps give clarity to make well-informed, clear, and decisive decisions.

Point 5   *Happiness* comes from within. Setting life goals, practicing *Inward* mindfulness, and putting more effort into your *Outward* relationships will help increase true *Happiness.*

Point 6   *Healthiness* enables us to reach our goals and destination. There are three areas we need to focus on that will significantly contribute to our *Healthiness*: eating, exercise, and sleeping.

Point 7   *Excellence* is a process of learning and involves your mind, your *Inward Knowledge*, and your competencies. It's a process of improving, not perfecting.

Point 8   It is important to assess your current levels of *PH2E* honestly to have a baseline measure for improvement. Each of the *Upward Living Life Gifts* will be scored from 0% to 100%.

Point 9   The *PH2E* Assessment at www.PH2E.com will give you a personalized score for *Peacefulness, Happiness, Healthiness, and Excellence* and show your areas for improvement.

Teach to Learn

The best way to deepen your understanding and, at the same time, share and stimulate new conversations with others is to teach. Share what you have learned with a friend, family member, coworker, or anyone else who will listen. Teaching is, by far, the best way to deepen one's understanding of new insights and concepts. Take any of the Points in the Captain's Log or this chapter as a starting point for thought-provoking discussions.

New Daily Voyage:

Activity:

Think of people you look up to as role models and assess their *PH2E*. Are their propellers balanced? How can this inspire you?

Ask yourself:

In your life right now, which *Life Gift* is at the highest level? At the lowest? What are the immediate steps you can take to increase your lowest *Life Gift* or balance out the levels of your *PH2E*?

Chapter 5

What is a *Dynamic Positive Culture?*

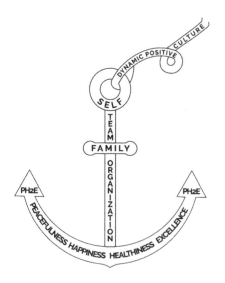

Spread love everywhere you go. Let no one ever come to you without leaving happier.

—Mother Teresa

Vincent filed his petition to become a United States citizen just before enlisting in the Navy. On August 9, 1918, he received his certificate of naturalization and was incredibly proud to be a citizen of the United States of America. He wrote to his family, sharing his Navy experiences and encouraging them to join him and his brother in America. In Italy, the family was proud of Vincent and decided to uproot themselves, grandparents included, to begin a new life in America. That decision would affect generations to come. Vincent's father, Dominick, and mother, Mary, along with his siblings, Joseph, Angelina, Thomas, and Catherine, started the process and, in 1920, finally arrived in America. The family was back together again!

In 1921, Vincent was honorably discharged from the 3rd Naval District in Brooklyn, New York. Vincent often said family is the most important and valuable gift in life. It provides a culture of support, learning, and love to everyone in the family and all of their close friends. He expected that when anyone entered their home, the guest would be treated like family and feel welcomed and taken care of. Vincent emphasized that everyone was always to be treated with respect. He believed if you want to be respected, you must respect others. Vincent created a foundation of love and respect and stressed the importance of having strong values. Through what he said as well as what he did, he created a *Dynamic Positive Culture* for himself, family, and anyone with whom he came in contact. Because of his example, everyone around him wanted to contribute to the *Dynamic Positive Culture* he created for the home and the family business.

Why a Dynamic Positive Culture?

Let's start by defining a *Dynamic Positive Culture*. To begin with, I define *culture* as a way of life and symbolic communication. In any culture, individuals' beliefs, behaviors, values, and symbols are connected to a set of shared ideals. I coined the word *"SelfCulture"* to describe your personal culture. Your *SelfCulture* is defined by your *Inward* and *Outward Living*. A positive *SelfCulture* is when a person's beliefs, behaviors, values, and symbols are in sync and aligned; in other words, when your *Inward Intentions* match your *Outward Actions*. Developing and understanding one's *SelfCulture* is a critical *Inward Life Anchor* that will be discussed in Chapter 11.

The goal is to develop a *Dynamic Positive Culture* in every environment of your life – *self, family, team, and/or organization*, which I refer to as your *4 Life Cultures*.

When identifying the culture for a *family, team, or organization* (*FTO*), you should be able to observe and see and feel it in artifacts hung on the walls, the physical layout of the rooms, the dress code, the manner in which people address each other, the smell and feel of the place, its emotional intensity, and other phenomena. If

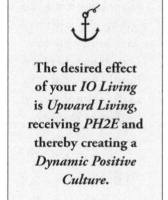

The desired effect of your *IO Living* is *Upward Living*, receiving *PH2E* and thereby creating a *Dynamic Positive Culture*.

the culture is effective, uplifting, and positive, you will feel and be propelled into one or more of the *PH2E's*.

The desired effect of your *IO Living* is *Upward Living*, receiving *PH2E*, and thereby creating a *Dynamic Positive Culture*. However, if your *IO Living* is *negative and ineffective*, you will produce a *Toxic Negative Culture*, described as *Downward Life Living*. In addition, if your *IO Living* is *neutral and mediocre*, you will produce a *Static Neutral Culture* described as *Wayward Life Living.* This will be explained using the *IO Living Culture Continuum* model, as described in Chapter 6.

A *Dynamic Positive Culture* for *family, team, and organization* (*FTO*) is when a group of people has a clear destination, and all members are heading toward it in a safe, enjoyable, and effective manner. The culture is guided by true north, universal, and natural principles where everyone has a mindset of continuously improving their mind, body, and heart. A leadership culture has integrity and inspires trust. A *dynamic* culture is energetic, lively, active, spirited, vibrant, compelling, and powerful. A *positive* culture is optimistic, confident, welcoming, encouraging, upbeat, supportive, and friendly.

A *Dynamic Positive Culture* for *family, team, and organization* is when a group of people have a clear destination and all members are heading toward it in a safe, enjoyable, and effective manner.

When others are in the presence of an individual who is radiating a *Dynamic Positive SelfCulture*, there will be high levels of trust. Others view you as having high integrity because your words and *Outward Actions* are consistent. Therefore, a *Dynamic Positive Culture* radiates an energetic, vibrant, optimistic, welcoming, supportive, unspoken, and symbolic communication. When you step into a *Dynamic Positive Culture,* you immediately sense an extremely high level of character and competence and feel welcomed.

Every organization, school, or business functions as it does because of the relationships within it. Therefore, if you want to improve the organization, school, or business, you need to improve the culture by enhancing the relationships within it. A dynamic leadership culture includes the knowledge, skills, tools, flexibility, and emotional security to counter any challenges that may arise and act to address them. The culture allows the relationships within it to flourish in ways that increase teamwork and synergy and enable the organization to reach new, unimagined heights. Dynamic cultures of leadership are based on collaboration and trust, not competition and fear.

When dynamic leadership is established, an organization becomes a learning community, continuously improving the mind, body, and heart. Organizations that grow a *Dynamic Positive Culture* of leadership promote shared decision-making and release the pressure to act individually in a vacuum. They help all stakeholders adjust to inevitable change by giving them the proper tools to make the adjustments necessary for the challenges and changes ahead. Dynamic leadership recognizes that everyone—every

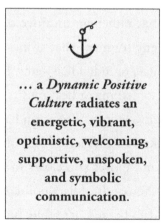

... a *Dynamic Positive Culture* radiates an energetic, vibrant, optimistic, welcoming, supportive, unspoken, and symbolic communication.

single stakeholder on an organizational chart—has unique talents. Each individual's talents must be nurtured and celebrated, and only when those talents are exercised is authentic, dynamic leadership realized.

In a *Dynamic Positive Culture* of leadership, everyone listens to one other, and trust expands. Empathic listening positively affects the culture and transforms it to a higher level that increases and improves relationships and quality of life in the organization. When that occurs, and an atmosphere of collaboration and trust embodies the organization, no topic is off-limits or too difficult to discuss. There are no longer any elephants in the room.

How do you know when you have a Dynamic Positive Culture?

When you have a *Dynamic Positive Culture*, you can feel it. Eugene Gendlin used the term "felt sense" to describe a bodily feeling or aura that isn't easy to describe in words. It's an *Inward* deep-down level of awareness. It's not a mental experience but rather, an intuitive one—an understanding of a person or environment that comes all at once, not based on a series of data or individual items. It comes in the same way that you taste something or hear music. It's a big feeling that is difficult to put into words. When you have a *Dynamic Positive Culture*, people know it. It's a big, unspoken, embodied feeling that uplifts you and moves you closer to higher levels of *PH2E*. There may be thousands of data points, but do not focus on any one piece of data because it's a big, bold, all-at-once feeling. When the aura feels positive and hard to label and put into words, you are most likely leading and living in a *Dynamic Positive Culture*. I was profoundly moved while I read Gendlin's book, *Focusing* and "felt sense" was defined. It can be illustrated by the following example.

Think of two people that have played a major role in your life. Let's call them Rose and Barney. You can substitute the names of the people you are thinking of as we illustrate "felt sense." Let your mind think about each of these important people in your life. Go back and forth, then dwell on one for a bit and think of the aura of Rose. When Rose steps into the room, what are the feelings you get as you think "all about Rose?" Do this now. Then switch to Barney and notice the completely different aura you feel. The "all about Barney" thoughts make you feel completely different. Both are positive but quite different.

Rose and Barney are both creating a culture in different ways. When you think of Rose, you are not thinking of all the positive data points about her and then putting them together to *Formulate* a feeling. You are not thinking about how tall she is, what her features look like, the pitch of her voice, or what food she likes. There are thousands of data points, but when you think of her, in an instant, the "all about Rose" culture is present, and you feel it in your body. That feeling is *Upward Living*. It's a natural law or what I refer to as the *IO Living Effect*. For Rose, the effect of her living a positive, nurturing, and effective life is *Upward Living*. This natural by-product of *Upward Living* leads to a *Dynamic Positive Culture*. In this case, Rose's *SelfCulture* is at the highest levels of the *PH2E*.

Let's continue. Think of yourself and how you felt talking to Rose, and then change to thinking about Barney. Didn't your insides change? You can feel the different sense within you. Think of being in a room with Barney and having a conversation when

Rose comes into the room. You now have the "felt sense" of both Rose and Barney.

What changed? The changes didn't come about by thinking but instead were driven by your feelings and their culture. Gendlin states that the senses that drove the changes are not emotions. They have emotional components but are bigger and much more complex than emotions and not easy to describe in words. This is what I call, their *SelfCulture*!

There are no shortcuts leading to a culture like Rose and Barney have that embodies the highest form of *PH2E*. It can only be created by living a *positive and effective* intentional life guided by natural laws, which will then produce *Upward Living,* thereby creating a *Dynamic Positive Culture.*

Culture is one thing, and varnish is another.

—Ralph Waldo Emerson

In 1914, 28 men and 69 sled dogs were trapped in the Antarctic's treacherous and uncharted seas. Their ship, the *Endurance,* was frozen and drifting with no control in the coldest climate on earth. Their lives depended on the leadership of their captain, Sir Ernest Shackleton. Their plight was epic, and their survival a testament to the capabilities of teamwork in the harshest conditions imaginable and the strong *Dynamic Positive Culture.* The expedition was undertaken to be the first land crossing of the Antarctic continent from the Weddell Sea to the Ross Sea, encompassing a total distance of 1,800 miles. Instead, the journey turned into over two years of nightmarish challenges requiring heroism from all involved and ended up one of the most amazing survival stories of all time.

Under the leadership of Sir Ernest Shackleton, the entire crew kept a *Dynamic Positive Culture,* which ultimately saved all 28 lives on the *Endurance.* On their journey through the Weddell Sea, Shackleton described the *Outward Environment* as a minefield of icebergs. Eventually, the ship became trapped and surrounded by ice. However, the crew's spirits remained high. The captain and the crew were well prepared for the journey and potential hardships and even managed to relax by playing soccer on the iceberg surrounding the ship. They decided to wait for the ice to break so the ship could continue on its journey in open waters.

They were 1,200 miles from civilization with no communication and no hope of outside help. However, the ice kept thickening, and after nine months, the pressure increased so much that it crushed the ship, and Shackleton gave the order to abandon it. He told the crew that they would head to the nearest supply depot 345 miles away. They headed out, but the ice blocked their path in every direction. *Inwardly,* he felt it was highly unlikely that they would survive, but *Outwardly* he was a strong leader and stayed positive. For the next six months, they camped on ice and traveled slowly. They hunted seals and penguins, but eventually, food got harder to find. Amazingly, Shackleton kept the culture of the crew positive.

They had two 22-foot small boats that they pushed on sleds with them. They made it to some waters, and Shackleton ordered the boats to sail to the uninhabited Elephant Island. They made it to the island, and the crew, which had not been on land for 16 months, was lightheaded but elated. Their only hope now was a boat journey to civilization.

Shackleton planned to sail 800 miles northeast to South Georgia, a dangerous voyage in a small, open boat. Shackleton and five other men left 22 men on the island and set sail into the dangerous waters to reach help. For 17 days in their small boat, they battled the *Outward* fury of the ocean waves and snowstorms. The weather was unstable, and the men didn't think they were going to make it. However, Shackleton kept the crew in good spirits and had a gift of being positive under the most challenging circumstances. He always adapted to the *Outward* conditions.

After 17 days, they finally saw the coast and found a safe harbor to land, but then realized they were on the wrong side of the island. The whaling station was on the other side, and to cross the island, they would have to pass through glaciers and mountains that no human had ever crossed. After a treacherous three-day journey, they made it to the whaling station. For the next three days, Shackleton and his men acquired supplies, a ship, and new crew members and left the whaling station to return to his men on Elephant Island.

It took three months to get back to the island, and when he arrived, all 22 men were alive. Theirs was an amazing journey that, without the *Dynamic Positive Culture,* would have surely ended in the loss of life. Shackleton had to *Evaluate* the situation constantly, *Calculate* and process the data collected, and *Formulate* a plan. He then had to *Communicate* his plan to his crew in a *positive and effective* manner. Lastly, he *Navigated* the plan. Each time he reached his destination, he re-evaluated the situation, and the cycle continued. I call this the *Life Map Cycle* for *family, team, and organization* (FTO). Throughout the book, the letters *FTO* are used to represent the words, *family, team, and organization*.

LIFE MAP CYCLE—FTO

We introduced the *Life Map Cycle* for you to use as an individual in Chapter 2. In this section, we will extend the *Life Map Cycle* for use with your *family, team, and/or organization* (*FTO*). As you will see, there is an additional dimension in this cycle—*Communicate*. After *Formulating* a plan, it must be *Communicated* to all members in the *FTO*. When the *Life Map Cycle* is used as an individual, and you have *Formulated* a plan to execute, there is no need to *Communicate* it to yourself since you have developed and understand the plan.

With *family, teams, and organizations*, the *Communication* stage is critical. It allows everyone to have a common understanding of the next steps to be undertaken. It's important that everyone in the group understands the plan and knows the language. The terminology related to the plan should be shared, so there is a *Common Language* among all members in the *FTO*. *Common Language* speeds progress and creates a bond for the group. *Create Common Language* is *Outward Life Anchor 9*, which will be discussed in Chapter 12. Many times, in *FTOs*, the *Communication* stage is neglected or executed poorly, which ultimately has a negative effect on the entire team during the *Navigate* stage.

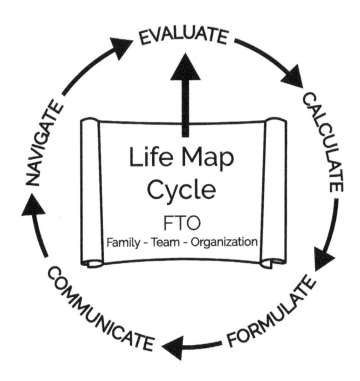

The Life Map Cycle FTO consists of Evaluate - Calculate - Formulate - Communicate - Navigate

The *Life Map Cycle FTO* is a process for *IO* and *OI Life Living* to develop a *Dynamic Positive Culture* in a *family, team, and organization*. It will help the group understand the reality of the situation and create a plan to execute. When each group member sees something, reads something, or experiences something, they may have their own opinion or *Life Map*. There needs to be a shared *Life Vision, Daily Mission,* and *Life Goals* in an *FTO*. Therefore, to get the team on the same page, each member must first *Inwardly Evaluate* the problem to be solved and try to understand it through a clear lens. The team needs to *Inwardly* take in the raw data without bias. This is a recording stage, like filming a movie about the issue.

Next, each member—individually or as a group—takes the raw data received and *Calculates* it by creating different scenarios with it, thinking and developing outside the box solutions. The *Calculate* stage should not be rushed. This is a critical stage where members of the *FTO Inwardly* individually or *Outwardly* as a group define and organize the data and begin to draw conclusions on what was heard, seen, or experienced.

Then, *Formulation* of a plan begins with the group. Based on the extensive work during the *Calculate* stage, a conclusion and plan are formed. Next, the plan is *Communicated* with all group members and anyone else in the *FTO* to keep the group together on track using a common map. How effective would a team be if everyone was following different maps? Lastly, the group will put into action the agreed-upon plan and *Outwardly Navigate* it in the world.

As the *family, team, or organization Outwardly Navigates* the actions, the group should be *Inwardly Evaluating* their actions and getting input from the people executing the plan. Then the process begins again. It's a continuous *Life Map Cycle,* which will grow the *family, team, and organizational* culture into a dynamic, positive, and successful group working together based on the same *Life Map.*

Life Map Cycle FTO
Simplified with Descriptions

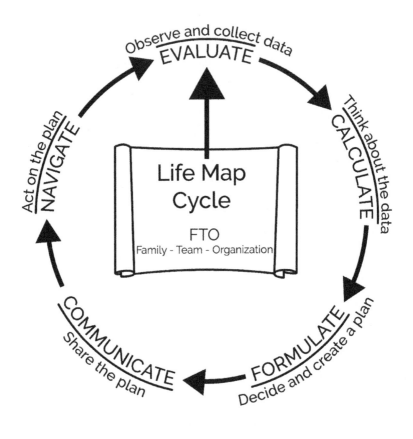

Communication is culture and culture is communication.

—Edward Hall

Your *SelfCulture* and the culture of your *family, team, and/or organization* are created by your verbal, nonverbal, and symbolic communication with every member of a group. In addition, how everyone communicates with each other defines your culture. How does the cultural environment feel in your life? *Outward Living* is all about communication with others. As you will read in Chapter 12, there are *Outward Anchors* focused on *positive and effective* intentional communication and creating an environment that will provide *Upward Living* for everyone, thereby moving toward a *Dynamic Positive Culture.* How would you describe your *SelfCulture* and the culture of your *family, team, and/or organization* ? Is it *Toxic, Static,* or *Dynamic?* In Chapter 6, we will discuss your *Inward* and *Outward Living* and the continuum of cultures that we all live in. By continually improving your *Life Map*s and living *Outwardly* guided by natural laws, you will accelerate your *Life Ship* full steam ahead toward your life destinations in a *Dynamic Positive Culture.*

Life Map Cycle FTO with Descriptions

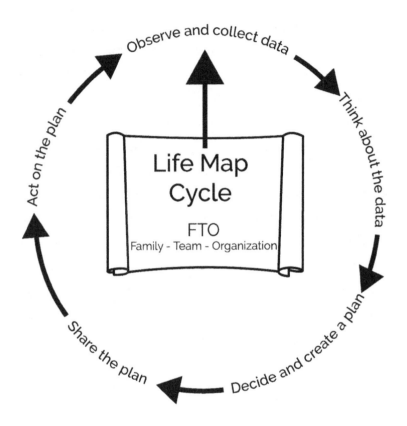

Captain's Log for Chapter 5

What is a Dynamic Positive Culture?

Captain's Log:

Point 1   A *Dynamic Positive Culture* for *self, family, teams, and organizations* occurs when all members have a shared, clear destination and are heading in the same direction in a safe, enjoyable, and effective manner. The culture is guided by true north, universal, natural law principles where everyone shares a mindset of continuous improvement.

Point 2   When a culture is dynamic, it is energetic, lively, active, spirited, vibrant, compelling, and powerful. A positive culture is optimistic, confident, welcoming, encouraging, upbeat, supportive, and friendly.

Point 3   The relationships within a culture are the most important piece of its functioning. If you want to improve the culture, you need to work on the relationships. Build a high trust culture based on collaboration and trust, not on competition and fear.

Point 4   The *Life Map Cycle for FTO's (family, teams, and organizations)* is similar to the *Life Map Cycle for Self* that was introduced in Chapter 2, with one major difference—the incorporation of the *Communicate* step.

Point 5   When you are leading a group, the *Communicate* step is a critical one because after you have *Formulated* a plan to execute, communicating it will allow everyone to gain a shared understanding of the reality of the situation and the need to implement the plan in a specific fashion.

Point 6   For *families, teams, and organizations*, a group may take in the data (*Evaluate*), then individually or as a group define and organize the data (*Calculate*). Next, they work to create a plan together (*Formulate*) and then ensure it is communicated to all members of the group and anyone else who is involved in or will be affected by the plan (*Communicate*). Finally, the group puts the plan into action (*Navigate*).

Point 7   The *Life Map Cycle* for *FTO* does not end with the *Navigate* step. Rather, it is cyclical, and the next step involves evaluating both *Inwardly* and *Outwardly* (based on input from people involved in the execution), and thus, the process begins again.

Teach to Learn

The best way to deepen your understanding and, at the same time, share and stimulate new conversations with others is to teach. Share what you have learned with a friend, family member, coworker, or anyone else who will listen. Teaching is, by far, the best way to deepen one's understanding of new insights and concepts. Take any of the Points in the Captain's Log or this chapter for thought-provoking discussions.

New Daily Voyage:

Activity:

Think of an initiative that was unsuccessful that involved a *family, team, or organization.* Can you identify where the breakdown in the *Life Map Cycle* was?

Ask yourself:

How can I improve the decision-making process with my *family, team, or organization* by incorporating the *Life Map Cycle*?

Chapter 6

The Life Living Continuum

Are You Living IOU, IOW, or IOD?

Only two sailors, in my experience, never ran aground.
One never left port and the other was an atrocious liar.

—Don Bamford

Family was the most important thing in Vincent's life. In later years, the stories he told all centered around family and the importance of tradition, customs, a sense of history, and a source of love and support. In 1925, Vincent married Maria in a double wedding ceremony with Vincent's sister Angelina marrying Maria's brother Anthony. Business was thriving for Vincent and his brother Sam. They wanted to expand the fruit and vegetable business, but the city was evolving fast, with farms sold and buildings constructed rapidly. With fewer farms and competition increasing, Vincent and Sam evaluated the situation. They decided to move to Long Island, where there were more farms to obtain produce and less competition from other merchants. So, in 1926, Vincent and Sam bought two lots on a main road in a small town named Baldwin. They each built a small building with a store on the main level and a place to live on the second floor. They opened a fruit and vegetable store in one of the buildings and rented the other first-floor store for additional income. Vincent was a positive and productive businessperson, always forward-thinking to determine the next move to improve business and his family members' lives. He said, "The day you stop thinking of ways to improve is the day you decline."

Vincent and Maria started a family and raised three sons—Dominick, Bartolo, and Salvatore—and one daughter, Virginia. Vincent's father, mother, and siblings also moved to Baldwin. Vincent's leadership created a *Dynamic Positive Culture* not only for himself but for his entire family. Everyone received the *Upward Life Gifts* and enjoyed their new voyage for many years to come.

Stop looking forward to things, look inward instead.

—Kamand Kojouri

IO Living Culture Continuum

Is your SelfCulture, Family, Team, or Organization Culture <u>*Dynamic and Positive*</u>, <u>*Static and Neutral*</u>, *or* <u>*Toxic and Negative?*</u>

The *IO Living Culture Continuum* displays the byproduct of your *Inward* and *Outward Living*.

Review this comprehensive continuum carefully.

It contains:

- The three levels of *IO Living*:
  Upward Living — IOU Life Leadership
  Wayward Living — IOW Life Drifting
  Downward Living — IOD Life Sinking

- The actions associated with each *IO Living*:
  Positive and Effective
  Neutral and Mediocre
  Negative and Ineffective

- What you receive from each *IO Living*:
  Life Gifts
  Life Impassivities
  Life Drains

- The byproducts for each *IO Living*:

  Life Gifts: PH2E—Peacefulness - Happiness - Healthiness - Excellence

  Life Impassivities: Apathy - Indifference - Unfitness - Mediocrity

  Life Drains: Anxiety - Unhappiness - Unhealthiness - Ineffectiveness.

- The culture that evolves from each *IO Living*:

  Dynamic Positive Culture

  Static Neutral Culture

  Toxic Negative Culture

Are you living a *positive and effective* intentional life, leading to *Upward Living*, and navigating toward a *Dynamic Positive Culture*? Or more times than not, are you *Downward Living* or *Wayward Living*? Are you feeling like you are in a rut, living by default day to day, drifting, creating a *mediocre* or even a *toxic* culture? Intentional *positive and effective* *Inward* and *Outward Living* results in moving to a higher level on the *IO Living Culture Continuum* for each of the four *PH2E Upward Living Life Gifts*.

You have 100% control on how you act and live *Inwardly* and *Outwardly*, however the byproducts or culture it creates act on you.

The *IO Living Culture Continuum* illustration shows the byproducts and culture of *Inward* and *Outward (IO) Living*.

When your *IO Living* is *positive and effective,* you are *Upward Living* and will receive the *Life Gifts* and enjoy the byproducts of *PH2E. IOU Living* will assist you in navigating toward a *Dynamic Positive Culture* for *yourself, family, team, or organization.* This level of living is considered *IOU Life Leadership.*

Next on the *IO Living Culture Continuum* is *Wayward Living,* which is living a life that is *neutral* and *mediocre* where the *Life Impassivities of Apathy, Indifference, Unfitness, and Mediocrity* are received. *IOW Living* creates a *Static Neutral Culture.* This level of living is considered *IOW Life Drifting.*

IO LIVING CULTURE CONTINUUM

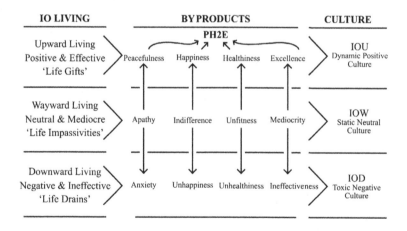

Lastly, on the lowest level of the *IO Living Culture Continuum* is *Downward Living,* which is when one lives a life that is *negative and ineffective* and then receives *Downward Life Drains of Anxiety, Unhappiness, Unhealthiness, and Ineffectiveness. IOD Living* creates a *Toxic Negative Culture*. This level of living is considered *IOD Life Sinking*.

You have 100% control of your *Inward Thinking* and *Outward Actions*; however, the byproducts or culture it creates act on you. The byproducts you receive are based on your *Inward* and *Outward Living*, which then determine your culture. *The IO Living Culture Continuum* displays the cultures that are created based on the byproducts we receive. You can't go out and grab the byproducts of the culture; they come to you based on your *Inward Thinking* and *Outward Actions*. If you want to change your byproducts or your culture, you need to start with your *Inward Living* then work on your *Outward Actions*. You will always be presented with obstacles during your *Life Journey*. However, *IOU Living* will provide you with the tools to get your ship back on course. Examine your *Inward Life Map*s and continuously strive for improvements and accuracy. Then, act *Outwardly* in a *positive and effective* intentional manner in accordance with your *Inward Thinking*. When you begin to do that, you will see the byproducts move to the highest level of *PH2E*.

At one time or another, we all receive *Life Impassivities* and *Life Drains*. *The IO Living Culture Continuum* is a mental model that will help organize your thoughts and *Inward* and *Outward Living*. It gives you a baseline of where you

The IO Living Culture Continuum is a mental model that will help organize your thoughts and *Inward* and *Outward Living*. It gives you a baseline of where you are and where you need to go.

are and where you need to go. The purpose of the *Continuum* is to provide a tool for intentional living when you are feeling negative, ineffective, neutral, or mediocre. The antidote to *Downward Life Drains* is living a *positive and effective* life. The *12 Essential Life Anchors,* explained in Chapters 11 & 12, will provide a framework for living *positively and effectively* so you can take control of your life.

Reaffirm your *Life Vision, Life Purpose*, and *Life Goals.* Having a purpose that evokes positive emotions is the way to undo lingering negative emotions, according to Barbara Fredrickson, an associate professor of psychology at the University of Michigan. In addition, Fredrickson's broaden-and-build theory suggests that positive thinking expands mindsets to deal with an array of negative issues.

Further, positive thinking broadens *Inward Thinking* and builds resources, such as resilience to combat *Outward* negative pressures, creating an *Upward* spiral moving closer toward the highest level of *PH2E.*

IOU LIVING PRINCIPLE
Inward - Outward - Upward

IOU LIVING
POSITIVE & EFFECTIVE

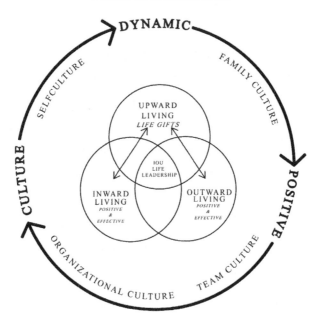

IOU Living is focusing *Inwardly* on positive things. It's a mindset of what is possible, what you can do, what is working, and the people who are with you and celebrating your achievements.

Life Leadership is living intentionally by your design and not the design of others, regularly receiving the benefits of *Upward Life Living* and receiving the *Life Gifts of PH2E*.

The goal, *IOU Life Leadership,* is shown in the center of the *IOU Living Principle Model* above. When living a life both

Inwardly and *Outwardly* in a *positive and effective* manner, the byproduct will be *Upward Living,* and you will thereby receive the *Upward Living Life Gifts of PH2E.* When this happens, as shown in the *IOU Living Principle Model,* you begin to navigate toward a *Dynamic Positive Culture* (shown on the outer edge) for yourself or when practiced with others in your *family, team, or organization.*

IOU Living is focusing *Inwardly* on positive things. It's a mindset of what is possible, what you can do, what is working, and the people who are with you and celebrating your achievements.

IOW LIVING PRINCIPLE
Inward - Outward - Wayward

IOW LIVING
NEUTRAL & MEDIOCRE

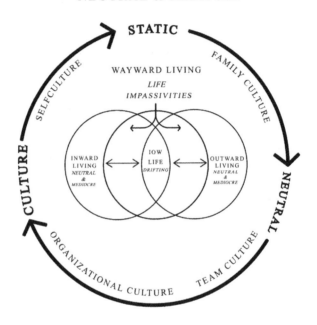

IOW Living stands for *Inward Outward Wayward Living*. *Wayward* is defined as "turning or changing irregularly." To live a *Wayward* life is living unintentionally with no clear *Life Vision, Daily Mission, Life Principles, Life Values*, and *Life Goals*. Therefore, you are living an irregular life. Your life may go up or down, or you may be moving straight ahead with no clear *Life Goal* and destination. This is *IOW Life Drifting*, as noted in the center of the illustration. You think everything is fine, and you are moving forward day by day, but, in fact, life is merely passing you by. Are you contributing in life, or are you just getting through each day? Are you living your life by default with an unbalanced propeller and little to no control of your ship? *Wayward Living* is unpredictable; you may feel like you are *drifting through life*, letting the tides, winds, and currents sometimes take you to the lower ends of life.

To live a *Wayward* life is living unintentionally with no clear *Life Vision, Daily Mission, Life Principles, Life Values,* and *Life Goals.*

Wayward Living results in receiving *Life's Impassivities*. You have not been invigorated in a long time. It seems as if you're living your life by default. Things are automatic, and you are on autopilot—you wake up, go to work, come home exhausted, watch TV, go to bed, and then it all begins again the next day. You have created a *Static Neutral Culture*: It can be difficult getting out of living a *Wayward Life*.

- You're neither stressed nor peaceful but rather apathetic.
- You're neither unhappy nor happy but rather indifferent.
- You're neither unhealthy nor healthy, but rather, simply feel unfit.
- You're neither ineffective nor effective, but rather, mediocre.

    (See these byproducts from *IOW Living* in the *IO Culture Continuum* illustration)

IOD LIVING PRINCIPLE
Inward - Outward - Downward

IOD LIVING
NEGATIVE & INEFFECTIVE

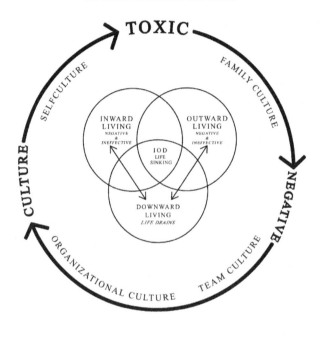

Some people are constantly scanning the world for things that are wrong or need fixing, which will ultimately lead to *IOD Living*. It's a mindset of continually thinking about what you don't have, what you need, what you cannot do, the people who are holding you back, and continually rehashing your setbacks.

Don't sell yourself short. You are worthy of having an *IOU Life*, but many times we limit our aims and quit our goals too soon. As soon as it gets difficult, we look for a way out.

When constant negativity and ineffectiveness are pressing onto you, and you let it get to you with no counter positive strategies, it's considered *IOD Living*. It can be *Life Draining* and creates a *Toxic Negative Culture*. You are living an *IOD Life Sinking* life.

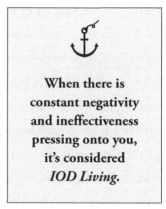

When there is constant negativity and ineffectiveness pressing onto you, it's considered **IOD Living.**

The Cistco Company was preparing for the annual presentation of its new products, which kicks off the new season. The morning started with a training on a new program that everyone would be using for the upcoming year. Several books, diagrams, and handbooks were distributed to each staff member. One part of the new program was an online resource that provided access to everyone's accounts. The facilitator explained the program, reviewed each handout, and shared the capabilities of this exciting new adventure for the Cistco teams.

The presenter distributed each employee's online username and password; however, there was a technical problem, and they couldn't access the online accounts. He asked the teams to take a 10-minute break as he tried to get the online resource to work. When the teams returned, he was still experiencing difficulty, so instead of wasting precious time, he decided he had plenty of other items to review. He described the online section without actually showing the technology, explaining that he would try to resolve the issue later in the day. The morning training was completed, lunch was served, and the afternoon task was for each team to meet in their departments, to discuss what they learned in the morning, and to prepare for the new season.

The Cistco manager walked around to observe each team's progress. The Team A leader shared the issues from the morning session, namely that they could not get online. The manager asked another Team A member, and that person shared another version of the same issue about not being able to get online. Each team member continued to offer negative comments, which affected their progress and thereby perpetuated their ineffectiveness.

Team A wasted valuable time on something over which they had no control. Their team culture was *Toxic* and *Ineffective*. Rather than focusing on reviewing the mounds of material in front of them, they chose to continue to lament the negative. It's a skill to put aside things you have no control over and instead concentrate on what you have 100% control over. Cistco's online issue is an example of an *Outward Inward* (*OI*) issue. In other words, it is an *Outward* issue coming to your *Inward Life*. You have no control over *OI* issues; however, you have 100% control over your *Inward* reactions to them. *OI* issues come to you from the *Outward World,* many times without warning. *OI* issues will happen to all of us every day for the rest of our lives.

You have no control over *OI* issues; however, you have 100% control over your *Inward* reactions to them.

Team B was also present in the morning meeting. Upon entering the room to check in with them, the manager could feel, hear, and almost taste their energy. The team members organized the material into various sections pertinent to their department. One member was using chart paper and drawing a timeline for implementation. Another team member was taking notes documenting the discussions. The team was clearly positive and working effectively, thereby creating a *Dynamic Positive Team Culture*. No one mentioned the morning issues. The manager was curious about their reaction to the lack of online access, so he asked them about it. They responded they were aware of the problem and accepted that the tech department would take care of it and put a solution in place. In this environment, the "felt sense" (as discussed in Chapter 5) was clear that this team was *Upward Living* and moving higher on the *PH2E* continuum.

You always have a choice about how you react to *OI* issues in life. You have 100% control of your *Inward Thinking* and 100% control of your *Outward Actions*. It may not be easy, but it's your choice to create either a *Dynamic Positive, Static Neutral,* or *Toxic Negative Culture*. Your actions for *yourself, your family, your team, or organization* will be cogs in the wheel that determine how the culture is defined.

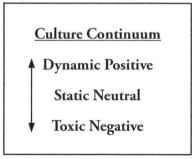

137

By practicing *IOU Life Leadership* and internalizing *The 12 Essential Life Anchors*, the byproduct of the *Upward Gifts* will provide you with a new outlook on life. It's an opportunity to rediscover yourself and simplify your thinking to begin to navigate toward a *Dynamic Positive Culture*. It all starts with you and your *Inward Being*.

You save yourself or you remain unsaved.

—Alice Sebold

THE 3 LIFE PRESERVING DIMENSIONS

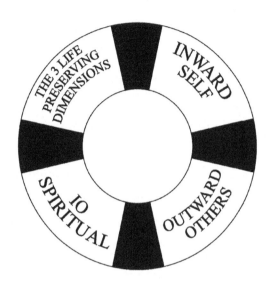

When you are *IOD Living*, spiraling downward, your ship is sinking, and constantly feeling negative *Downward Life Drains*, where do you turn to reverse this? When you are *IOW Living*, listless and drifting, what do you do to restart your engines and continue your journey?

There are *3 Life Preserving Dimensions* that can reverse course of your draining *PH2E* and move you in a better direction to receive *Upward Life Positive Gifts*.

There are *3 Life Preserving Dimensions* that can reverse course of your *PH2E* draining and move you in a better direction to receive *Upward Life Positive Gifts*.

1. **Inward Self Dimension**: This is your go-to *Life Preserver*. You always have it on hand as it is your *Inward Self.* You have all the tools to receive positive *Life Gifts* by reviewing your *Inward Life Anchors*. In the next chapter, we will discuss the many *Inward Life Anchors* we have, and in Chapter 11, we will examine *The 6 Essential Inward Life Anchors* that are foundational for *IOU Living*. If you were in a boat and off-course or drifting into an unknown area, what would you do? Check your location, start your engines, and get back on course. You would confirm your destination, take the captain's wheel, and turn the rudder toward the correct direction. In life, when you are off-course and drifting, you need to reaffirm your purpose and vision and get back on track to your destination or goals. The tools are within you; you simply have to take the time and utilize your *Inward* great gifts.

2. **Outward Others Dimension:** This *Life Preserver* is *Outward Others*, which may be a family member or a friend to support you when faced with adversity. You cannot depend that *Outward Others* will always be there, but there will be opportunities in your life when your *Outward* relationships will be there to support you. Remember that you have no control over anything related to *Outward Living* and relationships, but you can *Inspire* and *Influence* others. However, you always have 100% full control over your *Inward Living*. We should always be ready to be a *Life Saver* for others. If we carry that mindset, the world would be a better place where there

were *Life Preservers* thrown constantly to each other with the byproduct of receiving the *Upward Life Gifts*, thus moving us closer to higher levels of our *PH2E*.

3. **Inward-Outward Spiritual Dimension:** The *Spiritual Dimension* is an *Inward-Outward* relationship through meditation, prayer, nature, or music. It's a personal dimension for each person. Spiritual support can come in many forms and can have a major *Inward* impact on your confidence and motivation to solve a problem.

When *IOD* sets in and you begin to feel *Downward Life Drains* to any of your *Upward Life Gifts of PH2E*, your go-to *Life Saver* is always yourself, your *Inward Self Dimension*. Don't let those negative thoughts play over and over in your mind. Throw them "overboard!" You have a *SelfCulture, Life Vision*, and *Life Goals* that make up your *Inward Being*. You are unique to the world and have special skills and talents, and you have everything you need to receive the *Upward Life Gifts of PH2E*.

Walt Disney was fired from the *Kansas City Star* in 1919 because, according to his editor, he "lacked imagination and had no good ideas." Steven Spielberg was rejected by the University of Southern California School of Cinematic Arts multiple times. Sir Isaac Newton's mother pulled him out of school as a boy to run the family farm; he failed miserably. As a child, Albert Einstein had some difficulty communicating and learning traditionally. Vincent Van Gogh sold only one painting—"The Red Vineyard"—in his life, and the sale occurred just months before his death. Two years after Thomas Edison was fired from Western Union, pursuing inventing full-time, he received his first patent.

There are countless other examples of individuals faced with adversities, which could result in *Downward Negative Drains*. However, with a clear vision of what they wanted to accomplish and persistence, they turned to their *Inward Self Dimension* and overcame their obstacles. You can do the same! Any negative labels put on you by others only have the power to drain you if you let them. Their negative projection on you has no power; your response to it is your reality. You have no control over negative communications from the *Outward World*, but you have 100% control over your *Inward* reactions to them.

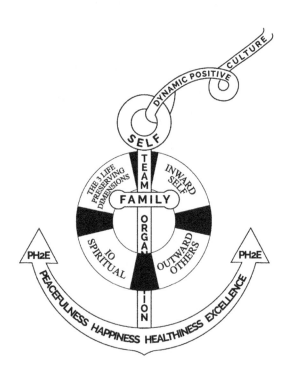

Between any *Outward* stimulus and your *Inward* response, there is a space, and in that space lies your *PH2E*. So, the real challenge lies in your *Inward Living*. It's imperative that we constantly and intentionally examine and strengthen our *Inward Self*, so we are ready for the challenges that inevitably come our way as we sail along our *Life Journey*. When a *Downward Life Drain* is directed toward you, you will have your *3 Life Preservers* waiting to neutralize it immediately and move on. You will also be ready at any moment to help others and well-prepared to *Outwardly* throw a *Life Preserver* to anyone in need of support.

Remember the *3 Life Preserving Dimensions*, and be ready to support *yourself, your family, your team, and organization*. You always have your go-to *Inward Self Life Preserving Dimension* and your *IO Spiritual Life Preserving Dimension* to support and help get your *Life Ship* back on course on your *Life Journey*. You can also look *Outward* to your high trust relationships and be ready to help them when their *Life Ship* is sinking, and *Downward Negative Drains* occur for them. A *Dynamic Positive Culture* has the *3 Life Preserving Dimensions* built into the fabric of its relationships and, when applied, will produce *Upward Living* and an increase in your *PH2E* levels.

The next chapter will discuss your *Inward Living* and assist you in connecting with your purpose and passion. We only get one opportunity to go through life, so don't waste another moment. Begin and plan your *Life Journey* by becoming an *IOU Life Leader*.

Captain's Log for Chapter 6

The Life Living Continuum

Are You Living IOU, IOW, or IOD?

Captain's Log:

Point 1   The *IO Living Culture Continuum* displays the byproduct of your *Inward* and *Outward Living*. You will naturally receive results based on your *Inward* and *Outward Life*.

Point 2   When you are living a *positive and effective* intentional life based on *The 12 Essential Life Anchors*, you will begin to navigate toward a *Dynamic Positive Culture* and receive the *Upward Living Life Gifts of PH2E*. This is *IOU Life Leadership*.

Point 3   When your living is *neutral and mediocre*, the effect will be a *Static Neutral Culture,* and you will receive the *Wayward Living Life Impassivities of Apathy, Indifference, Unfitness, and Mediocrity.* This is *IOW Life Drifting*.

Point 4   When you are constantly looking for what is wrong or needs fixing and always negative and thinking about what is holding you back, that will result in a *Toxic Negative Culture,* and you will receive *Downward Life Drains of Anxiety, Unhappiness, Unhealthiness, and Ineffectiveness.* This is *IOD Life Sinking*

Point 5   If you find yourself spiraling downwards and living either *IOW* or *IOD*, you can turn to your *3 Life Preserving Dimensions* to help you get back on track for your journey. These *3 Life Preserving Dimensions* are: *Inward Self*, *Outward Others*, and *Inward Outward (IO) Spiritual*.

Point 6   Your *Inward Self Dimension* is the *Life Preserver* always on hand and ready to help you. By practicing the *6 Essential Inward Life Anchors* (which are discussed in Chapter 11), you can quickly get back on track.

Point 7   The *Outward Others Life Preserver* may be a friend or family member who supports you when faced with adversity. While you cannot depend that they will always be there (because you don't have 100% control over their actions), there will be opportunities for you to reach out and receive support. You can also be an *Outward Others Life Preserver* for your friends and family to help them live *IOU*.

Point 8   The *Inward Outward (IO) Spiritual Dimension* is a *Life Preserver* you can access through meditation, prayer, nature, or music. It's a personal and individual dimension, taking shape differently for everyone. It can have a major *Inward* impact on your confidence and motivation to solve problems, change attitudes, and support you on your *IOU Life Journey*.

Teach to Learn

The best way to deepen your understanding and, at the same time, share and stimulate new conversations with others is to teach. Share what you have learned with a friend, family member, coworker, or anyone else who will listen. Teaching is, by far, the best way to deepen one's understanding of new insights and concepts. Take any of the Points in the Captain's Log or this chapter for thought-provoking discussions.

New Daily Voyage:

Activity:

Think about times in your life when you were living *IOU, IOW*, and *IOD*. As you remember those moments, reflect on the differences in how you felt. Relate those experiences to the *IO Living Culture Continuum*. In which situations did you feel more *PH2E*? Were you also more effective and on-track during these times?

Ask yourself:

How can I utilize the *3 Life Preserving Dimensions* to get back on track when I sense that my *Life Journey* has stalled?

PART II

What Is IOU Life Leadership?

Think About and Begin Planning Your Life Journey

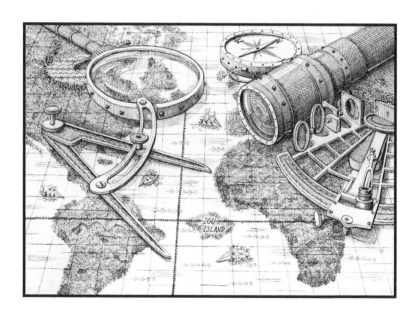

Chapter 7

Principle "I"

INWARD LIFE LIVING

Rarely do we find men who willingly engage in hard, solid thinking. There is an almost universal quest for easy answers and half-baked solutions. Nothing pains some people more than having to think.

—Martin Luther King, Jr.

It was 1942. Vincent was 47, and World War II was raging. America had been involved in this war since the bombing of Pearl Harbor and, by this time, was waging battles on both the

European and Pacific fronts. Vincent's first-born son, Dominick, enlisted in the Army and was stationed overseas. Vincent and his brother Sam owned a highly successful fruit and vegetable store in Baldwin, Long Island, and they were making $75-$100 per week when the average income was between $20-$30 per week. Vincent would later say that he was doing a lot of thinking about how he could help both the country and his son with the war.

He was concerned that his son would not get the proper supplies to do his job and remain safe, so after much *Inward Thinking*, Vincent took *Outward Action*. He enlisted in the Navy for the second time, even though he would only make $40 per week instead of the nearly $100 per week he was making at the store. Once again, he said the money didn't matter; what mattered was doing the right thing. When it was discovered that Vincent was one year too old to enlist, he negotiated with the recruiter and shared his expertise and prior experience with the Navy and shipping. The recruiters quickly understood that Vincent could be an asset, so they offered to have him stationed at the Brooklyn Navy Yard on the East River in New York. He thought it was a perfect solution since the Brooklyn Navy Yard was where supplies were shipped to Europe to benefit American soldiers—including his son Dominick.

When Vincent arrived for duty at the Brooklyn Navy Yard, four soldiers were in charge of the dock. Vincent took his orders from them, but he always said, "If I got orders and it was not the right thing to do, I would always speak up and not be intimidated by any senior officer. I was always respectful but would always give my two cents." He shared that if he saw something that would keep everyone on the dock safer and be more efficient, he would speak up. Amazingly, after two months, Vincent was put in charge of the dock. As the leader, he would position himself high up in the crow's nest to see all the activity. He would direct the supplies below and make sure they were correctly placed and balanced on the ships for safe passage across the Atlantic. He always treated everyone with respect and dignity because he believed that when you do, you get it right back.

It was apparent that Vincent took the time to think *Inwardly*, analyze his life in a positive way, and then determine what his next steps should be. Vincent modeled that for his whole life. He felt great satisfaction at the Brooklyn Navy Yard by contributing to the country while at the same time feeling he was helping his son. He had deep *Inward Thinking* that showed throughout his life. Through his stories he provided life lessons to his entire family and anyone else who would listen.

You are exactly where you are based on all of your *Inward Thoughts* and the choices you have made to date.

You have 100% control of your *Inward Living*. You are the *Inward* thinker and the *Inward* observer of the *Outward World*. You are in control of your *Inward Living* and must pay attention to your *Inward Thoughts*. The average person has about 49 thoughts per minute, according to the Laboratory of Neuro-Imaging at the University of Southern California. That adds up to a total of 70,000 thoughts per day! You are exactly where you are based on all of your *Inward Thoughts* and the choices you have made to date. Alternatively, you can play the role of the victim, stating that the *Outward World* is to blame for everything that may be wrong in your life—*I didn't get the job due to the economy*, or *I was angry because of some other person's actions*.

Have you ever said, "See what you made me do?" That is having a victim mentality, which has you believe there is nothing you can do; it's always someone else's or the world's fault. That's living a *negative and ineffective* life, which will lead to *IOD Living* and create a *Toxic Negative Culture*, which is the complete opposite of the *Dynamic Positive Culture* we all want.

There will always be adverse *Outward* circumstances that come to you, which you have no control over, but you must remember that you have 100% control over how you react to those things. You can choose to spiral downward into *Anxiety, Unhappiness, Unhealthiness,* and *Ineffectiveness*, or you can choose to act and respond in ways that will benefit you and move you *Upward* toward *PH2E*. It may not be easy, but it is entirely up to you.

There will always be negative *Outward* circumstances that come to you which you have no control over, but you must remember that you have 100% control over how you react to those things.

Take some time each day and intentionally reflect on your *Inward Being* and your *Inward Living*. That will give you the tools and power to control and react to the *Outward* negative events that happen to all of us. You can even proactively think about situations that might occur and determine your best reaction ahead of time. Be a victor, not a victim!

Carl Rogers, a famous 20th-century humanistic psychologist, believed that a fully functioning person is in touch with their deepest and innermost feelings and desires and is continually working toward becoming self-actualized. Fully functioning people live entirely in the moment and experience inner freedom. In a 1962 article, Rogers wrote,

> Such a person experiences in the present, with immediacy. He is able to live in his feelings and reactions of the moment. He is not bound by the structure of his past learnings, but these are a present resource for him insofar as they relate to the experience of the moment. He lives freely, subjectively, in an existential confrontation of this moment in life.

It is important to realize that the concept of a fully functioning person is an ideal to strive for and a continual process. It is not a destination or an end-product. Becoming a fully functioning person is about your *Life Journey*. It is a growth process that will continue throughout your life. People who think about becoming fully functioning or self-actualized as an end product believe that when they achieve a certain status, they will be done growing. *IOU Life Leaders* understand that this is not the case. In the same way that your *Upward Living Life Gifts* continue to grow, giving you ever greater amounts of *Peacefulness, Happiness, Healthiness, and Excellence*, so your self-concept will continue to evolve and grow.

Self-concept is generally understood as your individual perception of behavior, abilities, and unique characteristics. At its most basic, it is a collection of beliefs you hold about yourself. It can be conceived as a mental picture of who you are as a person and embodies the answer to the question, "Who am I?" In other words, it is your *Inward Being*.

According to Richard Crisp and Rhiannon Turner's book *Essential Social Psychology*, our self consists of attributes and personality traits that differentiate us from others such as introversion or extroversion. Our relational self is defined by our relationships with significant others, including siblings, friends, and spouses. Our collective self reflects our membership in social groups, such as our cultural and ethnic identity.

Traditionally, self-concept is considered more malleable when people are younger and still going through self-discovery and identity formation. In this paradigm, as people age, self-perceptions become more detailed and organized as people form a better idea of who they are and what is important to them. As they age, they become more entrenched in the ideas of who they are and are less likely to change their views. In contrast, an *IOU Life Leader* understands that continual growth and change are possible by developing the *Inward Being*. When you reflect *Inwardly*, you think about those aspects of yourself that are most important to you—your purpose and your passions and the *Outward Actions* you can take to help develop them. It is important to reflect on your *Inward Self* to continually grow and not get stuck in old ways of being.

Carl Rogers believed that there were three different parts of self-concept. The first, self-image, is how you see yourself and is a mixture of different attributes, including your physical characteristics, personality traits, and social roles. Your self-image isn't necessarily reality. Some people might have an inflated self-image, while others may perceive or exaggerate the flaws and weaknesses that others don't see. The second, self-esteem, can be thought of as how much you value yourself. Factors that may impact self-esteem include how you compare yourselves to others and how others respond to you. Sometimes, when people respond positively to behavior, you develop higher self-esteem, but when they respond negatively or when you compare yourself to others and find yourself lacking, it can have a negative impact on your self-esteem. Rogers' third aspect of self-concept is the ideal self or how you wish you could be. In many cases, the way you see yourself and how you would like to see yourself do not quite match up.

While *Inward Living*, it is important to develop your self-concept accurately. As you reflect more fully and with greater intention, your self-image or *Life Map* of yourself will become more accurate. Likewise, your self-esteem will become more stable. In other words, it won't be affected by the *Outward Actions* of others and how they respond to you. Finally, your *Inward Self* will align more closely with your ideal self as you reach new heights of self-awareness and understand on a deep level who you are. This is the essence of becoming a fully functioning person.

A fully functioning person understands that life is a journey striving for self-actualization. Abraham Maslow, an American psychologist, popularized self-actualization as reaching for the fulfillment of one's greatest potential. The understanding and definition of your greatest potential is a critical component when developing your *Inward Life Vision*. As we will discuss in Chapter 11, your *Life Vision* is the intersection of your life *Purpose, Potential,* and *Passion.* Therefore, having a clear mental *Inward* picture of who you are, your abilities, and your unique characteristics will lead to *IOU Life Leadership*.

You are a unique combination of attributes and personality traits.

The question is, *who are you?*

If you don't know who you truly are, you'll never know what you really want.

—Roy T. Bennett

Your "YOU" World

Your Own Understanding

The *Inward Principle* is your *Life Map*. It's your paradigm or your "YOU" World—**Y**our **O**wn **U**nderstanding of the world, which cannot be 100% accurate. As discussed in Chapter 3, The *Life Map Cycle* is used to examine your *Inward Being,* your opinions, or your *Life Maps*. You have a *Life Map* for everything in the world. If you didn't, you would be in a constant state of surprise. For example, when you walk into a grocery store, you don't expect to see an elephant standing there. You have a *Life Map* about what you think should be in a grocery store. You have a *Life Map* on politics, on how to raise children, on driving—on everything. All your *Life Maps* live inside you. It's your *Inward World*. You want to think all of your *Inward Life Maps* are correct, but how can they be? Two people describing the same event will have different descriptions because they have experienced it differently.

The *Inward Principle* is your *Life Map*. It's your paradigm or your "YOU" World—Your Own Understanding of the world, which cannot be 100% accurate.

Alfred Korzybski is correct when he stated that the map is not the territory. Our beliefs are our reality. Our *Inward Life Maps* need to be analyzed continually and modified to represent reality more accurately. Examining our *Inward Living* is a critical task to improve our *Inward Life Maps* and keep us on our *Life Journey*. The problem with our *Inward Life Maps* is that they are an abstraction of the real world. Therefore, there will always be inherent flaws. We need those abstractions to understand and organize the world *Inwardly*, but we rarely examine our *Inward Life Maps*. We continue to use our maps even if they are not always correct. This is true because we believe that to function in life, we need to have a map for everything. We can't be without a map for things in life, so we settle for any *Inward Life Map*, even if it is wrong. The world is what it is, and we try to put words and understanding to it, but the actual territory is beyond verbal explanation. As humans, we tend to simplify or make symbolic representations of what is going on in the world so we can think or talk about it. Is our *Inward Thinking* and living accurate? Does our *Inward Thinking* match life realities?

The world is what it is, and we try to put words and understanding to it, but the actual territory is beyond verbal explanation.

In the next chapter, let's examine the critical *Inward Anchors* with the goal of developing a structure to examine them and continually fine-tune them for accuracy.

Captain's Log for Chapter 7

Principle "I"

Captain's Log:

Point 1   You have 100% control of your *Inward Living*. You are exactly where you are because of your *Inward Thoughts* and the choices you have made to date.

Point 2   There will always be negative *Outward* events and comments that come to you over which you have no control. However, you do have 100% control over how you react to them. You can choose to spiral *Downward* into *Anxiety, Unhappiness, Unhealthiness, and Ineffectiveness* or you can choose to act in ways that will move you *Upwards* toward *PH2E*.

Point 3   A fully functioning person is in touch with their innermost thoughts and emotions and constantly working toward self-improvement. Fully functioning people live deeply in the moment and experience inner freedom.

Point 4   There are three different aspects of self-concept, which are all important parts of your *Inward Living*. Your self-image is how you see yourself; your self-concept is how much you value yourself; and your ideal self is how you wish you could be.

Point 5   Your *Inward World* is your *Life Map* that helps you navigate the world. It includes your beliefs and thoughts about relationships, *Life Principles*, *Life Values*, important concepts, and other critical aspects of your life.

Point 6   The map is not the territory, which means that our beliefs may not match reality. It is important always to reflect *Inwardly* and be willing to modify our beliefs to represent reality more accurately.

Teach to Learn

The best way to deepen your understanding and, at the same time, share and stimulate new conversations with others is to teach. Share what you have learned with a friend, family member, coworker, or anyone else who will listen. Teaching is, by far, the best way to deepen one's understanding of new insights and concepts. Take any of the Points in the Captain's Log or this chapter for thought-provoking discussions.

New Daily Voyage:

Activity:

Take some time to reflect on your *Inward Living*. Proactively think of situations that might occur and determine your best reaction ahead of time.

Ask yourself:

Do I react to events in ways that cause me to spiral *Downward*, to drift *Waywardly*, or to move *Upward*? How can I make more of my reactions *Upward* moving?

Chapter 8

Do You Know Your *I*'s?

Examine Your I's

What lies behind you and what lies in front of you pales in comparison to what lies inside of you.

—Ralph Waldo Emerson

Examine Your *I*'s

By examining your *I*'s, you will find the purposefulness of your life and gain greater self-awareness. Your *I*'s constitute your *Inward Living*, a place you spend a lot of time! Have you asked yourself, *What's my purpose in life?* If you have, how do you answer the question? To answer it, you first need to know your *Inward Being*. There are many *Inward Life Anchors* that we all have. When you *Inwardly* analyze your *I's* you can then begin to answer the question about your purpose.

As you will discover in the next sections, there are many *I's*. You have full control of your *Inward Thinking* and the ability to make course corrections with any of these *I's*. You shouldn't be an enigma to yourself. You have a unique purpose with special talents and skills to propel you anywhere you want to go. Self-examination is the key to finding your purpose and *SelfCulture*. As you reflect on each "*I*" in this chapter, you will begin to uncover your *Inward Being* in an intentional manner. Let's dive into your *I Living*!

By examining your I's, you will find the purposefulness of your life.

Happiness depends more on the inward disposition of mind than on outward circumstances.

—Benjamin Franklin

INWARD LIFE LIVING ANCHORS

Thinking, Opinions, and Your Life Maps

Your *Inward Life Anchors* are solid, grounded, immovable, timeless, and universal life principles included in all effective life plans for intentional living. For each *Life Anchor*, you have opinions and *Life Maps* you have developed and use when you live *Outwardly*. Therefore, *Life Anchors* are the laws of the universe, principles that do not change. We all have opinions or *Life Maps* we use to act on for each of our *Life Anchors*. Are your *Life Maps* accurate?

Your *Inward Life Anchors* are solid, grounded, immovable, timeless, and universal life principles included in all effective life plans for intentional living.

What *Inward Life Maps* are you using to guide your life? Are you even aware of your *Life Maps*? If you are, how do you know if they are correct? Understanding your *Inward Life Anchors* will help your *Inward Thinking* and will assist you in creating accurate *Life Maps* that will guide you to receiving your *Upward Life Gifts*. There are many *Inward* and *Outward Life Anchors*. In Chapters 11 and 12, we will discuss *The 12 Essential Life Anchors* in detail that lead to *Upward Living* and the *Upward Life Gifts*. Let's first look at your *I*'s or the *Inward Life Anchors*.

What we achieve inwardly will change outer reality.

—Plutarch

165

Principle "I" Inward

Your *I* is "YOU" as an independent person. You have 100% control over your *Inward Living* and how it impacts you. In fact, it's one of the few things in life you have control over, 100% of the time. The point is, you need to

Your *I* is "YOU" as an independent person.

live the *Inward Principle* by design and by intention. Do not live by default, reactively responding to whatever happens or based on the whims of others, because if you do, it will lead to a downward decline, and the byproducts will be *IOD Living* and receiving *Downward Life Drains*. If this happens, you need to look at your *Inward Living* and *Outward Living* and take control of it.

When you are in a pure *Inward Mode*, you are at peace. You are not affecting anyone *Outwardly*. However, you can also be alone and not in an *Inward Mode*. For example, you could be thinking about how you should be somewhere with someone, contacting someone, or doing something at that precise moment. By not doing what you are supposed to do for that other person, you are having an *Outward* effect on that other person. If that is the case, then it's a false *Inward* mindset. Remember, to be completely in an *Inward Mode*, you are not interacting with anyone. If you use this mode effectively, you will find it leads to peacefulness and self-improvement.

In an *Inward Mode*, you can analyze yourself. Imagine that you are standing outside yourself, observing your *Inward*

Thinking, and making choices to change. You have 100% control to change a negative thought and replace it with a positive, healthy thought. Dr. Caroline Leaf purports that when that process happens, your brain changes because it receives a positive neurochemical rush that will improve your intellectual capability and provide greater health and peace. You are thinking all the time, from the moment you are

When you are thinking *Inwardly*, there are three possibilities. You are either in an *I Now, I Later,* or *I Past Mode.*

born, throughout your entire life. You are thinking during the day when you are awake, and you are thinking when you are sleeping. What are you thinking about? Are your thoughts mostly positive or negative? Is your thinking controlled by the *Outward Actions* of others? Keep reminding yourself that you are not a victim of others, and you can control your reactions to negative *Outward Actions* from others. Intentional, focused thinking can bring about impressive *Inward* positive changes that will be beneficial in all areas of your life.

According to a study by Harvard Health Publications, practicing *Inward* mindfulness 10 to 15 minutes a day can improve your brain and health. Thinking about your *I's* is a brain-building action. Neuroplasticity, a term first used by Jerzy Konorski in 1948, describes the physical changes in your brain, forming new connections and pathways. These positive changes can happen for your whole life as long as you stimulate the brain.

When you are thinking *Inwardly*, there are three possibilities. You are either in an *I Now, I Later, or I Past Mode*. Let's examine the three subtypes of the *Inward Living*.

The ability to be in the present moment is a major component of mental wellness.

—Abraham Maslow

I Now—In the Moment

When you are in *I Now*, you are connecting with the world, your body, your mind, or your spirit. You are in the moment, relaxing, breathing, or meditating. In the *I Now*, we are mindful. You may want to take a walk in nature to think about something you have to do or a relationship you want to work on. If you choose that, you are not in the *I Now*, but rather in another *Inward Mode*, such as *I To-Do's* or *I Relationships*. There is a time and place for those and other kinds of *Inward Thinking*, but *I Now* focuses on the moment and what you are presently experiencing.

To connect to the world in the *I Now*, you connect with your surroundings. You see, feel, smell, listen to, and notice the details and energy of your current location. Your surroundings might be trees, the ocean, the sky, birds, a quiet room, or architecture. It is the world around you, right in front of you, and you focus on connecting with it.

I frequently practice a deep breathing technique to connect with nature and the *Outward World*. I enjoy photographing nature, mainly birds, (see my Instagram @naturemomentsbydrjoe) in beautiful, natural settings on Long Island, New York. Usually, when I do so, I'm walking quietly alone, taking in the natural beauty of the earth. I take a deep breath in while at the same time imagining the surroundings right in front of me going *Inward*, connecting with me. Then I exhale while imagining giving myself to the surroundings, like an *Outward Action*, in a sense, giving a piece

An essential *I Now Life Anchor* is your *I SelfCulture*. It's who you are at this moment.

of myself back to nature. I continue this *Inward* taking in and *Outward* giving back for about 30 seconds. The reward I always experience is feeling an incredible *Upward Lift of Peacefulness*. Not only do I receive an immediate *Upward Living Life Gift*, but it also lasts for hours afterward. For example, later I might be in a situation completely different than the natural setting. I might be driving in traffic, shopping, or with a large group of people, and yet, when I think back to that moment of *Inward* and *Outward* breathing and connecting with nature, I immediately feel that *Upward Peacefulness* again.

This *I Now* is a wonderful *Inward* connection to the world. You will find this technique helps you stay in the moment and prevents your mind from being distracted with other thoughts. There are many *Inward* thought techniques and programs to assist with your *I Now*. Find what works for you but understand that these programs and techniques are just one small part of the entire *Inward Living Principle*.

An essential *I Now Life Anchor* is your *I SelfCulture*. It's who you are at this moment. In Chapter 11, we will dive deeply into the foundational *Life Anchor* of *SelfCulture*, which incorporates the most essential *Inward Life Anchors* of *Life Vision*, *Daily Mission*, *Life Values*, *Life Principles*, and *Life Goals*.

I Later—In the Future

I Later is thinking *Inwardly* about later, as in any time other than the moment, even a few seconds later. What do you plan to do in the near and far future? We are usually in the *I Later Mode*, always thinking of what you need to do at a later point in your life—thinking about the things we need to do later in the day, people we are going to meet with later, or a project we are working on. Anything that we will be dealing with in the future is the *I Later Mode*. We need to spend time in the *I Later Mode*, but we can't ignore the *I Now Mode*, and we must balance our lives.

I Past—In the Past

I Past is reflecting on things that have occurred previously, even if they occurred only a few moments prior. It is thinking about the past, whether it's events, relationships, successes, or failures. It is thinking about specific pleasurable times, too. Remember to keep your balance. Don't stay in the past for too long because dwelling on the unchangeable past in excess can be unhealthy, especially if you are constantly dwelling on negative past experiences. However, it's important to think about your past because it's your history. Reflect on your childhood, your schooling, and your past relationships, whether they give you joy or sorrow. Always keep in mind that you have the choice of whether to let your past define you. Reflect on the positive moments of the past to celebrate and inspire you onward, and reflect on the negative aspects with the knowledge you have the power and ability to change and create a new present and future.

Remember, the *Inward Principle* is all about thinking *Inwardly*. This essential time for reflection yields tremendous dividends in our lives. Many activities can help structure our *Inward* time. One that I have found beneficial is the *10-Year Exercise*. This exercise is about using our past thinking to help us today.

Think about a situation that happened to you 10 years ago, which created anxiety or was a challenge. Maybe it was a job that created stress, or it could have been a relationship, a meeting, financial difficulties, or an illness. Looking back at it, how do you wish you handled it now that you are 10 years wiser? Perhaps you are asking yourself, *Why was I so nervous? Why didn't I think more clearly?* It may be that you couldn't change the outcome, but you didn't need to experience the stress and anxiety. Looking back, you can see that it was not as critical as you thought at the time. In fact, the stress and anxiety probably prevented you from handling the issue in the best way possible.

Let's use this exercise to help you now. Is there a situation you are currently dealing with that is causing stress and anxiety? Think about the 10-year rule: how will this event affect you 10 years from now? When you think back on the situation 10 years from now, how will you wish you handled it? Visualize yourself handling it with little to no stress and anxiety. You want to look back and say you reflected on all the possibilities and options, dealt with the situation, and then moved on.

I have used this *10-Year Exercise* technique many times as a leader. Whenever I knew I was going into a highly stressful situation, I paused and thought to myself, when I look back at this situation 10 years from now, how will I want to have handled it? Did I gather all the facts, pause, and respond calmly? If you want, you can start with less stressful events in your life and shorten the period. For example, in the past four weeks, how did I handle a stressful situation? Ask yourself the same questions as we discussed for the *10-Year Exercise*.

> *The longest journey is the journey inward.*
>
> —Dag Hammarskjold

INWARD LIVING LIFE ANCHORS

Inward Living can be characterized into many modes of thinking, such as:

I Gratitude

Taking the time to think *Inwardly* about the things we are grateful for is important living we should do regularly, and it is one of the simplest ways to feel happiness. Gratitude comes from the Latin word *gratis,* which means grace or gratefulness. During your *Inward Living,* you should acknowledge the goodness in your life each day. In positive psychology research, numerous studies show that being grateful leads to greater happiness.

One study by Emmons and McCullough asked a group of people to write about things they were grateful for at the end of the week. Another group wrote about things that irritated them, and a third group wrote about events that

Gratitude is a powerful positive *Inward* reset that will help you to refocus on what you have instead of what you don't have.

were neither positive nor negative. After 10 weeks, the group that wrote about the things they were grateful for reported feeling more optimistic and better about their lives than the other two groups.

Gratitude is a powerful positive *Inward* reset that will help you to refocus on what you have instead of what you don't have. It's a practice that grows in its effect the more you cultivate it.

It's not happiness that brings us gratitude;
it's gratitude that brings us happiness.

—Anonymous

I To Do's and Tasks

I To Do's and Tasks consists of thinking about tasks that need to get done, such as picking up the laundry, going food shopping, getting dog food, or working toward your goals.

One day, you will realize that material things mean nothing.
All that matters is the well-being of the people in your life.

—Leon Brown

I Relationships

Think about your relationships, such as with a spouse, child, parent, friend, coworker, student, community member, or extended family member. I call this your *Relationship Map*. When you are alone and *Inward Thinking*, think about the impact you have on your important relationships. What can you do to improve your relationships?

Write down all the roles in your life. My list looks like this:

- Son
- Grandson
- Father
- Brother
- Brother-in-law
- Spouse
- Friend
- Uncle
- Cousin
- Colleague
- Parishioner
- Leader

Then, write next to each role the names of individuals with whom you have each relationship.

It does not have to be a complete list. Just getting the list started by writing your *I Relationships* down can be a life-changing moment. You should first list all your family members, then the friends and colleagues who you frequently interact with, and then perhaps those with whom you need to interact more regularly. Your first list is an excellent start for your *Inward Relationship* thinking. Later, you should make a new list comprised of previous relationships that you want to reconnect with.

Next, put a "D" over the relationships that you connect with daily. Then, put a "W" over the relationships that you connect with weekly. Do the same for Monthly with an "M," "6" for 6 months, and "12" for yearly. When the list is complete, you will have in front of you your personal *Relationship Map*.

Look carefully over your *Relationship Map,* and the areas that need improvement will be obvious. Create a plan to connect more frequently with the people in your life that are most important to you.

I Learning

I Learning occurs when you are learning, reading, or writing about topics that will affect you in the near or distant future. It is a way you can invest in yourself to help you meet your goals.

Pay attention to what you are thinking, and then decide if those are thoughts that are creating the kind of life you want created, . . . And if it's not, then change your thoughts. It's really that easy.

—Jill Bolte Taylor

I Triggers

A trigger is something that sets your emotions off in a negative manner. What are the triggers that get you to a high emotional state? Are you doing anything about your reactions to them or just saying, "That's who I am, and I can't change it?" Are there triggers you are only minimally aware of or not aware of at all? Reflecting in this area can give you clarity about those areas and help you to grow. *I Triggers* is an important area to reflect on. Many of us have rarely or never thought about this aspect of *Inward Living*, which is important and can take many forms such as words, smells, glances from others, or actions. Write down your triggers and intentionally be aware of them, so when they occur, you can change your typical, possibly negative *Outward* response to a more positive one.

I Create

In this mode, you are creating something that excites you, such as literature, music, art, etc. There are many forms of creating something. The act of creating is usually connected to innovation and making something new.

I Self-Trust

In this mode, you think about the relationship that you have with yourself. Are you communicating with yourself in a positive or negative manner? Self-trust is respecting yourself and what you believe in—keeping your word to yourself. Building self-trust is just like building trust in other relationships. You need to take care of, encourage, and be in positive dialogue with yourself. Everyone needs to trust that they have the resources within them to help themselves. Carl Rogers, a humanistic psychologist, is attributed with creating the concept of Unconditional Positive Regard (UPR), which is defined as an acceptance of a person—regardless of how they are, how they behaved, or, whether they made a mistake, or struggled. In every situation, they were accepted. We all need to experience UPR toward ourselves and acknowledge it is acceptable to fail and struggle. Unconditional Positive Regard for yourself is the foundation for *I Self-Trust*.

I Health

I Health is the mode of continuous improvement in the areas of proper nutrition, exercise, and sleep. Exercise produces endorphins, which produce happiness. Plan to move your body every day, take a walk on a trail, or get into nature. Think about how to eat well and make sure to get enough rest.

I Service

How can you help others? *I Service* can mean donating your time, talents, or money—no matter how small your contribution may seem. The *I Service Mode* is planning and thinking about helping others. Remember, this is part of *Inward Living*, so *I Service* is only thinking and planning about giving service, it's *not* acting on it.

I Entertainment/Hobby

This mode includes thinking about things you like to do for fun. Perhaps it's going to the movies, watching television, attending a concert, playing a sport, baking, blogging, collecting something, or playing an instrument. The *I Entertainment/Hobby* area can be either an *Inward* or an *Outward* experience. If it involves another person, then it's an *Outward* experience; therefore, you are in a different mode of living, which is *Outward Living*.

I Spirit

I Spirit is thinking about your spiritual life, in whatever form you conceive it to be.

I Questions

When you are in this mode, you make a list of questions about things you always wanted to know. Write down questions of interest to you, possibly things you can live your life not knowing but would be interested to know, such as:

- How does electricity work?
- What's inside the walls of this house?
- How does the water come out of the faucet in my kitchen?
- Why is the sky blue?

Don't look up the answers when you write down the questions; simply make the list. In the *O Mode*, you will act on them.

This is a great exercise to discover things around you right now. There are so many more questions specific to you. Framing good questions helps you focus on the key aspects of the situation, circumstance, or problem.

I Problem-Solving

In this mode, you think about problems you are encountering— large and small—and work on possible solutions. Don't get stuck in thinking you can't solve the problem because it is too complex or difficult. Figure out a basic solution; you can refine it later. For example, when NASA worked on the problem of landing a person on the moon, they first had to solve the problem of how to get a spaceship to hit the moon. NASA purposely sent several spaceships called Rangers to the moon to take detailed images of lunar craters, rocks, and soil before literally "crashing" into the moon. The Rangers' missions were the first step in gaining information and using it to solve the problem of landing safely on the moon's surface.

I Problem-Solving is constantly making predictions about possible solutions to current problems. Even if your solutions are wrong, your *Inward* thoughts help you focus on the data you have and provide you with more accurate, possible solutions. Learning from predictions stimulates your brain to make reasonable assumptions based on what you do know. The more you learn about a topic, the better your predictions will be. All new ideas are slight variations of something that has already been developed.

Every problem has a solution; it just needs to be discovered. The solution may be the best course of action at a particular time. It may not completely solve the problem, but all you can ask for and execute is the best possible solution at the moment. Strive for the solution that solves the problem, or if this is not possible, look for the current, best solution that moves the problem closer to a solution.

I Body

Listen to your body—it is an amazing system. Your body tells you if there is some part that needs attention. Don't ignore it. Often, people don't listen or make the time to deal with and heal the inside pain. Taking some form of drug to mask the pain says to your body, *I don't want to hear you; stop sending the message of pain.* It is literally telling your body to be quiet! Self-medicating or even taking a doctor-prescribed medication will silence the body. Still, eventually, the body will send a new, even louder, and stronger message that there is a problem. Then, you will have no choice but to deal with it and be in *Environment 1—Urgent and Important.*

The inward journey is about finding your own fullness, something that no one else can take away.

—Deepak Chopra

The ESSENTIAL INWARD LIFE ANCHORS

As I mentioned at the beginning of this chapter, there are *6 Essential Inward Life Anchors* that lead to *Life Leadership*. There are also *6 Essential Outward Life Anchors,* for a total of *12 Essential Life Anchors.* We will discuss these *Essential Life Anchors* in Chapters 11 and 12.

The *Essential Inward Life Anchors* which assist us in living a *positive and effective* intentional life are:

1. *SelfCulture*
2. *Life Vision*
3. *Daily Mission*
4. *Life Principles*
5. *Life Values*
6. *Life Goals*

The *Essential Inward Life Anchors* will answer the following questions:

1. *Who am I?* This is your *SelfCulture*.
2. *What is my purpose in life?* This becomes your *Life Vision*.
3. *What am I trying to accomplish today?* This becomes your *Daily Mission*.
4. *What do I believe are the life laws?* These are your *Life Principles*.
5. *How will I act and behave?* These are your *Life Values*.
6. *Where am I going?* These are your *Life Goals*.

When you are *Living Inward*, it is just you and your thoughts. You do this work alone. With practice, it becomes the most peaceful time of your day!

Captain's Log for Chapter 8

Do you Know Your I's?

Captain's Log:

Point 1   Examine your *Inward Living* to find the purpose
of your life and gain greater self-awareness. This
will help you uncover your special talents and skills
that can propel you anywhere you want to go.

Point 2   You look *Inward* by asking: Who am I? (*SelfCulture*);
What is my purpose in life? (*Life Vision*); What
am I trying to accomplish today (*Daily Mission*);
What are my life laws? (*Life Principles*); How will
I act and behave? (*Life Values*); and Where am I
going? (*Life Goals*).

Point 3   There are three *Inward Modes: I Now, I Later,* or *I
Past. I Now* is when you connect with the world—
your body, mind, or spirit—in the moment and
relaxing. You connect with the world around you
through your five senses. *I Later* is thinking about
anytime in the future and planning what you will
need to do then. *I Past* is about reflecting on things
that previously occurred. It could be about events,
relationships, successes, or failures.

Point 4   There are numerous subtypes of the *Inward Mode,*
including *I Gratitude, I To Do's, I Relationships,* and
I Goals. It is important to balance your *Inward
Mode* by spending time reflecting on many of
these subtypes and not just one.

Point 5   *I Problem-Solving* is an important *Inward Mode* because you can think of problems you are encountering or have encountered and work on possible solutions. Be creative! Sometimes problems appear unsolvable, but look at them through a different lens, and come up with an out of the box solution.

Point 6   There are *6 Essential Inward Life Anchors* which will help you navigate your life effectively and live it by design: 1- *SelfCulture, 2 - Life Vision, 3 - Daily Mission, 4 - Life Principles, 5 - Life Values, 6 - Life Goals.*

Teach to Learn

The best way to deepen your understanding and, at the same time, share and stimulate new conversations with others is to teach. Share what you have learned with a friend, family member, coworker, or anyone else who will listen. Teaching is, by far, the best way to deepen one's understanding of new insights and concepts. Take any of the Points in the Captain's Log or this chapter for thought-provoking discussions.

New Daily Voyage:

Activity:

For one day, take note of how much time you spend in *I Now*, *I Later*, and *I Past*. Are you preoccupied with the past or future? Don't forget to balance the past and future focus with time spent taking in your present.

Ask yourself:

What *Inward Modes* can I identify in myself? Should I develop any others?

Chapter 9

Principle "O"

OUTWARD LIFE LIVING

A ship is always safe at the shore, but that is not what it is built for.

—Albert Einstein

Vincent lived his life *Outwardly* in a *positive and effective* manner with high integrity. Over the years, he bought various investment properties on Long Island. At one point, he decided to sell a valuable piece of property in a quaint residential area where new families were building their dream homes. A young, newly married couple offered to buy the property, so Vincent gave them a fair price. They thanked him and said they would give him an answer in a few days, then shook his hand and left. Shortly after that, a local bank heard that Vincent was selling the property and offered him three times the amount for which he had agreed to sell it to the young couple. Vincent told the banker, "I am waiting to hear from a young couple, and they will let me know if they want it in a few days."

The banker said, "You have no contract with them, and I'm offering you three times the amount."

Without missing a beat, Vincent replied, "But I shook their hand, and they are going to let me know if they want it." Once again, Vincent modeled integrity, honesty, and keeping your word with others. He believed that this would be a good property for the young couple to begin their life and have a family. *Outward Living* is about relationships and interacting with integrity toward others and the world. Vincent said, "It's not about getting more. Life is about being fair to humanity." Vincent's *Inward Living* of high integrity was felt by others through his *Outward Actions*. Due to his *Inward Life Principles*, and his intentional *Outward Living* of high trust with others, he and others received the byproduct of *Peacefulness* and *Happiness*.

Outward Living—Relationships and Trust

Outward Living is centered around your *Outward Actions* toward your relationships and building trust. A trusting relationship allows you to feel safe when vulnerable. A leading expert on trust, Stephen M.R. Covey states in *The Speed of Trust*, "Trust impacts us 24/7, 365 days a year. It undergirds and affects the quality of every relationship, every communication, every work project, every business venture, every effort in which we are engaged. It changes the quality of every present moment and alters the trajectory and outcome of every

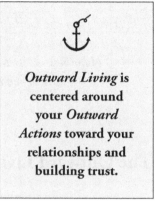

> *Outward Living* is centered around your *Outward Actions* toward your relationships and building trust.

future moment of our lives—both personally and professionally." Charles Feltman stated in *The Thin Book of Trust*, "Trust is choosing to risk making something you value vulnerable to another person's actions." Bryk and Schneider studied trust in school systems and concluded that a broad base of trust lubricates day-to-day functioning. Trust fosters a set of organizational conditions that make schools more conducive to the initiation of activities that affect productivity improvements. Bryk and Schneider's findings suggest that if you want to make noticeable improvements in your *family, team, or organization*, start by building trust.

Whether the relationship is with a friend, coworker, coach, spouse, sibling, or CEO, trust must be earned. Earned trust takes time to build, but lost trust can happen in an instant. Trusting relationships bring *Upward Living* and the *Life Gifts of PH2E* to you. You may not receive any of the *PH2E's* immediately; however, the alternatives of *Wayward* or *Downward Living* will certainly not bring the *Life Gifts*.

> *Everybody in the world is seeking happiness—and there is one sure way to find it. That is by controlling your thoughts. Happiness doesn't depend on outward conditions. It depends on inner conditions.*
>
> —Dale Carnegie

The Outward Living Principle

Outward Living is when you are interacting with other people and the world. As previously discussed, we have 100% control of our *Inward Living* and 100% control of how we react to

Outward Living is when you are interacting with other people and the world.

Outward Actions coming to us. We have varying degrees of influence and inspiration over others, but ultimately no control. Others have 100% control of their actions, and you can't make them act in the fashion you want. Even if you have positional power over them, such as a parent, boss, or teacher, you can only enforce consequences; you cannot control their actions. As soon as you walk away, there is no motivation for them to continue meeting your demands. Therefore, you truly don't have control over others. A better way is to *Inspire* and *Influence* others to see the benefits for both parties. When that happens, there is a higher level of success, coupled with a high level of trust.

We have 100% control over our *Outward Actions*, but we have no control over how others and the world react to our actions. That is an important distinction and needs to be repeated in our minds each day. The concept can be confusing because we think or assume our actions should create a particular reaction from others, but sometimes a completely different reaction occurs. We should not be surprised when that happens. In fact, we should expect it because of the *Outward Principle*.

Repeat the following to yourself every day for the next 30 days:

1. I have <u>No Control of the *Outward World*</u>.
2. I have <u>100% Control of my *Outward Actions*</u> to the *Outward World*.
3. I have <u>100% Control of *my reactions*</u> to the *Outward World*.

We judge ourselves by our intentions and others by their behavior.

—Stephen M.R. Covey

Inward Living to Outward Actions

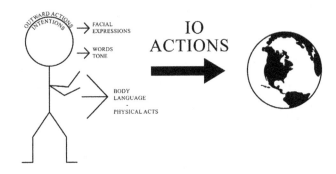

Inward Living to *Outward Actions* or *IO Actions* are when you interact with others and the world through your words, actions, and your *Hidden Outward Dimensions,* as discussed in Chapter 2. Be aware of all the possible ways you can *Outwardly* act toward others and the world. As you *Outwardly* act, other people and the world are acting on you. Therefore, when you are *Outward Living,* focus on and self-assess your actions and keep in mind that you can only try to *Inspire* and *Influence* others. As you will read in Chapter 12, there are *6 Essential Life Anchors* when *Outwardly Living.* When you incorporate them into your daily life, *IOU Trust* will exponentially grow. When this happens, *PH2E* will flow freely into your life.

To reach the highest level of *PH2E,* you need to focus on and examine what you have 100% control over. In the last chapter, we examined your *I's,* and in the next chapter, your *O's* will be examined. Living a *positive and effective* intentional life and continually focusing on what you have control over will propel you on your *Life Journey.*

An entire sea of water can't sink a ship unless it gets inside the ship. Similarly, the negativity of the world can't put you down unless you allow it to get inside you.

—Anonymous

The 3 Life Relation-Ships

Who's on your ship? Do you let negative people on board? Do you bring the world's negativity into your *Inward Living?*

When you are in an *Outward Mode*, you are in some way interacting with another person or nature. The *3 Life Relation-Ships* include the people you interact with during your lifetime. Let's review each *Relation-Ship.*

1. Inward Life Relation-Ship. On this ship, all the most important people in your life are accompanying you—your family members, your closest friends, and your *Inward* connection to your spirit. These people are deeply embedded in your *Inward Being.*

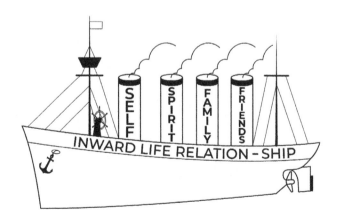

2. IO Life Relation-Ship. On this ship are your *Inward Outward* relationships. These are the people you interact with on a daily or weekly basis due to your work but who are not on your *Inward Life Relation-Ship,* such as your colleagues, mentors, and acquaintances. These people are more in the *Outward World,* but they do have some connection to your *Inward Life.*

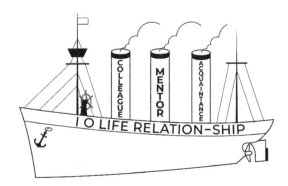

3. Outward Life Relation-Ship. On this ship are people in the *Outward World* who are strangers you notice but do not know. These people are entirely in the *Outward World* with no connection to you.

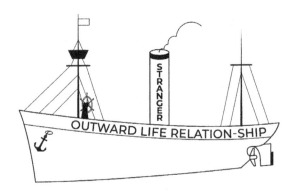

When you are navigating your *Inward Relation-Ship*, two other ships are always around your ship: the *IO Relation-Ship* and the *O Relation-Ship*. People can move from ship to ship. For example, on the *IO Relation-Ship* you may have a colleague who you become close to and with whom you develop a friendship. That person then moves to your *Inward Life Relation-Ship*,

Keep all people with negative thoughts off your *Life Ship*.

which has the people in your life you consider the closest to you. People in your life are ship hopping all the time. Be aware of this but know you always have 100% control of who you allow on your ships. Take a moment and think of the people on your *Inward Relation-Ship* and the people you know on the *IO Relation-Ship*. Keep all people with negative thoughts off your *Life-Ships*. Do not let someone force themselves onto your prestigious *Inward Life Relation-Ship*. That's what pirates do!

Nobody can make you feel inferior without your consent.

—Eleanor Roosevelt

Walk the Plank

You need to keep your *Inward Life Relation-Ship* in order. Think about who is on your *Inward Life Relation-Ship*. Is everyone on your *Inward Life Relation-Ship* the most important people in your life? Everyone on this ship needs to be positive and adding value to your *Life Journey*. If not, have them walk the plank—not literally, but in your *Inward* mind!

Take them off your *Inward Relation-Ship* and put them in a dinghy. A dinghy is a small boat or metaphor for a holding place for people you must interact with but are not supporting your *Life Vision* and *Life Goals*. Those people do not have to be on your ship. They can be on a dinghy, which is nearby but off your ship. You may have a family member you are not close to, or there may be someone with whom you have a conflict or negative interactions.

On your *IO Life Relation-Ship* you may have a mentor at work who is not supporting you and may even be undermining you. That person is a mentor in name only. These people are examples of who you need to mentally walk the plank and put them on hold in the dinghy. Hopefully, over time and through relationship building, you will welcome them back on your *IO Relation-Ship*. You have 100% control over who you want to walk the plank and go into the dinghy.

Who is on your dinghy?

Before you start throwing everyone overboard, let's review each of your *Relation-Ships*:

1 - Inward Relation-Ship

1. **Self** - It's you.
2. **Spirit** - Non-physical and invisible, could be a greater being, a greater feeling, a religion, a higher being

3. **Family** - Any individual related to you. A spouse, child, brother, sister, mother, father, grandmother, grandfather, cousin, uncle, aunt, etc.
4. **Friends** - A person with whom you have a close bond of mutual affection or esteem.

2 - IO Relation-Ship

1. **Colleague** - A person who you work with or of the same profession or business.
2. **Mentor** - A person who trains and guides you: An advisor, teacher, boss, spiritual leader, a coach
3. **Acquaintance** - Someone you know casually but is not a close friend

3 - O Relation-Ship

Stranger - A person you do not know or are not familiar with.

Letting go of negative people doesn't mean you hate them.
It just means that you love yourself.

—Anonymous

Who's on your Dinghy?

I'm sure you can think of someone, if not several people, who you would have walk the plank and into the dinghy. Before you do, I highly recommend that you write down or at least think about the people who are on each of the *3 Relation-Ships*. At first, make your list by name only. Let me explain. For the *Inward Relation-Ship*, list all the people you consider family and friends. Spirit should never walk the plank. Hopefully, your spirit is always with you, and you can go to it at any point for support and inspiration. After writing down all your family and friends, who would you put on the dinghy? Once you complete this task, the people left on your *Inward Relation-Ship* are your most important relationships you have and with whom you should have a high level of trust. These are the relationships you can comfortably share your *Inward Thoughts* with and *Outwardly* interact with *positively and effectively*. When this happens, the *Life Gifts of PH2E* come to you, and you receive *Upward Living*. This *Inward*, *Outward*, and *Upward Living* entwined with another person is *IOU Trust*.

Aligning Outward Living and Culture

We all want a *Dynamic Positive Culture* for *ourselves, our family, our teams, and organizations*. This can only be achieved by living *Outwardly* in a *positive and effective* manner with a clear vision. The vision and culture need to be aligned, and both are necessary. John Maxwell states this clearly in his writing on culture versus vision. Vision is about someday, and culture happens every day.

Everyone needs to focus on both the future and the present. If there is an established vision that is clear to everyone in the *family, team, or organization* without the appropriate culture, the vision will never be achieved. Likewise, if the *family, team, or organization* has an outstanding culture but no clear vision, everyone might really enjoy their time together but never go anywhere. We need to examine our *Outward Actions* continually, so they match our *Life Vision*. The *Outward Living* of *yourself, your family, team, and organization* needs a *Life Vision,* which provides a clear, shared, and intentional direction.

In the next chapter, we will examine the *Outward Anchors* with the goal of developing a structure to examine them and continually fine-tune them for accuracy. Others and the world do not see your *Inward Anchors,* but they do see your *Outward Living.*

Captain's Log for Chapter 9

Principle "O"

Captain's Log:

Point 1 *Outward Living* is when you are in the world and interacting with others and the world by your words and actions. At the same time, people are interacting with you.

Point 2 We have no control over the *Outward World*. In other words, we have no control over the thoughts and actions of others. We should not spend time focusing on what we have no control and only varying levels of influence over.

Point 3 We have 100% control over our *Outward Actions* toward the world. Remind yourself to be aware of your *Outward Actions*. They are based on our *Inward Living*, and we have 100% control over that, too.

Point 4 Our *Outward Actions* include our verbal and non-verbal communication, including facial expressions, words/tone, body language, and physical actions.

Point 5 The *3 Life Relation-Ships* can help guide you as you interact with the *Outward World*.

Point 6   Have non-supportive family members and friends
               walk the plank. Don't let their negativity influence
               your life. Get some cognitive distance from them
               by placing them on a dinghy!

Point 7   We need to examine our *Outward Actions*
               continually, so they match our *Life Vision*. If
               there is an established *Life Vision* that is clear
               to everyone in the *family, team, or organization*
               without the appropriate culture, the *Life Vision*
               will never be achieved. Likewise, if the *family,
               team, or organization* has an outstanding culture,
               but no clear *Life Vision*, everyone might really
               enjoy their time together but never go anywhere.

Teach to Learn

The best way to deepen your understanding and, at the same time, share and stimulate new conversations with others is to teach. Share what you have learned with a friend, family member, coworker, or anyone else who will listen. Teaching is, by far, the best way to deepen one's understanding of new insights and concepts. Take any of the Points in the Captain's Log or this chapter for thought-provoking discussions.

New Daily Voyage:

Activity:

Pick one person you will interact with today. Be mindful of your facial expressions, tone, and body language, and make them consistent with the message that your words wish to convey. Then, reflect on whether your message was received more clearly than in previous times when you weren't mindful of your *Outward* nonverbal communication.

Ask yourself:

Do I spend too much time focusing on the *Outward Actions* of others instead of my own?

Chapter 10

Do you Know Your *O's?*

Who you are is defined by your Outward Living.

—Dr. Joe Famularo

Examine Your *O's*

Between your *Inward Thinking* and *Outward Actions* there is a space in which you have 100% control. When that space expires, you act. Your chosen act becomes who you are and your world. Increase that space to help yourself make the best possible choices based on your *Inward Life Anchors.* Your life is a continuous *Inward-Outward* cycle.

Your life is a continuous *Inward-Outward* cycle.

Every *Outward Action* will have a positive, neutral, or negative consequence. You have 100% control of your *Outward Action* and no control over the consequence. Therefore, you need to examine your *O's,* or *Outward Living* continually.

As soon as you put any *Outward Action* (100% control) into play, the natural consequences of the *Outward World* will come to you (no control). Sometimes, *Outward* reactions from others will come right at you even when you have not done anything. However, there is always a reaction to your actions. Sir Isaac Newton's Law of Motion describes the response to actions. The law states that for every action in nature, there is an equal and opposite reaction.

Similarly, our actions are always followed by some *Outward Action* or consequence, which can be positive or negative. Sometimes, the reaction is expected, and sometimes it's not. Have you ever said something to someone with good intentions, and they react completely the opposite of what you may have expected? It happens to all of us, but why? Others define you by your *Outward Living*, not your *Inward Living*. Your intentions are inside of you, and no one but you knows what they are. The only way others see and understand your intentions is by how you *Outwardly* act. Do your *Outward Action*s match your *Inward Intentions*? In Chapter 2, we discussed nonverbal communications and the *Hidden Outward Living Dimension* in great detail. We can improve the match between intentions and actions by being aware of those communications and intentionally making adjustments that match our intentions. This section will focus on the *Outward Principles* referred to as your *Outward Life Anchors*.

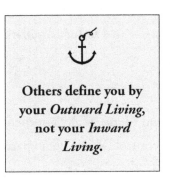

Others define you by your *Outward Living*, not your *Inward Living*.

Examine Your O's

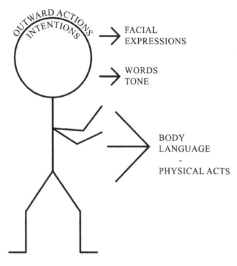

IOU Trust is the foundation of all lasting relationships. Trust is what bonds people together. We act *Outwardly* when we say or do something. Our mindset should always be focused on building trust. When we are in an *Outward Mode*, it is about relationships with people, nature, the environment, and the world. Remember, *Outward Living* is about relationships and trust. As Bryk and Schneider note, we build trust through day to day social exchanges, by consistently showing respect, competence, integrity, and personal regard for others.

IOU Trust is the foundation of all lasting relationships.

When we are trustworthy, we are vulnerable, open, and responsible. Brené Brown coined an acronym for trusting relationships, BRAVING, which stands for boundaries, reliability, accountability, the "vault" (holding confidences and not listening to gossip), integrity, being nonjudgmental, and generous. To have positive and dynamic relationships, you need trust as the foundation, and these BRAVING qualities will help you develop it.

Outward Living in a *positive and effective* intentional manner will create an environment that is safe, happy, and full of learning and growth. It's demonstrating high character and competence with an emphasis on developing collaborative relationships and trust. Executing the *Outward Life Anchors* will build your relationships and trust by promoting a *Common Language* consistent with your *Life Vision, Daily Mission, Life Principles, Life Values*, and *Life Goals*. Sharing traditions with others will connect people in a deep way. Traditions provide a sense of belonging, reinforce shared values, and define a group's identity. Also, you will *Outwardly* be continuously thinking of ways to improve your mind, body, and heart and have a *Mindset of Propelling PH2E*.

Remember that you have 100% control of your *Inward Living* and *Outward Actions*, but no control over how the *Outward World* reacts to you. When the *Outward World* acts on you or puts demands on you, you have 100% control over how you want to respond. As we discussed in Chapter 2, according to the *Life Leadership Matrix*, when the *Outward* demand is *Urgent and Important,* it puts your *Life Ship* in a sinking environment, which requires immediate attention (*E1*). You must deal with it now, or your *Life Ship* will sink. Even in this *Life Environment*, you have 100% control over whether to act or not. If you decide not to act, you will suffer the *Outward* natural consequence of your actions.

Influence vs. Control

You have no control over how your *Outward* relationships and the world react to you, but you do have influence. Influence is not control. In your relationships with others, influence may guide their actions, but ultimately, those people have 100% control concerning how they want to respond.

There is a continuum of influence that you have on others and the world. The greatest level is *High Influence*, which is the influence you have based on high trust with the people closest to you on your *Inward Life Relation-Ship*.

You can also exert significant influence out of fear. For example, where a parent tells their child to do something "or else," and the child chooses to do it out of fear, the parent is exerting *High Influence* but is ultimately not in control of their child. You cannot go inside the head and body of your child and control their movements to complete the task you are asking them to do. They will choose to do it or not and understand the

There is a continuum of influence that you have on others and the world.

consequences if they decide not to comply. Hopefully, there is a high trust relationship, and your child chooses to do it out of respect, understanding the positive relationship-building consequence of completing the task. In this case, they are not responding out of fear but out of respect. Be aware of the difference between using your positional authority to get others to do something versus using influence based on your relationship and persuasion.

Another example is a boss who has significant influence over his/her employees but no control. The boss can issue directives and instructions, but the employees choose how to respond. In a high trust employer-employee relationship, employees follow directives because they share a common *Life Vision* and *Daily Mission*, and they trust that the directive will benefit everyone. Even in the absence of high trust, employees may comply because they want to keep receiving their paychecks. The boss has *High Influence*, but ultimately, the employees choose whether to comply or not.

As those two examples demonstrate, there is an important difference between influence and control. Understanding this will shift your actions when you realize that you do not have control over others but can only exert influence.

Determine the level of influence you have over the different aspects of the *Outward World* and reflect on how you can increase your influence, which can be accomplished by understanding and analyzing your *Outward Life Anchors*. I will explain more about the *Outward Life Anchors* later in the Chapter 12, but first a word on the varying *Levels of Influence*.

The best way for us to perhaps influence others is to instead focus on ourselves by doing our best—then others will be influenced from our leadership by example.

—Lisa Kardos

3 Levels of Your Outward Influence

Be aware of things in your life you have *Outward High Influence* over, *Moderate Influence* over, and *Low to No Influence* over. Many people continually advocate and *Outwardly* spend their energy on *Low to No Influence* items. If you spend too much time in the *Low to No Influence* level and expect some change, you will quickly feel the emotions of *IOW* or *IOD Living*. You will feel the *Downward Life Drain of Anxiety*, the stress of not accomplishing anything. You will become the person who is constantly complaining and giving their opinion on things over which you have no influence. It's fine to talk and share opinions about *Low to No Influence* items, but when you are excessively stuck in the area, it begins to create a *Toxic Negative Culture*.

Aspects of life you have *Moderate Influence* over are the people and things with which you have limited contact, e.g., people you know and may see occasionally and may not have built the trust yet to have *High Influence*. You may advocate for a law or policy, and the people who can make the change may hear you, so there is a possibility you may affect their decisions. However, you are an outsider to them, so be aware of your level of influence in this area so you are

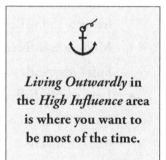

Living Outwardly in the *High Influence* area is where you want to be most of the time.

prepared that you may or may not get your desired results.

Living Outwardly in the *High Influence* area is where you want to be most of the time. You may feel you don't have much influence over things, but if you reflect on what you can control and influence, you will find an abundance of people and things you can have a high impact on. One area over which you have extremely *High Influence* is your health. However, it's one of the hardest in which to motivate yourself. You have *High Influence* over nutrition, exercise, and sleep. You also have *High Influence* over your closest friends and family members. You know the people in your life that you have influence over, and they have influence over you. The reason for this *High Influence* is because there is high trust. Influence increases exponentially when there is high trust. As you will read in Chapter 12, all *Outward Essential Life Anchors* are built around trust.

As you travel along your daily *Life Journey*, be aware of your influence level, and act *Outwardly* accordingly.

Levels of Influence

- **High Influence** - Your health, your close family members, friends, and colleagues
- **Moderate Influence** - Acquaintances, some laws, some businesses with which you have dealings
- **Low to No Influence** - The rotation of the earth, the sun, moon, galaxy, the weather, natural disasters, the past, strangers

Here is an exercise you can do to understand the different levels of influence. Think of a recent problem or issue in the news over which you have *Low to No Influence*. Think about why you have *Low* or *No Influence* over the issue. What position would you need to hold to raise your *Level of Influence*?

Now think about a problem or issue over which you have *High Influence*. Feel the difference in your influence in this situation versus the *Low to No Influence* situation.

Are you spending more energy in the *High Influence* areas or the *Low to No Influence* areas in your life? We should be spending our time where we can have an impact. Where are you putting your energy each day? Are you focusing on your *Inward Living* where you have 100% control and the areas and relationships of your *Outward Living* where you have *High Influence*?

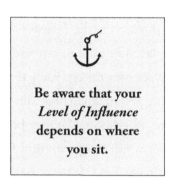

Be aware that your *Level of Influence* depends on where you sit.

Be aware that your *Level of Influence* depends on where you sit. If you are an attorney who argues cases before a court, your influence level will be higher on influencing court decisions than most people. Based on your position, job, and relationships, you have various levels of influence. Reflect and be aware of where you have *High*, *Moderate*, and *Low to No Levels of Influence*. When you do, you will feel like you have more control over your life, and you will!

> *A leader is one who knows the way, goes the way and shows the way.*
>
> —John Maxwell

211

LEADER RELATIONSHIPS

We have 100% control of our *Inward Thinking* and our *Outward Actions*. We have no control over others or the world. *Life Leadership* is living a *positive and effective* life by design—your design. We should always interact with others in a respectful manner, building trust that will create many dividends in the relationship. We live a life of leadership with the ultimate goal of receiving the *Upward Life Gifts of PH2E*. However, we are all placed in roles in our lives where we have positional leadership roles over others, such as a parent leading a child through their life and gradually releasing more independence on their journey to adulthood. We may be the leader of a group of people on a team in an organization for a particular project or an ongoing assignment. You may be a leader of a sports team. Another role is the leader of an organization with many departments and teams that report to you. I call these leadership roles, "*Leader Relationships*." Successful leaders understand the areas you have 100% control over and the areas over which you have no control.

It was a rare Saturday with a blank calendar box on the refrigerator. I had no practices or games to drive the children to, no tutoring, no lessons, no events—nothing. It was a perfect day to visit my mom, their grandmother. I walked into the playroom where my son was relaxed and playing video games. He'd had a long week. He always works hard in school and competes at a very high level as the captain of the high school varsity soccer team while only a junior; he is a real leader on the team. I know he doesn't have a lot of downtime, but we all value time spent with family.

I said, "At five, we're going to Grandma's for dinner."

He immediately said, "No, I don't want to go."

I tried to *Inspire* him and said, "We'll have a good time. We're having Grandma's lasagna!"

He said, "No, I'm not hungry. I'm not going. I'm staying home."

Next, I tried to *Influence* him and said, "It's important for the family to be together. You haven't seen Grandma for a while, and it's good to spend time with her."

He replied, "I said I'm not going. I'm staying home!"

After several more back and forth comments, I shifted to *Consequences.* "Give me your phone, turn off the video games, and turn off the television."

At that moment, I realized I had no control and could not force my son to go to my mother's house, but I did have control over the *Consequences* imposed if he chose not to go. This mindset actually settled my emotions a little, but I still felt I could not back down.

As I was beginning to reach out to take my son's phone, I realized my son's emotions were still heightened, so I said, "I'm going to walk out of the room and give you 15 minutes to think about the situation and how you want to handle it. When I come back, I'll ask you again if you're going,

We have 100% control over our actions and no control over others and the world. We can have influence but no control.

and whether you say yes or no, the natural *Consequences* of either will follow."

I left the room. At first, I was incredulous that he was not doing what he had been told because he had never been so oppositional. Then I realized I have no control over him. I can't go inside him and make his legs move or control his mind to do what I want. What I do have is 100% control over the *Consequences*. Just thinking in those terms brought a peaceful calm over me. We have 100% control over our actions and no control over others and the world. We can have *Influence* but no control. When we are in a *Leader Relationship* such as a parent, what we have control over is to *Influence* and *Inspire*, as well as 100% control over the *Consequences* of the actions and decisions of our children.

When the 15 minutes were up, I walked back into the room and asked, "What have you decided?"

He told me he would go. I simply said thank you and walked out, knowing it wasn't a good time to discuss it any further. I was incredibly proud of his introspection and positive choice.

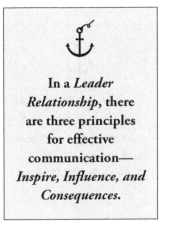

In a *Leader Relationship*, there are three principles for effective communication— *Inspire, Influence, and Consequences.*

When it was time to go to Grandma's, his attitude was fine, and I chose not to discuss it with him. I often want to give the "big lesson" story but realized I should refrain because my son had already learned the "big lesson" through his *Inward Thinking.*

It's always important to tell ourselves that we have 100%

control of our *Inward Living* and no control of others and the world. We do have *Influence*, can *Inspire*, and when in a *Leader Relationship*, we have 100% control of the *Consequences*.

Leader Relationships are relationships that are positionally at a higher level such as a parent to their child, a coach to a team, a lead manager to their team members, a teacher to their students, or a CEO to their employees. A *Leader Relationship* has no control over the individual(s) to whom you are *Outwardly* communicating your intentions. In a *Leader Relationship*, there are three principles for effective communication—*Inspire, Influence,* and *Consequences*.

LEADER RELATIONSHIPS

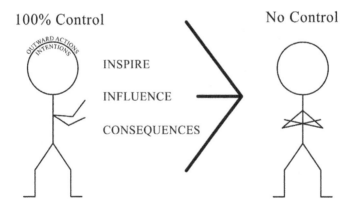

100% Control   No Control

INSPIRE

INFLUENCE

CONSEQUENCES

My daughter came home very unhappy. "There is something I need to tell you, but I don't know how to. I don't think I did the right thing."

She had our attention, and we told her to tell us what happened. She said that she had gotten a third hole pierced in her ear for an earring. Our daughter had asked for a third hole for the past year, but we wanted her to wait until she is older. She was 16, and we had explicitly told her we didn't want her to do it yet. She had willfully disobeyed our wishes.

We were very unhappy with her decision but tried to stay calm. It wasn't the third hole in particular that made us upset. Instead, it was about her disrespecting our wishes and going behind our backs. At that point, had she asked again, we may have given her permission. We were disappointed she purposely went against what we had clearly discussed for the past year. We asked her to take the earrings out, but she refused. We tried to *Inspire* her by appealing to her emotions and explained that her actions showed disrespect toward us. She didn't understand or agree and wouldn't take them out.

Next, we tried to *Influence* her by explaining why we were against a third hole and how we felt for her it was neither appropriate nor necessary at 16 years old. We discussed that our relationship was built on trust and respect. When that didn't work, we were planning to move to *Consequences*. For starters, we would take her phone away. However, before we had to inform her of the *Consequences*, she shared that she was extremely sorry and decided to take the new earrings out. We knew the holes would close up in a few days, and then we could discuss it again in the future. She knew her mother and I were extremely disappointed in her.

Here is the point. We had no control to force her to take out the earrings. We can't crawl inside of her and control her hands to do what we desire, nor are we going to hold her down physically and take them out. However, what we do have is 100% control of *Consequences* for her since the parent/child relationship is a *Leader Relationship*. In a *Leader Relationship*, we can try to *Inspire, Influence*, or share the *Consequence* to get the desired results. Before jumping to the *Consequence* step, it's important to go through the *Inspire* and *Influence* stages first. If we proceeded directly to *Consequences*, it would have caused high emotions and resentment and would have been very difficult to explain the problem with her actions. After all, the most important factor is the life lesson, not the punishment or *Consequences*. Later that day, it was clear she had learned an important life lesson and was sorry for what had happened. She took the earrings out herself, having learned from the conversations during the *Inspire* and *Influence* levels, not from the *Consequences*.

When you are in a similar situation, remember to go through the *Inspire* and *Influence* stages before implementing the *Consequences*. *INSPIRE* is to motivate with the heart. *INFLUENCE* is to reason with the mind. *CONSEQUENCE* is the cause and effect of an action.

When we are in the role of a *Leader Relationship*, we need to think of these three principles:

INSPIRE

To *inspire* is to motivate and is defined as to breathe life into. *Inspire* is the first level when trying to motivate any individual or group. It is associated with the heart.

INFLUENCE

Influence is reasoning, giving the facts, and explaining why it's important and the benefits to do a certain task or begin the journey. It is associated with the mind.

CONSEQUENCES

Every action or inaction has a *consequence*. There are natural *Consequences* in the world, and there are *Consequences* created by the leader of a *family, team, or organization*. The *Consequences* need to be fair and developed with the integrity of the *family, team, or organization* in mind.

Too many times, we jump right to *Consequences*. It's difficult not to do that when you feel loyalty or that clear rules or policies have been violated. However, remember that *Outward Living* is about relationships and building trust, so make sure to attempt to *Inspire* and *Influence* first in a calm way. If you find yourself often moving to *Consequences, Inwardly Reflect* on your *Life Maps* to shift your thinking and find alternate ways to *Inspire* and *Influence*.

An effective leader *Inspires, Influences,* and makes sure the *Consequences* are clearly established in the culture. When these principles are explained and practiced within any group, the culture will be on a clear path to becoming dynamic and positive.

The only things I regret, and the only things I'll ever regret are things I didn't do. In the end, that's what we mourn. The paths we didn't take. The people we didn't touch.

—Scott Spencer

IO INACTIONS

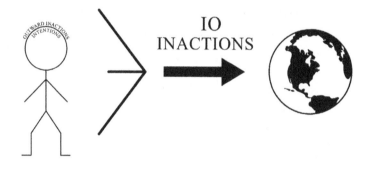

We have discussed many times that *Outward Living* is when you affect another person or the world. *IO* or *Inward Outward Inactions* are situations when you (*I - Inward*) should be doing something (*O - Outward*); however, for whatever reason, you don't do what you were supposed to do. Therefore, you are affecting someone due to your *Inaction*. For example, you made plans, and your friend is waiting for you to go out for dinner. You are at work and forgot about your plans because you are involved in a special project and are almost done. Due to your *Inaction* by not going to your friend's house to pick them up or making a call, you have affected your friend waiting for you. Your *Inactions* place you in an *Outward Mode*. In this case, you don't even realize you are in an *Outward Mode* because you forgot about your appointment. Nevertheless, due to your *Inaction,* you have affected another person.

IO or *Inward Outward Inactions* are situations when you (*I - Inward*) should be doing something (*O - Outward*), however, for whatever reason you don't do what you were supposed to do.

All of our *Outward Actions* come from our *Inward Being.* Therefore, *IO Inactions* start with an *Inward Intention.* An *Inward Intention* that you are supposed to do *Outwardly* but don't necessarily perform is an *IO Inaction. IO Inactions* can produce *Downward Drains* for you and the other person involved. Be aware of your *IO Inactions* and how they can affect your relationships. As discussed earlier in this chapter, your *Outward Actions* and *Inactions* will define who you are.

In the next two chapters, we will discuss in detail your most important *Life Anchors—The 12 Essential Life Anchors* that will assist you in navigating your *Life Journey.*

Captain's Log for Chapter 10

Do You Know Your O's?

Captain's Log:

Point 1   Every *Outward Action* has a consequence, both positive and negative. You have 100% control over your action and 0% control over the consequence that come to you.

Point 2   Trust binds people together and is the foundation of all lasting relationships. Strive to build an environment that is safe, happy, full of learning, and based on collaborative, trusting relationships.

Point 3   While you have no control over the reactions of your *Outward* relationships and the world, you do have *Influence*, which varies on a continuum of *High, Moderate and Low to No Influence.*

Point 4   In *Leader Relationships*, we can *Inspire, Influence,* and/or provide *Consequences*. We need to design what we want to exert in any situation. *Inspiring* is motivating, *Influencing* is reasoning, and *Consequences* are the cause and effect of an action.

Point 5   *IO* or an *Inward Outward Inaction* is a situation when you (*I—Inward*) should be doing something (*O - Outward*), however for whatever reason you don't do what you were supposed to do, and therefore you are affecting someone due to your *Inaction*.

Point 6   Our *IO Actions* and *Inactions* define who we are.

221

Teach to Learn

The best way to deepen your understanding and, at the same time, share and stimulate new conversations with others is to teach. Share what you have learned with a friend, family member, coworker, or anyone else who will listen. Teaching is, by far, the best way to deepen one's understanding of new insights and concepts. Take any of the Points in the Captain's Log or this chapter for thought-provoking discussions.

New Daily Voyage:

Activity:

Think about your significant relationships and reflect if there is high trust. If not, what specific actions can you take to develop such trust?

Ask yourself:

What are the *Outward* subtypes I spend the most time in? Is this the way I want to spend my time? Do I do this by design or by default?

PART III

Executing IOU Life Leadership

Launch Your Life Ship
&
Navigate Your Life Journey

The 12 ESSENTIAL LIFE ANCHORS

The only ship that can safely navigate out of distressed and troubled water is an IOU Life Leadership.

—Dr. Joe Famularo

The 12 Essential Life Anchors are embodied in the life of Vincent, who was a great *Life Leader*. Through the stories he shared about his life and sailing the seas, Vincent provided many principle-centered life lessons. He always had a clear vision and purpose in everything he did. He lived a long *Upward Life* receiving *PH2E* and thereby created a *Dynamic Positive Culture* with whomever he came into contact in his life.

The 12 Essential Life Anchors are immovable, timeless, universal life principles that will transform your life both *Inwardly* and *Outwardly*.

By now, you should be familiar with the *I and O Modes* that, when lived in a *positive and effective* manner, lead to the byproduct, the *U* or *Upward Life Gifts*, which will be one or more of the *PH2E's* (*Peacefulness, Happiness, Healthiness, and Excellence*). The question you should be asking yourself is, how do I live *Inwardly* and *Outwardly* in a *positive and effective* intentional manner?

Part III will review *The 12 Essential Life Anchors* for living the *IOU Principle* in a *positive and effective* intentional manner. In the image of the captain's wheel (shown on the next illustration), the center displays an anchor, which is a symbol that is strong, stable, and grounded. *The 12 Essential Life Anchors* are immovable, timeless, universal life principles that will transform your life both *Inwardly* and *Outwardly*. Imagine yourself in the center of the wheel and the anchor within you as a life guide to *IOU Living*.

The 12 Essential Life Anchors are the framework for *Life Leadership*, akin to how notes harmonize together make up a musical score. There are *6 Inward Life Anchors* and *6 Outward Life Anchors*. The next section will focus on the *Inward Living Anchors*, which comprise your thinking, or what I call your *Inward SelfCulture*.

You are always living in one of two modes—*Inwardly* when you are alone thinking, or *Outwardly* when you interact with another person or the world. In Chapter 1, your *Daily Voyage Exercise* was to determine what percentage of your day you spend *Inwardly Living*. Most people are *Inwardly Living* the majority of the day. Are you living by your design or the design of others? You have 100% control of your *Inward Living*, and by taking the time to create your *Life Maps*, you will feel a sense of control and purpose as you travel on your *Life Journey*.

IOU LIFE LIVING WHEEL

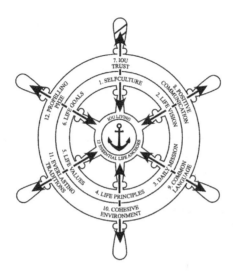

You owe it to yourself and others to understand and live by the *IOU Life Living Wheel.*

When the captain rotates the wheel on a ship, it turns the rudder and thus sets the course for the journey. The *IOU Life Living Wheel* is a synergy of *The 12 Essential Life Anchors* that will assist you in setting the course and navigating your *Life Journey.* The result is *Upward Living,* which is the byproduct of the synergy of living the *Inward* and *Outward Principles* in a *positive and effective* manner. The anchor is a critical piece of equipment, which can stabilize a ship. The deeper life meaning of the anchor is a symbol of security, stability, and groundedness. A *Life Anchor* helps you live in tune with your *Inward Being.* In times of difficulty, you can pause and reflect *Inwardly* on your *Inward Anchors—SelfCulture, Life Vision, Daily Mission, Life*

227

Principles, Life Values, and *Life Goals,* which are your safe harbor. The anchor in the center of the *IOU Life Living Wheel* represents YOU, with *6 Inward Anchors* that point in symbolizing your *Inward Thinking,* your *Inward Opinions,* and your *Life Maps.* The *IOU Living Wheel* also has *6 Outward Anchors* that point out that symbolize your *Outward Living* and your *Outward Actions* with others and the world. The *IOU Life Living Wheel* represents *IOU Living,* a foundational framework for *positive and effective* intentional living based on universal life principles leading to a *Dynamic Positive Culture* for *you, your family, your team, and your organization.*

The anchor in the center of the *IOU Life Living Wheel* represents YOU, with *6 Inward Anchors* that point in symbolizing your *Inward Thinking,* your *Inward Opinions,* and your *Life Maps.* The *IOU Living Wheel* also has *6 Outward Anchors* that point out that symbolize your *Outward Living,* and your *Outward Actions* with others and the world.

It's time to take charge of your life, lift the anchor, hoist the sails, and turn the captain's wheel to set the rudder in the direction of your life dreams!

Effectiveness vs. Efficiency

Do you strive for effectiveness or efficiency? Always strive for effectiveness first. Your ship could be running smoothly, engines fined tuned, and all hands-on deck ready for *Outward* obstacles in the water or stormy weather with the entire crew working to their optimum levels. In this scenario, everyone is extremely efficient 24/7. However, is the ship on course, off-course, or even on the wrong course?

Most importantly, is it on the right course? There is only one person who sets the course—the captain. You can be efficient and not be effective if you are not on the right course. This is analogous to leading your *Life Journey.* As an *IOU Leader,* you set the right course and continually adjust it to keep your *Life Ship* aligned to your *Life Vision.* Your ship could be efficient with everyone working hard and feeling

**The *IOU Leader*
strives for effectiveness
first, not efficiency!**

positive, but if it's heading in the wrong direction, you will not be successful or reach your goal. The *IOU Leader* strives for effectiveness first, not efficiency! Let's dive in and examine *The 12 Essential Life Anchors* that will provide a foundational framework to guide your life, focusing on effectiveness and thereby guiding you toward a *Dynamic Positive Culture* for yourself and others.

Chapter 11

THE 6 INWARD LIFE ANCHORS

Thinking - Opinions - Life Maps

INWARD LIVING

*The person that is always looking Outward for happiness,
at some point stops and looks Inward and discovers the
Life Gifts are within them.*

—Dr. Joe Famularo

IOU LIFE LIVING WHEEL

INWARD LIVING
LIFE ANCHOR 1

SELFCULTURE

The Principle of Self-Identity

At the center of your being, you have the answer: you know who you are, and you know what you want.

—Lao Tzu

The *SelfCulture Life Anchor* is your foundational *Inward Life Anchor*. Culture typically relates to the environment of a group of people or an organization. Think of the last time you entered one of these environments, such as when you entered the home of a friend or a family member. How did it feel? Let's say you're at the first meeting of a new project team or sports team. When you initially meet with these teams, how did it feel? Now think about times when you entered a business or school environment how did you feel? How would you describe the characteristics and nuances of the environment? What vibe was projected? Was it warm, welcoming, and friendly? In the same way that groups have a culture, so do individuals.

I have coined the term *SelfCulture* to describe your personal culture, which is the feeling people get when in your presence. Perhaps you have never reflected on your *SelfCulture*, but reflecting on it provides an opportunity to define how you want to be and how you want to be perceived by others. It's your personal brand and the lifestyle you live by design. It is who you are in every way—your authentic self! *SelfCulture* focuses on the *Principle of Self-Identity*; it's your *Inward Being*, who you are at the deepest level. If you don't create your *SelfCulture*, the *Outward World* will create it for you. Your *SelfCulture* can either bring others toward you or drive them away from you.

You design your *SelfCulture*. What do you want someone to see and feel when they step into your *SelfCulture*? It's your aura, your look, your brand, your style, and your "I am." It is who you are right now, and the good news is you have 100% control over it. However, if you don't intentionally examine and improve it, you may go through life not knowing how your *SelfCulture* presents when *Outwardly* interacting with others.

No one can create your *SelfCulture*; it's all up to you. It's like creating your self-portrait. Can you easily answer the following questions?

- Who are you?
- What do you do?
- What makes you unique?
- Why should others care?
- How would you describe yourself?
- What do you stand for?
- How do you describe the ideal you?
- What are your unique talents, personal qualities, and accomplishments?
- How do you want to be perceived?
- What are you passionate about?

It is probably difficult to answer these questions automatically, as it is for most people. However, think about it. It's about you! You need and should be able to craft a brief paragraph about your most important asset—you! Take some time to think and write a description using the questions above as a guide. Don't put any constraints on yourself. Your paragraph will be your *SelfCulture*, a description of who you are and who you want to be.

- I am ambitious and driven
- I am a natural leader
- I am an excellent communicator

- I am a team player
- I look for positivity in all things
- I am flexible
- I am reliable
- I am motivated
- I am a self-starter
- I am dependable
- I am collaborative

Now, take a minute and ask yourself the following question: Do your actions match your description? Examine your social media. Do your posts match the *SelfCulture* you described?

Think about *Outward Actions* from the past week that did not fit with your *SelfCulture*. If there are posts that don't match your *SelfCulture*, delete them and be mindful that future posts match and are aligned to the culture that you want others to see and feel. Remember, you are defined by others based on your *Outward Actions*.

Your *SelfCulture* tells your story! It's your *Self-Identity*. You can either create and develop your *SelfCulture* or let it develop out of your control, possibly influenced by others with a different agenda. Your *SelfCulture* is vital for both your personal and professional lives.

As you go through the *Life Anchors*, you will continually return to your *SelfCulture* and refine it to exactly what you want it to be. The *Life Anchors* will guide you to examine what's important to you as you proceed on your *Life Journey*.

In 1954, Kenneth Pike coined two words to describe opposing perspectives—*emic* and *etic*. The *emic* perspective is the study of a subject from an insider's perspective. The *etic* perspective is the study of a subject from an outsider's perspective. The *emic* and *etic* perspectives are developed from the study of language arts. *Emic* comes from the word "phonemic," which is the study of the meaning of the parts of words. *Etic* comes from the word "phonetic," which is the study of the sounds of words that have no meaning.

When defining your *SelfCulture*, do you take an *emic* or *etic* perspective? If you take an *etic* perspective, you are taking an external view, listening to your *Outward* language and actions, and comparing yourself to others. If you define yourself in terms of your differences from others, you make a peripheral assessment and make judgments based on it. That approach will not lead to developing a *Dynamic and Positive SelfCulture*. On the other hand, if you take an *emic* perspective, you ask questions and integrate your answers with your beliefs and principles. You get the hidden nuances in your own individual language and *Inward Thinking* that would be missed if you took an *etic* perspective.

The keys to brand success are self-definition, transparency, authenticity and accountability.

—Simon Mainwaring

Visual Brand for Family, Team, School, Organization

A visual brand is a symbol that represents *you, your family, team, or organization.* It's part of your *SelfCulture.* It is everything you're promoting, such as your beliefs and vision. When people see your visual brand, it should be like looking at a rich, detailed landscape. How many paragraphs would it take to describe everything you can take in with your eyes in an instant? As the saying goes, a picture is worth a thousand words. How many ideas can you get by looking at rolling hills or mountains with trees, birds, a creek, or wildflowers growing across the valley? How many experiences can you envision in that setting? That is the power of the visual brand, which is a single image that sums up your message and is instantly associated with you or your organization.

The visual or the logo should represent your Life Vision, Daily Mission, and Life Values. The best scenario is to develop a visual or logo with all shareholders in your organization. However, if you already have one that's deeply embedded in your culture, you should rebrand it and connect it to the newly developed Life Vision and Daily Mission.

Think of the Nike logo and the instant recognition whenever the Swoosh is seen accompanied by the instant recall of their slogan, Just Do It. How about the iconic G for Google? Or the New York Yankees emblem? These are all examples of powerful visual brands.

Once you determine your brand, you must make sure that visuals are placed everywhere and constantly reinforced. Think of the powerful message that gives. Each time a visual is seen, it is like instantly giving a thousand lessons or saying a thousand words. The lessons are easily comprehended and loaded with background knowledge connected to them.

For as long as I can remember, I've always used a visual for my endeavors. For example, when I was 16 years old, I started a guitar school and created a brand called "The Guitar Experience," which I registered with the US Trademark Office.

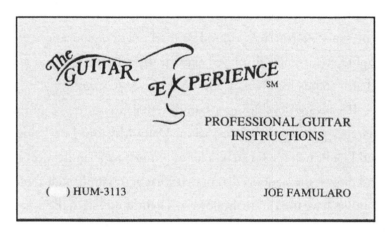

When I became the principal of an early childhood center, I led the staff in developing a set of values and a visual brand. Our symbol became a star. Adults were considered "Star Polishers," and students were the "Stars" that needed love and care to develop. When I became superintendent of the same district, the first thing I did was lead in developing our organization's *SelfCulture*. I engaged all stakeholders in formulating a vision, mission, core values, and logo. At the time, the logo was "A Commitment to Excellence." Our new vision became "A Community of Learners" to emphasize the collaboration between all stakeholders. This vision was made prominent in our redesigned logo, and therefore, became an integral part of our visual brand and *SelfCulture*. In fact, the district was recognized by FranklinCovey as a *Leadership Lighthouse District*, one of two districts in the world with this prestigious designation.

It is critical to match your visual brand to your Life Vision, Daily Mission, Life Values, and Life Principles. They all must align to project a single consistent message. When people see the visual brand, it should call to mind everything your organization represents. As you walk around your school or organization, you should see artifacts displayed that clearly reflect the brand and what it stands for, thereby adding to the *SelfCulture*.

If you are developing a family visual brand, make sure it matches your family's Life Vision, Daily Mission, Life Values, and Life Principles. It can be a lot of fun to have a family meeting and discuss the symbols that match what your family is all about. Families have used animals, flowers, a lighthouse, stars, the ocean, a boat, a word, or the first letter of their family's last name. It can be anything you want. You might even want to have your symbol proudly displayed in your home or have inspirational words or quotes hanging in prominent locations as reminders. The discussion and process is extremely powerful and will bring your family closer together. When someone in your family feels it needs to be revisited, have the discussion again. My wife and I have made this a practice with our family at the end of each year for over 20 years, and it has proven to be an effective tool for creating a more positive family *SelfCulture*.

*Personal branding begins the moment you begin
to discover yourself.*

—Bernard Kelvin Clive

Your Personal Brand

Your personal brand may not be a symbol, but it can be in your mind. You may not display it, but it's a good exercise to think about it and go through the process of creating it.

Your *Outward Actions*, including your body language represent a form of your personal brand to others. Are your *Outward Actions* and body language consistent with how you want to be seen in the world?

You have 100% control of the following:

- Your look (hairstyle, clothing, colors)
- Your *Outward Actions* (words, tone, facial expressions, body language, physical acts)

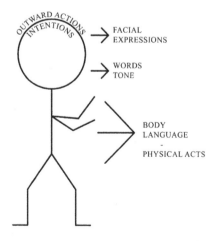

Socrates is credited with saying, "An unexamined life is not worth living." Examining our lives—or thinking—is the key to knowing ourselves and how to live. When we examine anything, the result is that we understand it better. Wouldn't we want to understand ourselves and our *Outward Actions* better? We are with ourselves 24 hours a day. By examining our *Inward Living*, we can understand what influences us, what we influence, the choices we make *Outwardly*, and why we make those choices. I am not saying you need to climb a mountain and spend days meditating (although I wish I had time to do that). It's about examining your behaviors, your life patterns, and the things that affect you in both a positive and negative manner. By taking some time to notice and think about your *SelfCulture* and your *Inward Living*, you will take responsibility for your *Outward Actions* and be in a position to make marked improvements to your life.

THE SELFCULTURE MODEL

The Principle of Self-Identity

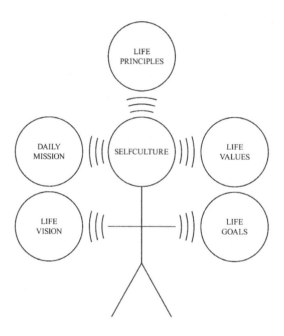

Your *SelfCulture* is your *Inward Being*, your *Self-Identity* and projects who you are *Outwardly* to the world—your Life Vision, which is your *Purpose, Potential,* and *Passion* in life; your Daily Mission, which are your daily actions; your Life Principles, which are your beliefs, opinions, and *Life Maps*; your Life Values, which is your character and how you behave toward yourself and others; and your Life Goals, which set your daily directions and aspirations.

Life Anchor 1—SelfCulture is comprised of *Life Anchors 2* (Life Vision), *3* (Daily Mission), *4* (Life Principles), *5* (Life Values), and *6* (Life Goals), which will be discussed in the following sections. After identifying your *Inward Life Anchors 2-6*, your *SelfCulture* will be clearly defined by *your* design and on *your* terms. The *Inward Anchors* comprise a framework based on universal principles. You will be able to examine your *Inward Being* intentionally, take control of your life, and become a *Life Leader*.

Life Leadership is about leading yourself, leading others, and leading with others. As John Wooden stated, "It's better to be out in front with a banner than behind with a whip." When others enter your world, do they feel your culture is supportive, collaborative, and trustworthy?

Notice others' *SelfCulture*. As you get together with different friends, family, and coworkers, what is the "feeling" you get when you first see them? Is the culture sustained, or does it change after the first hello? How do you describe the feeling? How does it differ from another person's *SelfCulture*? Describe each *SelfCulture* on the *IO Living Culture Continuum* model as *Dynamic and Positive, Static and Neutral,* or *Toxic and Negative* as we reviewed in Chapter 6.

Remember that this is a continuum, so you can say it's between *Dynamic and Static* or a little above *Toxic*. When you first meet someone, their most overt behaviors will be apparent. You need multiple meetings over time to determine the underlying values, thought patterns, and *Life Maps* driving their behaviors. We cannot judge another person's *SelfCulture* based solely on what we see (an *etic* perspective). It's also what we feel, hear, and observe (an *emic* perspective). Only by interacting with people over time and experiencing their *SelfCulture* from both an *Inward* and *Outward* perspective can begin to uncover what underlies their values and *Life Maps*. Be aware of this because, as you *Outwardly* interact with others, they use these same cues to determine your *SelfCulture*.

You can only define your *SelfCulture* by observing with your own eyes and mind. Does your *Inward Being* match your *Outward Actions*? Does your perceived image match your actual image? What do you want your image to be? It can be instructive to ask whether you would want to be around yourself.

Take control and define your *SelfCulture*! As you read about the following five *Essential Inward Life Anchors*, they will assist you in defining yourself clearly. If you have never taken the time to think thoroughly about your purpose, Life Vision, Daily Mission, Life Principles, Life Values, and Life Goals, then how will you be able to describe your *SelfCulture*? When you have examined and internalized all of the *Inward Life Anchors*, your *SelfCulture* will be centered around universal life principles, as shown in the *SelfCulture* model.

SelfCulture
Anchor Planning

<u>Questions for Self and/or for the FTO as a group:</u>

What are my life aspirations? _____

_____

How would I describe myself? _____

_____

How would I like to experience my life? _____

_____

Describe the ideal me. _____

_____

How do I want to be perceived? _____

_____

How do I want people to feel when they are around me, enter my home, or enter my workplace?

_____

_____

Download all the _IOU Anchor Planning_ pages
Free at: www.iouanchors.com

INWARD LIVING
LIFE ANCHOR 2

LIFE VISION

The Principle of Life Living

Your vision will become clear only when you can look into your own heart. Who looks outside, dreams; who looks inside, awakes.

—Carl Jung

A *Life Vision* is the creation in your mind or imagination of an aspired practice or condition. *Life Vision* is the principle of *Life Living*; it's your desired SelfCulture actualized.

Think of a *Life Vision* statement as a lighthouse shining in the darkness guiding you on your *Life Journey*. What is your *Life Vision?*

We are all so busy. How many times have we heard, "Time is flying by," It's hard to believe it's [insert holiday name] again?" or "Where did the time go?" We are going somewhere, but is it by our *Life Map* or someone else's map? *Life Anchor 2* is about setting our destination. First, we must think about our individual *Life Vision*. Remember, we have 100% control over our *Inward Living* and, therefore, can modify, edit, and change our *Life Vision* or any of the *Inward Life Anchors* at any time. The beauty of *Inward Living* is the flexibility and control we have.

When you have a clear *Life Vision*, it helps you live *Outwardly* and engage people because you know where you are heading in life. A *Life Vision* is inherently future-oriented. Think about the vision painted by Martin Luther King Jr., "I have a dream that my four little children will one day live in a nation where they will not be judged by the color of their skin, but by the content of their character." There was also President John F. Kennedy's vision for the 1960's United States space program—landing a man on the moon.

In both cases, the vision drove the development of a mission, strategy, and tactics. It represented a clear view of the desired future. Similarly, once your *Life Vision* is defined and articulated, you can begin to build the other dimensions of the planning process: *Life Anchors 3, 4, 5,* and *6,* which will become the foundation for your intentional *Life Living* leading to your highest levels of *PH2E.*

My current *Life Vision* statement is *"To help and inspire others to find and develop their Inward talents and passion which lead to PH2E, with the hope that they Outwardly do the same for others, and ultimately receive Upward Living. All my Inward Thinking and Outward Actions are guided by the natural laws of life."*

This is my big picture of life. It's my purpose and gives me a direction in life but does not give specific actions. The Daily Mission, as we will discuss in the next section, is the day-to-day actions that I take that keep me pointed in the right direction, focused on my *Life Vision.* Because your Daily Mission defines your actions, it may change by the month, week, or day. The *Life Vision* should be a statement that lasts longer. I have had the same *Life Vision* statement for three years now. I have modified it several times, but the general big picture purpose has been stable.

Developing Your Big Picture Life Vision

When developing and identifying your *Life Vision*, you need to think about your big picture. For example, imagine yourself driving down a beautiful country road, with rolling hills and spectacular natural beauty. Admire the peacefulness and tranquility of the environment. As you turn a corner, you spy a huge billboard further down the road. It's the only billboard around. You can't quite make it out. As you get closer, you can see that it's a picture.

That picture is your future. It's where you want to be, your *purpose*, and the reason you exist. It utilizes your unique talents and deep *passions*.

What is that picture? What are you doing in it? How do you feel in the picture? Think big and be bold! That's your *Life Vision*!

Think about where you want to be in five or more years. What do you want to have accomplished? Add five years to your age right now and say the following, "I am [current age plus five] years old right now. I am enormously proud of what I have accomplished in the past five years." What did you accomplish? Think about it and write it down.

Some examples might be:

- I have positively developed my relationships with my family and friends.
- I have helped and supported my colleagues at work to create a positive work environment for all.
- I am a teacher and have inspired and continually inspire my students to reach their potential.

You need to take some time to answer these questions and write down the answers. Put them in your phone and hang them on the walls of your home and at work. I put my *Life Vision* and Daily Mission statements on my phone in the Reminders App. My *Life Vision* comes up on my locked home screen every day and provides a reminder for my actions that day.

Developing the Life Vision for the FTO

Life Vision statements are important not just for individuals but also for families, teams, organizations, districts, and schools. I continue to use the term *"Life"* when developing the vision for the *family, team, and organization* because it's the "life" of each of these groups. The *Life Vision* is the *Purpose*, *Potential*, and *Passion* of the group. All groups should take the time to discern their *Life Vision* by answering the following questions:

Why do we exist?

What is our purpose?

Where are we going?

After discussing those questions, all stakeholders should feel that they belong to this safe, happy, learning, and effective environment. The *Life Vision* declares to everyone that they are in a culture dedicated to continuous improvement and learning.

The first step to developing a *Life Vision* statement is to discuss and be clear why a *Life Vision* statement is important. Make this clear to all stakeholders, so everyone understands what is being developed. Before you can create the actual *Life Vision*, everyone needs to work from a clear definition. This shared understanding is critical to the rest of the process.

In the simplest of terms, a *Life Vision* is a statement of where a group wants to be in 5-10 years. It describes where the group is going and what it is moving toward. Similarly, a mission statement is a specific action, what the group or individual does day to day to progress toward their vision. I call this your Daily Mission since it is what you will be focusing on daily. Developing your Daily Mission will be discussed in the next section.

If you currently have a vision statement in place, the first thing to do is reexamine it. When was it developed? Who developed it? Is the vision statement in line with the beliefs and goals of the current members of the *family, team, or organization*? Every member of the organization should be able to recite a *Life Vision* statement. If they cannot, it's time to collaborate with all stakeholders to develop a new one. Add some life to your current vision statement. Keep it short and concise. You will find this to be an extremely powerful experience. In fact, the process of developing it can be more powerful than the actual statement itself.

When developing a *Life Vision* statement for a *family, team, or organization*, it's important to involve all stakeholders. If there is no involvement, there will be no commitment to the *Life Vision*. When done correctly, it will result in all stakeholders understanding and being a part of the identity of the group and organization.

I have facilitated the development of *Life Vision* statements for many groups, teams, and organizations. With a school district team, we agreed upon a vision of "A Community of Learners." We defined who was in the community and how we would create an environment where everyone is continually learning and improving. The process was a great team-building exercise.

In addition, I have facilitated the development of *Life Vision* statements with many other groups. For example, as a soccer team coach, I helped the players came up with "Unity, Loyalty, Friendship, and Competitiveness." As president of a county-based organization of superintendents, we developed a *Life Vision* statement, which was, "Lead for the Success of all Students in Nassau County." When I was a principal in an early childhood center, the vision we developed was "A Community of Rising Stars." My neighborhood civic association determined its *Life Vision* statement would be "A Great Place to Live and Raise a Family." When I was 16 years old teaching guitar lessons, the *Life Vision* was "Fun, Inspiring, and Creative Learning." As a reading teacher and principal, I developed the *Life Vision*, "Read Only the Days You Eat!" Every word in each of the *Life Visions* carried tremendous meaning. When developing a *Life Vision* statement, the group needs to define what each word means to the *family, team, or organization.*

Finally, I have lived this process with my own family. For the past 20 years, at the end of every calendar year, our family gathers and develops our family *Life Vision* statement. Each year we revise it and select a symbol that represents us. It has been a rewarding and important process that has benefited everyone in the family. It unifies us and clarifies our *Purpose, Potential,* and *Passion* as a family. We ask:

- What is the purpose of our family?
- How do we want people to feel when they enter our home?
- How should we treat each other?
- How should we support each other?
- What are the responsibilities of each family member?
- What are the kinds of things we want to do as a family?

One *Life Vision* statement developed by our family is, "We Lead Each Other, We are Attentive to Each Other, We are Thoughtful Toward Each Other." One year, my daughter found a framed statement that we previously discussed, and everyone agreed upon it as the *Life Vision* for the following year. It hangs in our kitchen, and it reads:

WE ARE FAMILY
We are thoughtful
WE HAVE FUN
We show gratitude
WE MAKE MISTAKES
We say grace and "I'm sorry"
WE SHARE AND GIVE
We seize the moment
WE WORK HARD
We laugh and cry together
WE ARE BLESSED

Whatever the family decides on, it's vital that everyone is involved and contributes. I have learned to let my children take the lead and not try to focus on perfection. Whatever is developed is fine. It's more about the process.

As part of your *Inward* focus, you must think through and identify your personal *Life Vision*, Daily Mission, Life Principles, Life Values, and Life Goals. Take time to reflect deeply and determine what you strive for, what you want to be, and what you stand for. What drives you to personal growth and fulfillment?

When we move into the *Outward Anchors*, we will discuss how to make sure your actions match your *Life Vision*. The goal is for your actions to take you to your *Upward*, peaceful, big picture billboard! I'm sure there are many times you are lost and off-track, on another road that is leading you somewhere unknown. It is so simple, but we are neither reminded enough nor have a system or tools to keep us on track. Living and thinking the *IOU Principle* every day will keep you on track and is a simple way to remind you where you are heading and confirming to yourself that you are on the right road to your *Upward PH2E* big picture billboard or *Life Vision*.

THE LIFE VISION MODEL

The Principle of Life Living

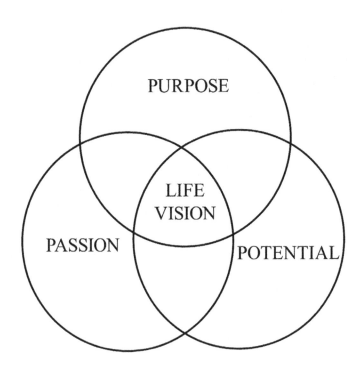

Your *Life Vision* is the intersection of your *Life Purpose, Unique Talents and Potential,* and *Life Passion,* and you have 100% control over it. We spend our precious time on many things in life; however, we must take the time to reflect on our *Purpose, Potential,* and *Passion.* Everyone needs a *Life Vision.* It's your big picture. In the darkness of night, it's a distant lighthouse beacon that keeps you on track for your *Life Journey.*

Below are some examples of a *Personal Life Vision* in the form of "To be a [insert goal] and [insert what you will do.]"

- To be an Occupational Therapist and help people with life skills.
- To be a Teacher and help children become life-learners.
- To be a Parent and raise a family in a loving environment.
- To be the Leader of a business and create an environment where everyone is excited about its mission.
- To live a life helping others to see their greatest potential.

Reflect on the questions in the *Life Vision Anchor Planning* section. Take your time, think about them separately, together, over an hour, a week, or months, but think about them! It's *Your Life Vision!*

Life Vision
Anchor Planning

Questions for Self and/or for the FTO as a group:

What do I want to be known for? _____

_____

What do I want to have accomplished in five years? _____

_____

Purpose

What is my purpose of existence? _____

_____

What gives my life meaning? _____

_____

What is the purpose of my *family, team, or organization?* _____

_____

Potential

What are my unique skills, talents, and strengths? _____

_____

What are my *family, team, or organization's* skills, talents, and strengths? _____

_____

Passion

What excites, motivates, and drives me? _____

_____

If I had a free day to do whatever I wanted to do, what would I do?

_____

_____

What do I enjoy doing for others? _____

_____

What collectively does your *family, team, or organization* enjoy doing? _____

_____

_____

Download all the *IOU Anchor Planning* pages

Free at: www.iouanchors.com

INWARD LIVING
LIFE ANCHOR 3

DAILY MISSION

The Principle of Intentional Actions

The secret of your success is determined by your daily agenda.

—John C. Maxwell

Vision and Mission statements are often confused and melded into one. While there are various definitions of "Vision" and "Mission," I have added the word "*Daily*" before the word "*Mission*" to emphasize that it is something done every day as contrasted with "Vision" which is a long term aspiration. It can change as often as you want. Your *Daily Mission* is an *Intentional Action* you do that moves you closer to your Life Vision (big picture) and your Life Goals (achievable in the short term).

You must recite your *Daily Mission* statement every day. You are in control. For example, "I will *Listen Wholeheartedly* to everyone I speak with. When I do, I will feel the *Life Gift of Happiness.*" Keep it short, one or two sentences. Also, add the byproduct that you will receive, namely one or more of the *PH2E's*.

Say it, post it, live it.

- I will learn something new each day. **Excellence**
- I will respect my colleagues and boss. **Peacefulness**
- I will use my talents to help others. **Happiness**
- I will exercise for 30 minutes today. **Healthiness**
- I will inspire others with my actions. **Happiness**
- I will not fear mistakes. **Peacefulness**
- I will find things to be thankful for today. **Peacefulness**
- I will project positivity to everyone I interact with today. **Happiness**
- I will eat healthily and monitor what I eat. **Healthiness**

Your *Daily Mission* statement will ensure you prioritize your energy on what's important and aligned to your Life Vision. You may also have more than one *Daily Mission* for a particular day. Remember you have 100% control over your *Inward Anchors*.

As an educational leader, I am responsible for many stakeholders, including students, staff, parents, community members, and administration teams. As an educational leader, one of my *Daily Mission* statements in school is "Safe – Happy – Learning." These three words encapsulate much meaning. The first word, "Safe," signifies everyone's safety is my first order of importance. For anything else to happen, everyone needs to feel safe. There are daily items we must take to make sure we are always focused on safety and continually finding ways to improve it. Once there is a feeling of safety, the second word of my *Daily Mission* is "Happy," which focuses on everyone's *Outward* interactions. As an organization, we strive for *positive and effective* relationships. We have created an environment that promotes Positive Communication, Common Language, and Everlasting Traditions, propelling the organization toward *Happiness*, thereby shifting toward a *Dynamic Positive Culture*. The last word of my *Daily Mission* statement is "Learning." Everyone needs to feel safe and happy for learning to occur. If students feel unsafe and unhappy, it will be difficult for them to learn. When safe and happy occur, the byproducts are *PH2E*.

Let me compare my Life Vision statement to my *Daily Mission* statement to see the difference. As I shared in the last section, my personal Life Vision statement is "*To help and inspire others to find and develop their Inward talents and passion that give them*

PH2E, with the hope that they Outwardly do the same for others, and ultimately receive Upward Living. All my Inward Thinking and Outward Actions are guided by the natural laws of life." My Life Vision is a big picture style vision. It's not specific but has a clear destination. My *Daily Mission* supports and is aligned with my Life Vision. I have revised both my Life Vision and *Daily Mission* many times, whenever I feel like it. Remember, you have 100% control of your *Inward Life Anchors.*

Since you have control over your *Daily Mission*, you can change and modify it every day, week, or month, whenever is needed. It's important that you see it and say it every day. Put it on your phone as a reminder to pop up once or several times per day. Even if you are off-course during the day, when you reaffirm your *Daily Mission* by seeing it, it will give you an *Upward* lift and refocus your energy to get back on course in your *Life Journey.*

In every day, there are 1,440 minutes. That means we have 1,440 daily opportunities to make a positive impact.

—Les Brown

I have often used *The Daily Mission Model* comprised of the *Who, What,* and *Byproduct* (*Upward Life Gifts of PH2E*) to develop a specific *Daily Mission.*

THE DAILY MISSION MODEL

The Principle of Intentional Actions

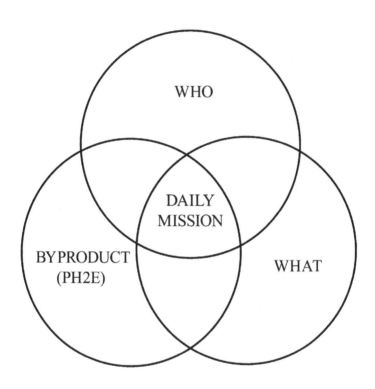

The *Daily Mission* Model is the intersection of *Who* you want to affect, *What* you will do, and what *Byproducts* you hope to produce for the other person and yourself. This model involves deciding your "*Who*," "*What*," and the "*Byproduct*" of one or more of the *PH2E*'s.

Let's drill down into those three areas.

The Who

Each day I think about the *"Who."* *Who* do I need to attend to? It may be a person or a group. I may need to interact with someone I have neglected personally or someone at work.

The What

Once you decide who, *"What"* is it that you feel you need to say or do? The *"What"* is the *Outward Action* you will take.

The Byproduct

Our goal is to receive the *PH2E's* in life, and we know we can't just grab them. Therefore, we need an intentional plan to act *Outwardly* in the hope of receiving one or more of the *PH2E's*. Here is where you anticipate the *Byproduct* that you hope to receive when you complete your *Outward Actions* according to your designed plan.

For example, if you neglected to make a needed call to a loved one or a friend, you then decide how to remedy it with the hope of a *Byproduct of Happiness* (*H*), or a feeling of *Peacefulness* (*P*) in your *Inward Being*. It does not always work out as planned, but without an intentional effort, it never will.

Another example may occur at work. You need to present a project to a team and are prepared and feeling confident. You know the *"Who"* and *"What"* of the presentation. The *"Byproduct"* you hope to receive is *Excellence* (*E*).

Another example pertains to yourself. The *"Who"* is you, the *"What"* is going to the gym to work out. The *"Byproduct"* is receiving *Healthiness* (*H*). You may already exercise all the time, but you will feel a tremendous sense of accomplishment if you think about working out as one of your *Daily Missions*. Designating it as a *Daily Mission* also amplifies the *Byproduct*, in this case, *Healthiness*. As a result, you will feel more in control of your life as if you were actually on a ship heading on course toward your *Life Journey* destination.

Your *Daily Mission* can be specific or general, but it needs to be actionable. It is based on the *Principle of Intentional Actions*. It drives you *Outwardly* to do something aligned to your Life Vision. You must take time for yourself to plan. As you plan, make a list of *Daily Missions* with a *PH2E Byproduct* for each one. You will find that your *Daily Missions* can be repeated, even for weeks or months. It's up to you; you have 100% control of designing and implementing your *Daily Missions*.

Once you practice identifying and creating *Daily Missions* several times, you won't have to think about the process. It will come naturally, and you will Propel your PH2E. Start off with only one *Daily Mission,* and as you get more comfortable with developing and implementing them, you can add more. This is intentional living by *your* design!

Daily Mission
Anchor Planning

<u>Questions for Self and/or for the FTO as a group:</u>

What do I want to accomplish today/tomorrow/next week that is aligned to my *Life Vision*?

_____

_____

Who do I want to affect with my *Daily Mission*? Is it myself, someone else, or a group?

_____

_____

What is that I need to say or do to accomplish my *Daily Mission*?

_____

_____

What *Byproduct* of the *PH2E* (decide on one or more) do I hope
to receive when I accomplish my *Daily Mission*?_____

_____

_____

Download all the _IOU Anchor Planning_ pages
Free at: www.iouanchors.com

INWARD LIVING
LIFE ANCHOR 4

LIFE PRINCIPLES

The Principle of Life Realities

*It's a law of life—check it, and you'll see it holds true
in every situation of life.*

—Indira Gandhi

A *Life Principle* is a foundational life law that is universal, timeless, and true in any society. We can't change principles, such as the principle of positivity. There is an essence of being positive that's undeniable. You may have a different view or opinion concerning what being positive is, but the principle is unchangeable. *Life Principles* are natural laws that apply to everyone and the world's *Life Realities*. We should strive to understand *Life Principles* in their purest sense. However, we all have opinions, points of view, beliefs, and perceptions that distort the reality of *Life Principles*. We must be aware of these distortions of our *Life Maps*. We act *Outwardly* to others and the world based on our *Life Maps*. We all believe our *Life Maps* are 100% true and apply them continuously. Our *Life Maps* define and guide our *Inward Thoughts* and *Outward Actions* based on how we interpret *Life Principles*. It is normal to use our history, background knowledge, and experiences when developing our *Life Maps*, but are you *Inwardly Thinking* about your *Life Maps* with the aim to improve continually and get closer to the principle?

We have *Life Principles* about friendship, family, service to others, and many other topics. *Life Principles* are not a skill because skills only work for particular situations, whereas *Life Principles* can be applied in many situations. There are no shortcuts with *Life Principles*. For example, in the principle of learning, you can't skip learning the foundational background information, introductory terminology, and theories and only read the last page and expect to understand and learn the concept. Instead, in the *Life Principle* of learning, we must learn each step sequentially and build upon previous information to get to a full understanding and proficiency.

If you are not sure if it's a *Life Principle*, ask yourself if there is a shortcut where you can bypass the foundational skills and concepts and still get the results without doing the work. If there is, then it's not a principle. For example, if you were a beginner guitar player and just started to learn how to play, would you think that after a few lessons, you would be able to play some of the greatest guitar solos note for note? The answer is obviously no. You cannot master playing an instrument unless you first learn the foundational skills and concepts. That is the *Life Principle* of learning.

We all have interpretations of *Life Principles*, but are they accurate? Using the *Life Map Cycle* discussed in Chapter 3 will help make your *Life Principles* more accurate and closer to the "territory."

Life Principles are laws that serve as a basis for our *Inward Thinking* and *Outward Actions* and are fundamental ways you commit to act in your life. Therefore, they are more externally focused in contrast to values, which are more internally focused. Your *Life Principles* guide your *Inward Thinking and Outward Actions*. *Life Principles* can be written as "I believe" statements. Here are some examples.

I believe in the:
- *Life Principle* of being family-oriented
- *Life Principle* of being goal-oriented
- *Life Principle* of the farm

- *Life Principle* of the golden rule
- *Life Principle* of forgiveness
- *Life Principle* of change
- *Life Principle* of failing your way to success
- *Life Principle* of giving
- *Life Principle* of humility
- *Life Principle* of continuous improvement
- *Life Principle* of love
- *Life Principle* of living positively
- *Life Principle* of prioritizing
- *Life Principle* of living by the compass, not the clock
- *Life Principle* of preparation
- *Life Principle* of spirituality
- *Life Principle* of persistence
- *Life Principle* of discipline
- *Life Principle* of creativity
- *Life Principle* of living in the moment
- *Life Principle* that less can be more
- *Life Principle* of fearlessness
- *Life Principle* of simplicity
- *Life Principle* of the process
- *Life Principle* of personal responsibility
- *Life Principle* of modeling
- *Life Principle* of mastering the basics
- *Life Principle* of relationship building
- *Life Principle* of self-confidence
- *Life Principle* of synergy
- *Life Principle* of 3rd alternatives (thinking outside the box)

- *Life Principle* of compassion
- *Life Principle* of empathy
- *Life Principle* of humanitarianism - promote human welfare
- *Life Principle* of loyalty
- *Life Principle* of moderation
- *Life Principle* of gratitude
- *Life Principle* of it's never too late
- *Life Principle* of being open-minded
- *Life Principle* of living each moment to the fullest
- *Life Principle* of growth mindset
- *Life Principle* of surrounding myself with good people
- *Life Principle* that I have 100% control of my responses and actions
- *Life Principle* of meditation
- *Life Principle* of being appreciative
- *Life Principle* of being dependable
- *Life Principle* of living a balanced life
- *Life Principle* of personal Life Vision
- *Life Principle* of personal Daily Mission
- *Life Principle* of being goal-oriented
- *Life Principle* of Life Values
- *Life Principle* of wholehearted listening

Your *Life Principles* should be timeless, always present, never change, and never ignored. If you ignore them, you will be living an *IOD Life* and receive the *Downward Life Drains* of *Anxiety, Unhappiness, Unhealthiness, and Ineffectiveness.*

After you have taken time to think about and identify your essential *Life Principles*, ask yourself if you are living them. If you are, you will feel the *Upward Living Byproducts* and the satisfaction of living intentionally and balanced by your own design. Another important question is, are your principles 100% correct? Frankly, the answer is no, but it is not about having perfect principles. It's about continuously moving toward *Upward Living*. It's the journey, not the destination.

Here are some ways I live my *Life Principles*. I believe in the *Life Principle* of abundance as opposed to scarcity. In a scarcity mindset, you believe there are finite opportunities to succeed, and when someone else is successful, there is less room for your success. That is a fear-based mindset. An abundance mindset is believing there is enough for everyone to succeed, which is a plentiful, peaceful mindset.

I believe in the Life Value of human kindness and adopted some guiding *Life Principles* to act on it. For example, I look for opportunities to be helpful to people in public. When I'm riding the train, I try to be observant of people who might need a seat (I think a lot of people on the train or bus would give up their seat for an elderly person or a woman who's pregnant, but they don't pay attention enough to turn their kindness into action). When I'm driving, I try to keep my emotions in check, reminding myself most people don't intend to be rude when they drive. Like many of us, they have many stressors and worries and being patient with them and refraining from impulsive expressions of anger is a huge step in the right direction to live in kindness.

We are so distracted with life issues that it's easy to lose sight of our *Life Principles*.

At some point, after you have thought about and identified your top *Life Principles*, write them down. After a few weeks, ask yourself if you have acted in accordance with your *Life Principles*—not just mentally, but *Outwardly Acted* by them. Many times, we believe in a *Life Principle* but don't act on it. In fact, we may completely ignore a deeply held *Inward Life Principle* or even act contrary to it. Be observant!

In the future, think about other ways you could live the truth of your *Life Principles*. Start simple, start small, and be sure to store your *Life Principles* in a conspicuous place. The next time life gets tough, or you are faced with a difficult decision, look to your *Life Principles* to help show you the way.

THE LIFE PRINCIPLES MODEL

The Principle of Life Realities

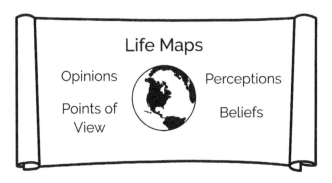

The *Life Principle* Model is a representation of the personal *Life Maps* that drive our *Inward Thoughts* and *Outward Actions*. Remember, *Life Principles* are natural laws and always correct, while *Life Maps* are how a person defines and acts on the *Life Principles*. Our *Life Map*s are how we see the world and our interpretation of *Life Realities*. We all have *Opinions, Points of View, Perceptions*, and *Beliefs*, but are they correct? Accept that they are not; begin examining your *Inward Living* today and adjust, as necessary. Use the *Life Map Cycle* we discussed in Chapter 3 as a guide to identify and examine your many internal *Life Maps*, which are filled with beliefs and opinions. It's a relief knowing we don't have 100% accurate maps, and it's ok to make adjustments or even change them. Whenever you adjust or change your *Life Map*, you will immediately feel an *Upward Living Lift* moving closer to timeless, universal *Life Principles*. Celebrate it! It's a process that will last a lifetime.

Life Principles
Anchor Planning

<u>Questions for Self and/or for the FTO as a group:</u>

List two-four of your most essential *Life Principles*.

_____

_____

Reflect on the *Life Principles* you wrote above. How are the *Life Principles* you listed always correct?

_____

_____

Determine your key *Life Principles*. Then, ask yourself, "How do my *Life Maps* (opinions, points of view, perceptions, beliefs) distort my *Life Principles*?"

_____

_____

Download all the *IOU Anchor Planning* pages
Free at: www.iouanchors.com

INWARD LIVING
LIFE ANCHOR 5

LIFE VALUES

The Principle of Life Character

Values are like fingerprints. Nobody's are the same, but you leave them all over everything you do.

—Elvis Presley

Your *Life Values* determine your behavior. Some examples are dedication, loyalty, and honesty. *Life Values* describe how you want to behave based on your *Inward Character* to fulfill your Life Vision and Daily Mission. Your *Life Values* are the centerpiece of your SelfCulture and are based on the *Principle of Life Character*. When identifying and developing your *Life Values,* think about a person in your life with high character who you trust and makes you feel special. It could be a teacher, a family member, or a friend. How did this person make you feel? What *Life Values* did that person project to you?

There are many *Life Values* we should be practicing *Inwardly and Outwardly*; however, it is important to choose three high priority *Life Values* and focus on them every day for a set period. After that, you may choose to focus on a new set of *Life Values.* At times, you may have specific *Life Values* you decide to keep in the forefront for years.

A list of *Life Values* is below. Although you will probably agree with all of them, pick your top three. Otherwise, you will just have a long list of feel-good words. With three, you will be able to reflect on these *Life Values* daily. It may be easier to begin with your top 10, narrow the list to five, and finally to three. May sure to select the *Life Values* that you commit to acting on.

Life Values:

- Dependable
- Reliable
- Loyal
- Committed

- Open-Minded
- Consistent
- Honest
- Efficient
- Innovative
- Creative
- Good-Humored
- Compassionate
- A spirit of adventure
- Motivated
- Positive
- Optimistic
- Passionate
- Respectful
- Courageous
- Persistent
- Dedicated
- Respectful
- Integrity
- Trustworthy
- Teamwork
- Positivity
- Optimism
- Passion
- Courage
- Education
- Perseverance
- Service to others

My current *Life Values* are:

1. Respect
2. Trustworthiness
3. Dedication

Identify your Life Values

What are yours? Write them here:

1.
2.
3.

Identify Your Family, Team, or Organization's Life Values

The process is the same for *FTO's*. When identifying and developing *Life Values* with a group, the *family, team, or organization* needs to discuss and agree on the *Life Values*. What are the intentions and character of the group? Ask how everyone wants to be treated by each other. It's a statement of how the *FTO* will behave.

The US Navy Core Values

Vincent was proud to have served in the United States Navy. The Navy's bedrock core values from the American Revolution to this day are *honor*, *courage*, and *commitment*. Vincent unambiguously lived these values throughout his life. His stories always included at least one of them.

When he spoke of honor, he always said you must conduct yourself in the highest ethical manner with all your relationships—whether the person was a superior or subordinate. Always be honest and truthful.

When he spoke of courage, he always met the demands of his job and mission, even when it was difficult. He said you need the courage and mental strength to do what's right, even in the face of personal or professional adversity.

When he spoke of commitment, it was about being committed to positive change and continuous improvement. He used to say, "Let me tell you, once the order is made, I am fully committed to take action to complete the order." It was about giving full attention and focus after weighing all the options and making a decision. Vincent lived a life of high character and was extraordinarily committed to everything he did.

THE LIFE VALUES MODEL

The Principle of Life Character

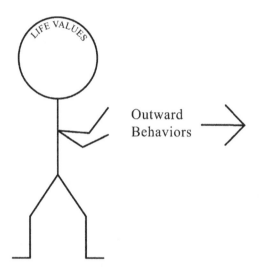

The *Life Values* Model represents your *Outward Behavior* based on your *Inward Life Character*. It reminds you to be aware of how you behave and treat others in your *Outward* mode. It starts *Inwardly* by identifying the *Life Values* by which you want to live, then moves *Outwardly* to how you behave as you travel on your *Life Journey*.

Life Anchors 2, 3, 4, and *5* comprise the hull of your ship. These anchors—Life Vision, Daily Mission, Life Principles, and *Life Values*—are your foundation, being, and SelfCulture. Take the opportunity now to build your ship solidly, by your design, and make it ready for your *Life Journey* to *PH2E*.

Life Values
Anchor Planning

<u>Questions for Self and/or for the FTO as a group:</u>

Think of a person who made or makes you feel special. Write down how it feels.

_____

_____

Write down the *Life Value* the person projected to you.

_____

_____

Write down three high priority *Life Values* to focus on over a set period of time.

_____

_____

Download the _IOU Anchor Planning_ pages

Free at: www.iouanchors.com

INWARD LIVING
LIFE ANCHOR 6

LIFE GOALS

The Principle of Life Aspirations

A man without a goal is like a ship without a rudder.

—Thomas Carlyle

Your *Life Goals* turn the propeller that moves your ship to improve and make real and positive changes in your life. Your life is full of journeys, but are they random with no clear destination? Setting *Life Goals* will give you a clear destination. Your goals should be aligned to your Life Vision and Daily Mission. They should be based on and reflective of your SelfCulture, Life Principles, and Life Values. *Life Goals* are based on the *Principle of Life Aspirations.* An aspiration is a strong hope, dream, or goal that has a positive *Upward* connotation. Setting *Life Goals* is a powerful tool that guides and takes you where you want to go in life. Your *Life Goals* need to be specific with clear, measurable outcomes. It should be obvious when you have arrived, and your goal has been met. Make your *Life Goals* specific with a timeline, assessment tools, and a method of accountability.

In terms of our nautical analogy, you are the captain of your ship, setting the destination for your *Life Goals.* When you reach the destination, you anchor at the port, and you prepare for your next *Life Goal,* enjoying both the preparation and the journey. When you are on open waters, you will continuously get pushed and pulled by the tides, currents, and, at times, stormy weather. There will be many *Outward* obstacles getting in your way and pushing you off-course. You must continuously put yourself back on course to reach your goal. Without a clear *Life Goal,* the *Outward* obstacles will push you in off-course directions that may even be negative and pull you to ineffectiveness. You will not be able to adjust your direction because you never set the goal or destination.

Identifying goals fuels your daily actions. Set big goals and think big picture. If the goal is small and unexciting, your focus will drift, and you'll lose interest in the goal and abandon it. Average goals produce average attention, which means you may only think of the goal once a week, month, or year. If you are taking the time to identify and set a goal, make it exciting and something you will think about daily. The excitement fuels your engine for the journey. The more you are excited about your goal, the richer the fuel will be. The richer the fuel, the more effective your engine will run, which means you will be more likely to reach your destination —your goal. The book, *The 4 Disciplines of Execution* encourages you to set Wildly Important Goals or WIGS. A WIG is a goal that matters most to *yourself, family, team, or organization.* It's your top priority and is based on the discipline of being focused. Thoughts of your goal need to wake you up each morning and inspire you to think about what you can do to move closer to your destination. Let's get your propeller turning at optimum speed and enjoy the ride!

The goal needs to motivate you to take *Outward Action.* For many years, as the head of a multimillion-dollar educational organization, I've set goals for myself, the organization, leadership teams, and thousands of staff members. The shared team goals helped us move toward a *Dynamic Positive Culture* for the entire organization. The key to setting successful *Life Goals* is to challenge yourself and others and not be persuaded by negative people who will say you can't achieve the *Life Goal* because it will be too hard to accomplish. Be a *REBEL* to those sentiments. Be a *REBEL* to the lack of confidence creeping into your mind and saying you can't do it. Be a *REBEL*, start setting meaningful *Life Goals* with purpose and take control of your life's direction.

Simply setting a goal without a system to guide it will likely lead to failure. Setting a *Life Goal* is a process with an end in mind. The following section will discuss a strategy for setting goals and ensuring you achieve them.

THE LIFE GOALS MODEL
The Principle of Life Aspirations

Creating REBEL Goals

Set your goals and plan like a *REBEL*! Get out of your rut and think big, be bold, and plan for something that excites you. Whether you are setting a goal for yourself or as a group in a *family, team, or organization*, be a *REBEL*!

REBEL stands for:

Rudder - Engine - Buoys - Evaluate - Lifeline

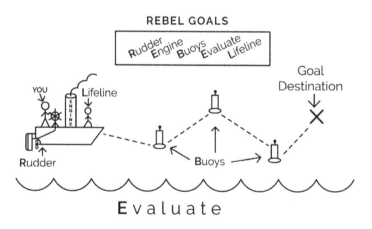

Rudder. Set your *Rudder* to your destination. It's your *Life Goal*. When the captain's wheel on a ship is turned, it adjusts the rudder to your destination. By setting the *Rudder*, you are pointing the ship in the direction of a new endpoint. Your new destination is your *Life Goal*. Therefore, the first step is to determine your *Life Goal*. This is *Inward Living* because it's a time to think about what you want to achieve. Give it a name and write it down.

A simple example of a *Rudder* is a *Life Goal* to lose 10 pounds. Give your *Life Goal* a fun name:

- 20 Pounds Goodbye
- Project Read
- Jobs, Jobs, Jobs
- Fun Time with the Family
- Relationship Rally
- Degree for Me

Engine. The *Engine* drives your ship forward by turning the propeller. It's the system that moves you toward your destination. The *Engine* is the *Outward Actions* you need to take to move you toward your *Life Goal* destination. You have 100% control of your *Engine*. If the *Rudder* is to lose 10 pounds, the *Engine* could be exercising three times per week and eating healthily.

Buoys. The *Buoys* guide your journey. On the waterways, buoys are guides that help ships navigate the waters by helping with direction and assisting in avoiding dangers and obstacles that could interrupt your journey. In terms of a *Life Goal*, the *Buoys* are your checkpoints. They will help you with direction and progress toward meeting your *Life Goal*.

If the *Rudder* is to lose 10 pounds, and the *Engine* is to exercise and eat healthily, the following may be the *Buoys*:

- **Buoy 1** - In week 2, I will lose 2 lbs.
- **Buoy 2** - In week 4, I will lose 2 lbs for a total of 4lbs.
- **Buoy 3** - In week 6, I will lose 2 lbs for a total of 6lbs.
- **Buoy 4** - In week 8, I will lose 2 lbs for a total of 8lbs.
- **Buoy 5** - In week 10, I will lose 2 lbs for a total of 10lbs.

Evaluate. *Evaluate* your progress and make necessary adjustments. As you are heading along on the journey toward your *Life Goal*, there will be many *Outward* forces taking you off-course. In boating, you can encounter storms, tides, and other obstacles. In terms of *Life Goals*, other people, nonrelated responsibilities, and unexpected events will distract you. You may have to readjust your *Rudder*, stoke the *Engine*, and change some *Buoy* locations to reach your destination or goal. It is fine to adjust your goal midstream. Too many people keep pushing forward to complete the goal even if it is no longer pertinent. Many times, a simple adjustment is all that is needed to make the goal meaningful again. The *Evaluate* stage is the time to make those adjustments.

If you set your *Rudder* to lose weight, you need to *Evaluate* if you are meeting your *Buoy* checkpoints. If not, you need to adjust your eating habits or increase exercise.

Lifeline. Who's on your ship? Your crew takes the journey with you to support and keep you on course. A *Lifeline* is an accountability partner who can encourage and give honest feedback to help you complete your goal. Find someone you trust to talk with about your challenges and progress.

You must have a *Lifeline* partner because there are many opportunities for you to stop striving for your goal. Your *Lifeline* partner is someone you can speak to about your goal on a schedule, whether it's once a week or once a month, someone who understands you and your goal, and someone you trust and respect for their honest feedback. *Lifelines* are partners who provide support, keep you on track, and motivate you. Listen to the advice and/or encouragement that they offer.

Small to Big Goals

Goals are designed to motivate and focus the team and you. If you are overwhelmed by diving into a big goal, start small and build your capacity to set larger and longer-term goals. If you are not used to setting and achieving goals, begin with small goals you can achieve in one week. Train yourself to be successful. Start with a task you need to complete by the end of the week. For example, "I need to go through some important paperwork," "I will call a friend by the end of the week that I have been meaning to get in touch with for some time," or "I will reorganize a closet in the house." Make it small, but make sure you do it. The whole point of these small goals is to set the goal and then accomplish it. Make it a habit to set attainable goals and complete them. The purpose is to exercise and prepare your brain for more meaningful *Life Goals* that keep you on your *Life Journey*. Think about a few things you need to do then turn them into goals. Start the statement with, "My goal is to. . . ." This simple exercise will help you set *Stretch Life Goals,* as described in the next section.

Your goal should be just out of reach, but not out of sight.

—Denis Waitley and Remi Witt

The Goal is Setting Stretch Goals

There are three types of goals you can set—*Comfort Goals*, *Stretch Goals*, and *Delusional Goals*.

It's important to identify and set the right type of goal. It's a tricky balance of setting the "just right" goal that moves you to a higher level when completed. If you achieve a goal and don't see any noticeable improvement in your life, you may not feel goal setting is worth the effort. I call these types of goals *Comfort Goals*, which do not bring out your best performance. You will be on autopilot and simply go through the motions.

A *Stretch Goal* is one with the "just right" amount of difficulty. The *Stretch Goal* has precisely the right amount of challenge that is achievable. The goal needs to be just out of your reach, but when you stretch yourself, you can grab it! Be willing to reset your goal if necessary. According to Martin Seligman, one of the founders of positive psychology, achieving a *Stretch Goal* will give you a sense of accomplishment, fulfillment, and produce happiness. Setting and achieving an appropriate goal is an essential element in one of Seligman's theoretical models of happiness. Having goals and achieving them will build self-esteem and increase well-being and happiness.

A *Delusional Goal* is one that is too difficult. A goal can be big, ambiguous, and futuristic, but also needs to be realistic for the moment. I want to be clear that it's ok to set a goal to be the

301

CEO of a company and not have any experience or skills in that industry. What's delusional is thinking you are going to get that job with one goal. You need to set many other *Stretch Goals* that will help you work your way toward that CEO position.

Strive for setting *Stretch Goals* that are just out of your reach—not too easy, not too difficult, but exactly right. Russian psychologist Lev Vygotsky developed the Zone of Proximal Development, which is a tool widely used in education. The Zone of Proximal Development (ZPD) is a great tool to emphasize the importance and understanding of *Stretch Goals*. The ZPD is the space immediately outside your current capacity that you can reach with a little work. In the following diagram, the center represents your current abilities. If you set goals in this area, they will be *Comfort Goals*. Just outside your current abilities is the ZPD, or your *Stretch Goals*. Outside your ZPD or *Stretch Goals* is the *Delusional Goals* area, or as Vygotsky purports, the frustration area or the level you cannot achieve yet. If you try, it will cause you anxiety. Setting goals in your "zone," or setting *Stretch Goals* will inspire, satisfy, and propel you forward, giving you the best chance to reach your destination.

What kind of goals are you setting?

If plan "A" doesn't work, the alphabet has 25 more letters—
204 if you're in Japan.

—Claire Cook

Failures are Productive Struggles

Everyone fails to achieve some goals. We need to think of failures as productive struggles giving us important information and valuable lessons to improve our lives. Don't throw the information away but rather use it to set up the next *Life Goal*. That's what successful people do.

Thomas Edison held over 1,000 patents for different inventions. Yet, he viewed failures as opportunities for growth. When things didn't work out, he was quoted as saying, "I have not failed 10,000 times, I've successfully found 10,000 ways that will not work." He also said, "I can never find the things that work best until I know the things that don't work."

We must have that type of attitude as we move on our journey with our *REBEL Goals*. REBEL goals help us make the necessary adjustments during the *Evaluate* stage. Take time to evaluate progress and think about difficult areas being faced. Determine the productive struggles and make the adjustments necessary to the next checkpoint, then move the following *Buoy* to a new location and continue on the journey. If you don't evaluate your goals and make adjustments, the goal will simply fade away and never be completed.

Obstacles are those frightful things you see when you
take your eyes off your goal.

—Henry Ford

My oldest daughter, a successful Division 1 collegiate track athlete and a CAA Champion reflects on a life learning lesson from high school.

"Heat. Waves of sunlight burning so intensely, I feel my skin flush. Sweat glistening on my forehead, I walk slowly onto the track and up to the starting line of the New York State qualifier track meet. The official raises his gun, and I take my stance, eyeing the first of ten hurdles arranged around the perimeter of the track. 'On your mark,' the official calls out, signaling the moment to move up to the line. 'Set,' he yells. I prepare myself for motion. There is a moment of total silence as I feel my heart beating in my ears and my stomach dropping in anticipation. An explosion pierces the quiet, and I'm off. First hurdle, second hurdle, third hurdle cleared. Fourth, I begin to pull away from the group. Fifth, I continue to gain speed. My mind is reeling because I realize a personal record is within reach. I'm positive I'll make finals as I clear the sixth hurdle. I'm convinced I'll break the school record as I leap across the seventh. Already looking past the eighth hurdle, I'm visualizing the finish line, imagining my coach and teammates congratulating me and most importantly, proud of attaining a goal for which I had worked so hard. Then—
I fall.

All the success I anticipated instantly evaporates, leaving me dazed on the track, watching the rest of the girls race by me. Composing myself, I finish the race and walk off the track in shock. I notice my coach's look of pity and become utterly distraught. *What happened? How could this happen?* I was on a straightaway to the finish line, fewer than fifty meters from my goal, and yet, suddenly, it is all over. I return home with my family, and instead of waking up the next day and heading to finals, I sleep in.

As I wake up, I relive the race in great detail. I realize the problem wasn't my form, endurance, or approach to the eighth hurdle. Instead, I was distracted, out of the moment, and my concentration slipped. I think about how my friends and family commended me on the great character I demonstrated by getting up and finishing the race. Although their intentions were good, their sentiments did not provide solace at the time of the race or even now. I can't put my finger on it, but I know there must be a greater lesson than just, "Pick yourself up when you fall."

My daughter learned that the most challenging part of any journey are distractions. One key to success is how you choose to deal with the inevitable *Outward* life distractions, fight impulses, and remain focused on the small steps (or hurdles) along the way. You must clearly outline the steps required to attain each goal, focus on the task at hand, resist the urge to get ahead of yourself, and handle distractions and obstacles as they arise. Don't lose sight of the present by focusing too intently on the finish line. At the same time, don't allow the everyday hurdles to distract you and cause you to lose sight of your *Life Goal*.

Decide to identify and develop both *Inward* and *Outward Life Goals* based on your *I*'s and *O*'s. These are personal *IO* growth *Life Goals*. Your *Inward Goal* will be centered around one of the *6 Inward Life Anchors*, while your *Outward Goal* will be centered around one of the *6 Outward Life Anchors*. The next chapter will discuss your *Outward Life Anchors*. After internalizing them, set *Life Goals* around them.

Life Goals
Anchor Planning

Questions for Self and/or for the FTO as a group:

Set a **REBEL** *Goal:*

_____

_____

Rudder—Write down what you want to accomplish in the end. What is your goal destination?

_____

_____

Engine—Write down specific actions you need to take to move toward your destination.

_____

_____

Buoys—Write down two-four measurable check points you must meet along the journey toward your destination.

_____

_____

Evaluate—Write down questions you can ask that will evaluate your progress. Do you need to adjust your goal slightly? Do you need to modify your goal significantly? Is your goal achievable? Do you need to change your goal?

_____

_____

Lifeline—Write down the person you can count on to keep you accountable.

_____

_____

Write down a *Comfort Goal* that is easily achievable with little effort.

_____

_____

Write down a *Stretch Goal* that is attainable with the right amount of challenge to achieve it.

_____

_____

Download all the _IOU Anchor Planning_ pages

Free at: www.iouanchors.com

Captain's Log for Chapter 11

The 6 Inward Life Anchors

Captain's Log:

Point 1   The *SelfCulture Life Anchor* is your most foundational *Inward Thinking Life Anchor* and is your authentic self. It is the feeling people get when in your presence, your personal brand, by your design. It is important to take an *emic* or inside perspective when reflecting on our *SelfCulture* to shift toward a lasting *Dynamic Positive Culture*.

Point 2   A visual brand can help encapsulate the *SelfCulture* for *you, your family, team, or organization*. It is a powerful way to express your uniqueness to the world.

Point 3   A *Life Vision* is the creation in your mind or imagination of a practice or condition to which you aspire. It is a practice, a way of living, and your desired *SelfCulture* actualized. When you have a clear *Life Vision*, it helps you live *Outwardly* and engage people because you know where you are heading in life. A clear *Life Vision* also drives the development of a mission, strategy, and tactics. Think "Big Picture." What is your billboard? Where are you heading? What is your *Purpose, Potential, and Passion*?

Point 4   Your *Daily Mission* is an action that moves you closer to your *Life Vision* and your *Life Goals*. Say it every day and work on it every day. Your *Daily Mission* answers the questions *Who, What*, and what is the *Byproduct*?

310

Point 5   *Life Principles* are foundational laws that are true in any society. It's the reality of life that is universal and timeless. *Life Principles* are unchangeable, and we should strive to understand *Life Principles* in their purest sense.

Point 6   *Life Values* determine how you behave to fulfill your *Life Vision* and *Daily Mission*. Choose three high priority *Life Values* and focus on them for a set period.

Point 7   *Life Goals* are the vehicle to improve and make real and positive changes in your life. Setting *Life Goals* will give you a clear destination, and should be aligned to your *Life Vision* and *Daily Mission* and reflective of your *SelfCulture*.

Point 8   Set your goals and plan like a *REBEL*! Remember to set your *Rudder* toward your destination and give your goal a name. Your *Engine* contains the actions you will use to get there. *Buoys* are your checkpoints. They will help you with direction and progress in meeting your goal. *Evaluate* your progress and make necessary adjustments. Also, make sure you have a *Lifeline*, an accountability partner to keep you motivated to continue to your destination.

Point 9   *Life Goals* fuel your daily actions and motivate you to take *Outward Action*. There are three levels of *Life Goals*—*Comfort Goals*, *Stretch Goals*, and *Delusional Goals*. Aim to set *Stretch Goals* that move you forward but are attainable with just the right amount of difficulty.

Point 10   Always keep in mind that failures are productive struggles. Everyone fails. The important thing is that we get back up and try again after making any necessary adjustments.

Teach to Learn

The best way to deepen your understanding and, at the same time, share and stimulate new conversations with others is to teach. Share what you have learned with a friend, family member, coworker, or anyone else who will listen. Teaching is, by far, the best way to deepen one's understanding of new insights and concepts. Take any of the Points in the Captain's Log or this chapter for thought-provoking discussions.

New Daily Voyage:

Activity:

Set a *REBEL Goal* right now. Define your *Rudder, Engine, Buoy(s)*, how you will *Evaluate*, and your *Lifeline(s)*.

Ask yourself:

Are my current goals *Comfort, Stretch,* or *Delusional?* How can I modify them to make them *Stretch Goals?*

Chapter 12

THE 6 OUTWARD LIFE ANCHORS

Actions - Relationships - Trust

OUTWARD LIVING

Twenty years from now you will be more disappointed by the things that you didn't do than by the ones you did do. So, throw off the bowlines. Sail away from the safe harbor. Catch the trade winds in your sails. Explore. Dream. Discover.

—Mark Twain

"Anchors aweigh!" Vincent yelled as he told us a story about when the ship was leaving port. "Anchors aweigh" is a phrase that is yelled to notify the captain that the anchor has been raised and the journey can begin. "Weigh" means to heave, hoist, or raise. When the anchor is raised from the ocean floor, the ship becomes under the control of the captain, who must hold on to the ship's wheel, setting the rudder to its next destination. The captain is now living *Outwardly*.

The *Outward Life Anchors* all involve interactions with others or the world (i.e., nature and nonhuman living creatures). Your *Outward Living* with others represents your actions, relationships, and trust-building. Whenever you move out from your *Inward Living* and interact and affect other people, nature, or nonhuman living creatures, you are *Outward Living*. This chapter will discuss the *6 Outward Anchors*, which are universal, timeless principles that will help grow a *Dynamic Positive Culture* for *family, team, and organization* (*FTO*).

The *Outward Life Anchors* all involve interactions with others or the world (i.e. nature and nonhuman living creatures).

When you enter the *Outward World* and interact with others, there will be some level of pressure. However, as John Wooden has said, the only pressure that is meaningful is the pressure you put on yourself. Do not worry about outside forces or let them get to you. On the other hand, do put appropriate "pressure" on yourself to do the best job you are capable of doing. If not, you are cheating your *Inward Self* and everyone around you.

John Wooden was known as the best college coach of all time with 10 NCAA Championships, including seven consecutive titles. You would think he must have spoken to his players about winning, but several of his former players, including those who later played in the NBA, stated that he never discussed it. Instead, Coach Wooden spoke about life and interacting with others. When we interact *Outwardly* with others, we

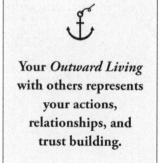

Your *Outward Living* with others represents your actions, relationships, and trust building.

need to remind ourselves we have no control over their actions and how the world interacts with us, but we have 100% control over our reactions to those interactions. Realizing and internalizing this point can be a life-changer.

In Chapter 11, we focused on your *Inward Living*, your *Inward Being*, and purpose; your *Inward Life Anchors* of Life Vision, Daily Mission, Life Principles, Life Values, and Life Goals, all of which make up you—your Self Culture! All of the *Inward Anchors* are pointed inward to the center anchor of the *Life Living Wheel*. Imagine the center anchor is you—strong, stable, and grounded in *6 Inward Life Anchors,* which are immovable, timeless, universal life principles of *Self-Identity, Life Living, Intentional Actions, Life Realities, Life Character,* and *Life Aspirations.* Now it's time to raise the anchor, leave port, move your ship into the *Outward World* and focus on the *6 Essential Outward Life*

Anchors. Notice how the arrows of the *Outward Life Anchors* are pointed out from the center anchor on the captain's wheel to each handle. The captain needs to grab the handles and steer the ship through the *Outward* elements of the waves, tides, and storms. Let's examine our *6 Essential Outward Life Anchors*, which focus on our interactions with others and the world.

IOU LIFE LIVING WHEEL

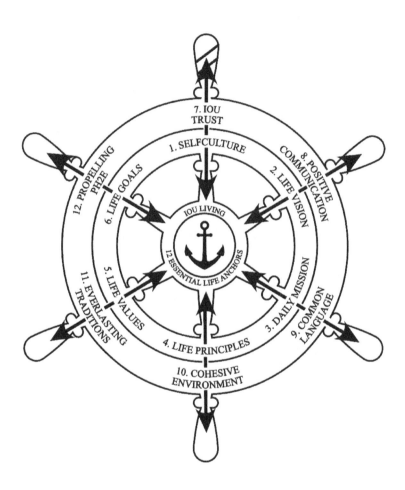

OUTWARD LIVING
LIFE ANCHOR 7

INSPIRE IOU TRUST

The Principle of Life Relationships

The first job of a leader—at work or at home—is to inspire trust. It's to bring out the best in people by entrusting them with meaningful stewardships, and to create an environment in which high-trust interaction inspires creativity and possibility.

—Stephen M.R. Covey

A *Dynamic Positive Culture* must foster trust. Your *Inward SelfCulture* needs to foster trust. Your *Family Culture* needs to foster trust. Your *Team Culture* needs to foster trust. Your work or *Organizational Culture* needs to foster trust. I purposely repeated the phrase "needs to foster trust" in each sentence to emphasize the importance of promoting and having trust in all of our *Outward* relationships. The first *Outward Life Anchor* is *Inspire IOU Trust*, which is short for *Inspire Inward-Outward-Upward Trust*. This signifies you first need to trust yourself *Inwardly* before you can trust others *Outwardly*. In addition, you need to be *Inwardly* trustworthy before others can trust you. When you have *Inward* and *Outward Trust*, you will be *Upward Living* and receive the *Life Gifts of PH2E*.

Trust is central to our *Inward* and *Outward Living*. Trust affects us every moment of our lives. When there is trust, there is a connection between what we believe based on our *6 Essential Inward Life Anchors* and our *Outward* relationships with others. *Inspire IOU Trust* is based on the *Principle of Life Relationships*. We trust what other people tell us, and therefore we *Outwardly Act* based on their words and commitments. In the same way, other people trust us based on our commitments, integrity, and actions. In trusting relationships, the byproduct is *Upward Life Living* and increasing the *PH2E* levels for all involved.

Trust will grow when your *Outward Actions* are consistent with your *Inward Thinking*. It becomes clear to others if you are sincere, honest, and genuine. If you have not taken the time to think about your *Inward Life Anchors*, your *Outward Actions* may appear to be insincere, skeptical, and disingenuous, even though you have the best intentions. Stephen M. R. Covey explains that there are people who may have good intentions and sincerely seek the welfare of others, but their *Outward* execution of intent is poor. There are also people who have poor *Inward Intent* and insincere *Outward Behaviors*. In both scenarios, the people will judge themselves by their *Inward Intent*, while others will judge them by their *Outward Behaviors*. To *Inspire IOU Trust*, you need to be aware and match your *Inward Intent* with explicit *Outward Behaviors*. If not, the lack of explicitness may cause others to see your interactions as an unsafe place and would not be vulnerable and take risks. Therefore, they will not want to engage and *Inspire IOU Trust*, since the solid foundation of trust is lacking. *Essential Life Anchor 7, Inspire IOU Trust*, is the foundational *Life Anchor* for all of the remaining *Outward Life Anchors*. Without it, there is no foundation to build upon with the other *Outward Anchors*. Without trust, loyalty, and commitment, your byproduct will be *Living IOD* and *Downward Life Drains*.

Every high *IOU Trust* relationship is permeated with respect, where each person genuinely listens to each other. The principle of listening will be discussed in greater detail in Essential Life Anchor 8 (Practice Positive Communication). John Wooden stated that it's better to trust in someone and be occasionally disappointed than not to trust and be miserable all the time. Living a life of trust brings peace and gives you a better chance to succeed in life, physically function better, and enjoy the fruits of your decisions. In other words, practicing *Essential Life Anchor 7 - Inspire IOU Trust* will result in greater rewards of *PH2E*.

When trust is inspired between two people, the byproduct is an *Upward Lift of PH2E* for both parties. To inspire someone means to excite, encourage, or to breathe life into their efforts. When you *Inspire IOU Trust*, you are authentically leading from your heart and mind. All of the other *Essential Outward Life Anchors* are within *IOU Trust*. When you are living *Life Anchor 7*, you are Practicing Positive Communication (Life Anchor 8), have Created Common Language (Life Anchor 9), have Constructed a Cohesive Environment (Life Anchor 10), have Established Everlasting Traditions (Life Anchor 11), and are Modeling a Mindset that Propels Your *PH2E* (Life Anchor 12).

Trust is the glue of life. It's the most essential ingredient in effective communication. It's the foundational principle that holds all relationships.

—Stephen R. Covey

Five Levels of Trust

Think about someone you trust at work. Now, think about a family member you trust—a spouse, a sibling, a child, or a cousin. Is the trust level the same? Probably not, however, we say we trust various people in our *Outward* interactions all the time. *Anchor 7*, to *Inspire IOU Trust* is the highest level of trust to achieve. When you have all three areas in the *Inspire IOU Trust* model, you have arrived at the highest form of trust.

Not all trust is *IOU Trust*. There are five levels of trust to be aware of in your relationships. When you are, you can act *Outwardly* accordingly.

1. **IOU Trust.** Your closest relationships. The highest form of trust, where you *Inspire, Influence* and have *Alignment on Life Principles*. This person is on your *Inward Life Relation-Ship*.

2. **IO Trust.** Close relationships. A high form of trust where you *Inspire* and *Influence* each other. You have *Alignment on most Life Principles*, but some may be unclear. This person is on your *Inward or IO Life Relation-Ship*.

3. **Trust.** Relationships in which you believe that the other person has high character and high competence, but you may not yet know many of their deeply held *Life Principles*. This person is on your *IO Life Relation-Ship*.

4. **Low Trust.** The relationships that you're developing and building. This person is on your *IO* or *Outward Life Relation-Ship*.

5. **No Trust.** The relationships that are taking advantage of you, have not kept their commitment to you, are manipulative, or are not respectful toward you. This person should be on the dinghy!

Strive for level 1, *IOU Trust*. This is the highest form of trust. It starts with you to *Inspire* it in others. As the saying goes, "Shoot for the moon, and if you miss, you will land among the stars." If it misses, you may still have a high form of trust, which is vital and is the glue for all relationships.

You are no better than anybody else,
but nobody's better than you.

—Katherine Johnson

Know Who You Are and Inspire Trust

As our society moves into the *Leadership Age*, this book aims to help you know yourself better as a *Life Leader* and rediscover your *Purpose*, *Potential*, and *Passion*.

An inspiring *Life Leader* was Katherine Johnson, a mathematician for NASA who calculated and analyzed the flight paths for many spacecrafts on their mission into space and to the moon. In 1953, she began working at the National Advisory Committee for Aeronautics with a group of African American women who manually computed complex mathematical calculations. Despite segregation and many other difficult circumstances, Katherine persevered, showing her talents and *Inward* drive, and insisted on participating in high level briefings only attended by men. She eventually was invited to attend those meetings, and everyone quickly recognized her extraordinary talents and saw that she made significant contributions to the team.

In 1962, NASA was ready to launch the spaceship Friendship 7 with the hope of placing the first American in orbit. John Glenn trained for months preparing for the mission. The relatively new IBM computer calculated the space capsule's trajectory from the moment it lifted off at Cape Canaveral until splashdown near Bermuda. However, John Glenn personally asked Katherine to recheck the computer's flight trajectories for his orbital mission before launching. Glenn is quoted as saying, "If she says they're good, then I'm ready to go." Glenn's request showed the tremendous trust he had in Katherine Johnson, not only to safeguard NASA's reputation, but most notably, for the safety of the astronauts' lives. Katherine calculated the trajectory numbers manually to confirm the IBM computer's calculations. It took Katherine a day and a half to complete the calculations, which she figured two decimals points beyond the computer's numbers to confirm the trajectories were correct.

Johnson was also instrumental in the success of Apollo 11, which involved the first landing on the moon. She calculated the Eagle's landing on the moon and its syncing back to the Lunar Module so the astronauts could return home. Katherine Johnson overcame racial and gender discrimination and became a critical person in the success of NASA's space explorations. She was a *Life Leader* and a *Life Changer* for the US Space Program and millions of Americans.

Katherine Johnson *Inspired IOU Trust* in the men with whom she worked. Developing trust was a process described in her autobiography. When she first started in NASA's East Computing Wing, an engineer wanted Katherine to analyze some flight test data. She discovered an error in one of the calculations and was nervous about how to approach the engineer. After thinking *Inwardly* and taking a deep breath, she said to the engineer, "Is it possible you could have a mistake in your formula?" Everything stopped, and you could hear a pin drop before the engineer looked over the work Katherine did and agreed that he made an error. In fact, that error has been in the formula for years. From that moment on, all the engineers went to Katherine every day for calculation checks. She went beyond the equations and started to ask questions to stretch their thinking. Even though they seemed annoyed, she didn't stop challenging them, no matter what rank they held. After a few months of Katherine's constant questions, the engineers saw the value she had to offer. She inspired and influenced them and even became good friends with many of the engineers once *IOU Trust* was established. From this trust, Katherine received *Upward Living* and the *Life Gift of Happiness.* She stated, "I truly loved going to work every single day, and when you love what you do, it doesn't feel like work!"

> *Most of us consider trust to be built slowly,*
> *with verification, and in degrees.*
> *. . . [T]rust is created by a combination of things and,*
> *while the end result is almost magical,*
> *the process cannot be rushed.*
>
> —Mac Richard

Building *IOU Trust*

Outward Living is all about your *Life Relationships.* In fact, the three *Life Relation-Ships* discussed in detail in Chapter 9 describe the relationships we all have in our lives. It is normal and appropriate that each relationship has different levels of trust. The question is, how do you move your relationships to the highest level possible? The following *IOU Trust* Model is a guide that will inspire you and others to move to the highest level *Life Relation-Ship*. The people on your *Inward Relation-Ship* embody integrity, credibility, reliability, authenticity, and compassion. You *Inspire* and *Influence* each other and have *Agreement on Life Principles*. *Agreement on Life Principles* means that you have similar points of view, perceptions, and beliefs, and therefore you have similar *Life Maps*.

THE IOU TRUST MODEL

The Principle of Life Relationships

INSPIRE IOU TRUST

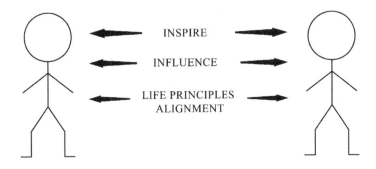

IOU Trust is defined as the highest form of trust due to the *Upward Living* you receive when you interact with the other person. When you have *IOU Trust* with someone, you receive one of the *PH2E's* consistently. Three areas need to be in place for *IOU Trust* to occur.

The first is two-way, reciprocal *Inspiration* between you and the other person, both emotionally and intellectually—emotionally where there is high character and intellectually where there is high competence. Both individuals *Inspire* each other. As Stephen M. R. Covey has written, both character and competence are vital for a trusting relationship. Character includes the motive for your *Outward Actions* toward others. What is your intent? Competence includes your skills and capabilities.

The second area is *Influence.* Is there a two-way *Influence?* Does the other person *Influence* you in any way, and do you have any *Influence* on the other person? When you have *Influence,* there is trust because to accept the *Influence* of another person, you must have trust in them. Why would you do something they are advocating if you don't trust them?

The third area is *Life Principle Alignment.* This is a must! If both of you are not aligned in your Life Principles, then you have different *Life Maps.* If you have a strong Life Principle regarding family and the other person has the opposing view, it would be difficult to attain *IOU Trust.* There may be trust but not in its highest form—*IOU Trust.*

Inspire IOU Trust
Anchor Planning

Questions for Self and/or for the FTO as a group:

Think of the one or two people with whom you are closest. Do you experience *IOU Trust* with them? How do you *Inspire* each other, *Influence* each other and how are you *Aligned on your Life Principles*?

_____

_____

Now think of other people with whom you are close. Reflect on how your trust level is not as high. Can you see where you differ on some *Life Principles*? Write about it.

_____

_____

List key people you have on your *Inward Life Relation-Ship*. Is there anything you can do to raise the level of trust you share with them?

_____

_____

Think of people with whom you have *Low Trust or No Trust*. Can you identify why? What can you do to either grow trust or send them to the dinghy?

_____

_____

Download all the *IOU Anchor Planning* pages
Free at: www.iouanchors.com

OUTWARD LIVING
LIFE ANCHOR 8

PRACTICE POSITIVE
COMMUNICATION

The Principle of Outward Understanding

*The most important thing in communication
is hearing what isn't said.*

—Peter Drucker

If you ask anyone what skill is most important and necessary for communication, the usual response is an *Outward* skill, such as speaking clearly, getting to the point, or staying on topic. These are all related to speaking. However, *Life Anchor 8, Practice Positive Communication*, is about much more than speaking. At its heart is active listening and understanding others before speaking. *Practice Positive Communication* is based on the *Principle of Outward Understanding*. In the 13th century, Francis of Assisi was credited with coining the famous phrase, "Seek first to understand then to be understood." Stephen Covey incorporated this as Habit 5 in *The 7 Habits of Highly Effective People*. Many people underestimate the importance of listening and are on the defense in conversations, trying to make sure the other person understands them. We need to pause intentionally, listen with our whole heart first, and then speak as effectively as possible.

Practice Positive Communication is the mindset you must have when listening and speaking to others. When the person you are talking to feels your positive energy, they become more comfortable and relaxed. *Practicing Positive Communication* will enhance every one of your relationships. Will Rogers said, "I never met a man I didn't like." I'm sure there may have been a few people less likable than others, but his positive mindset resulted in others being comfortable with him and allowed him to communicate freely with everyone.

When a boating journey begins, a good captain has to know the conditions of the seas, which is the *Outward Environment*. The captain needs to study the tides, currents, winds, and waves to have a smooth and successful journey. I refer to this as

Outward Listening. Once the ship is at sea, the captain reads or *Outwardly Listens* to the waves in front of the vessel and makes slight adjustments, so the ship remains steady and on course. The captain is observing or *Outward Listening* to the waters and then steers by turning the captain's wheel or speaking and responding with his *Outward Actions.* The goal of this *Outward Action* of listening is a smooth and successful journey.

When listening to another person, you must carefully read and listen to the other person's words and body language as if they are the waves of the ocean, so you respond appropriately and receive positive results by moving the conversation and relationship to higher levels of IOU Trust. The ability to read others' emotions and nonverbal communication increases understanding and elevates relationships, which is listening wholeheartedly, or what I refer to as *WholeHearted Listening.* *WholeHearted Listening* is when we don't judge or jump to conclusions and neither agree nor disagree but listen for understanding with our whole heart and mind.

Let's examine the **4 Levels of *Outward Listening*** with the goal of improving your communication with others in a positive manner.

The 4 LEVELS OF OUTWARD LISTENING

- **WholeHearted Listening**
- **HalfHearted Listening**
- **Reply Listening**
- **Distracted Listening**

Level 1. WholeHearted Listening

At this level, your whole heart and mind try to understand the other person. You neither agree nor disagree with what is being said but seek to understand from the speaker's perspective.

Grasping the speaker's perspective might be difficult, especially if it differs from yours. However, this must not stop you from listening deeply with your whole heart. It will help if you first calm yourself down and prepare to listen. If you are "hyped up," anxious, or distracted, you are not going to be a *WholeHearted Listener*. It is also important to pay attention to both verbal and nonverbal cues from the speaker.

Use clarifying statements to confirm that you understand the speaker's intentions. Clarifying statements may include:

- What I'm hearing is . . .
- It sounds like you . . .
- It seems that you . . .
- So, you are . . .
- You seem . . . (use an adjective) . . . frustrated, angry, confused, thrilled, nervous, scared, happy, etc.

Try using these clarifying statements in your next conversation, especially when the speaker presents with high emotions. Your goal should be to understand, not to judge, agree, or disagree.

Level 2. HalfHearted Listening

At this level, you try to understand what the other person is saying, but instead of deep listening, you evaluate, judge, and draw conclusions based on their comments. If you recall the *Life Map Cycle*, it's as if you have jumped to *Formulating* your opinion before carefully *Evaluating* and *Calculating* what the other person is trying to say. This occurs because you are only *HalfHeartedly Listening*.

Level 3. Reply Listening

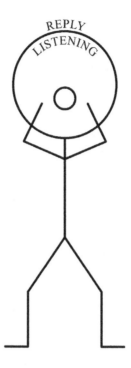

At this level, you are slightly paying attention to what the other person is saying and hear enough to get the gist of the person's thoughts but are only listening to give a reply. You have *Formulated* your response and are waiting for the opportunity to speak. In fact, you are waiting for a period, a comma, or a breath from the other person to jump in with your thoughts. Stephen Covey stated that "Most people do not listen with the intent to understand; they listen with the intent to reply."

Level 4. Distracted Listening

At this level, you are not really listening, but only pretending to listen while you are thinking of something unrelated to what the other person is saying. To make it appear as though you are listening, you make a few replies, such as: "Yes," "Uh-huh," or "Right."

Two Levels of Outward Speaking

When we *Outwardly Listen* to others, we have only met half of *Life Anchor 8 Practice Positive Communication*. The other half of *Practicing Positive Communication* is speaking. Your tone, words, and body language all communicate either trust or distrust.

Level 1 - High Tide Safe Talk

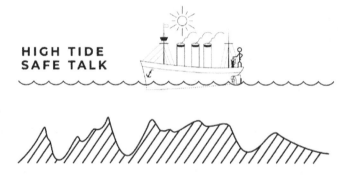

HIGH TIDE
SAFE TALK

Is your communication positive, safe, and IOU Trust building? When *Positive Communication* occurs, you create a safe environment comparable to when you are navigating a boat during high tide. High tide is the safest time to navigate a vessel in waters because the water is at its highest level, well above any dangerous obstacles in the ocean, such as sand bars, shipwrecks, or rocks. Some areas are actually only passable during high tide. This is analogous to communicating with others. You want to have conversations where the other person feels safe and is open and unconcerned about getting hurt. I call this *High Tide Safe Talk*.

High Tide Safe Talk occurs when you create an IOU Trust environment where the other person feels comfortable communicating their deepest joys and concerns. Consider your communication style. Are your words *High Tide Positive?* Do people feel safe to be vulnerable and reveal themselves without fear of being judged? Do people feel empowered after your conversations? Do your conversations build and strengthen relationships? In *High Tide Safe Talk*, other people want to board and stay on your ship. They perceive you as their lifeboat and believe your ship will rise above any dangers lying ahead.

When you intentionally implement *Wholehearted Listening* and *Hide Tide Safe Talk*, the other person is open, comfortable, and feels high trust. The relationship moves to the highest level possible. This is *Life Anchor 8 Practice Positive Communication!* Noted author and researcher Brené Brown has written extensively about courage and vulnerability. She uses the phrase "Let's rumble" to refer to having an open mind and heart to serve the needs of all participants instead of any individual's ego. Regarding listening, she suggests listening with the same passion with which you want to be heard.

You have to wait to engage in *High Tide Safe Talk*. In the ocean and bays, high tide occurs about every 12 hours at a different time each day. Nothing can be done to bring about high tide; we just have to wait. Similarly, when you want to have an emotional discussion with someone, you need to wait for the right time. Do not try to discuss details when high emotions are present, or the other person is in *Life Environment 1*. Wait for "their" high tide, so the environment is safe. You may be able to help them get there, but you can only discuss the issue when they are ready. Then you can navigate both of your concerns in a safe way.

Level 2 - Low Tide Unsafe Talk

Low tide is the opposite of high tide, where it can be extremely dangerous to boat. If you are in unfamiliar waterways, you can run aground on a sandbar and get stuck, or even worse, hit an obstacle such as a rock or sunken boat. Low tide boating can be very unsafe. *Low Tide Unsafe Talk* is when you create an environment where the other person feels unsafe, and therefore, shares minimally. That occurs when your speaking is negative, unsafe, or judgmental. Do your words and body language result in the diminishing of your relationship? If so, you are *Low Tide Unsafe Talking*. When this occurs, people shut down and do not board your ship because it's too dangerous. If they are there already, they may want to jump ship! They feel unsafe and wonder if your ship will hit something and be unable to complete its journey.

The following are two examples demonstrating the difference between *Low Tide Unsafe Talk* and *High Tide Safe Talk*:

Example 1:

You notice that John usually gives 100% effort, but his results are starting to slip. His productivity is dropping, and you notice he is arriving late several times a week. You decide to talk to him, and the conversation goes like this:

Supervisor: I notice your results are falling. What's going on?

John: I know I need to focus better and get more data to produce better results.

Supervisor: I see. Do you need help with this project?

John: No, I got it. You will see better results ASAP.

Supervisor: You've been coming in late. Do you think that might have anything to do with your productivity dropping?

John: Yes, I will correct that. I'm sorry. I'll be on time.

That was an example of *Low Tide Unsafe Talk*. From the supervisor's first question, there was no opportunity for John to feel comfortable sharing any issues that might be affecting his performance and preventing him from improving results. There was no relationship building.

Example 2:

This supervisor notices the same issues with John, but leads the conversation differently:

Supervisor: I've noticed that you've been distracted lately and wonder if there is anything on your mind. Is there something I can help you with?

John: Yes, I know. I have a lot going on at home lately.

Supervisor: Can I help you with it?

John: Thank you, but my mom needs to go to the hospital for treatments, and I have to drive her every morning. Sometimes the treatments run late.

Supervisor: I'm glad you shared that. You've always gone above and beyond in your work. Don't worry, just get here as soon as you can.

John: I've worked it out with my sister to take Mom starting on Monday.

Supervisor: I'm sure this has been affecting your progress on the project. Shall I put Bill on the project with you?

John: I can finish it in a few days; however, if Bill can get the data on last month's outcomes, that would expedite my completion.

Supervisor: Absolutely, I'll get him on it.

Which conversation do you think will get better results and build trust and a stronger relationship between John and his supervisor? The results are the same in both the *High Tide Safe Talk* and *Low Tide UnSafe Talk* scenarios. However, in the *High Tide Safe Talk*, not only do you get results, but you Inspire IOU Trust, which will pay multiple dividends to benefit John and the organization. If *High Tide Safe Talk* continues throughout John's career, how do you think he will feel about work? He will undoubtedly be loyal and fully committed to the organization's Life Vision, Daily Mission, and Life Goals.

Practice Positive Communication is an *Outward* connection to others and the world. Whatever our *Inward Intentions* are, it's our *Outward Communications* that others see and hear. It can be frustrating if we cannot accurately express our *Inward Intentions*. How many times have we said, "That's not what I meant," or "You're not understanding me," or "Let me clarify?" We only know we have been misunderstood when we get feedback from the other person in response to our message. As the old saying goes, the single biggest problem in communication is the illusion that it has taken place. When delivering important messages to others, we should practice asking clarifying questions such as, "Does that make sense?" "Are we on the same page?" or "Should I explain it another way?"

Practice Positive Communication is a skill that requires intentional practice and attention. As your listening skills improve, miscommunication decreases. Listening at the highest level, *WholeHearted*, will make other people feel respected and valued, build IOU Trust, and a strong *Inward-Outward Relationship*, resulting in a *High Tide Safe Talk Environment*. This creates the space and freedom for two-way listening and speaking at the highest level, which propel the *Upward Living Life Gifts of PH2E*. Begin *Practicing Positive Communication* by listening *WholeHeartedly* and creating a *High Tide Safe Talk Environment*. You will immediately feel your SelfCulture and the culture of your *family, team, and organization* grow *Dynamic* and *Positive*.

The Positive Communication Models

The Principle of Outward Understanding

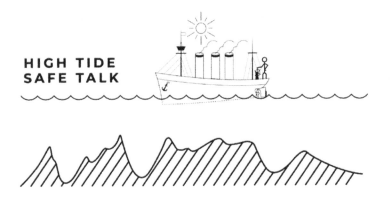

**HIGH TIDE
SAFE TALK**

There are two models to *Practice Positive Communication*. The first is to practice *Wholehearted Listening*. In your next conversation with another person, try listening wholeheartedly with your whole heart and mind, neither agreeing nor disagreeing with what is being said, but rather trying to understand from the speaker's point of view.

The second model is creating a *High Tide Safe Talk* environment when speaking to another person. Be aware of the environment you are creating. Does it feel safe for others to communicate their deepest joys and concerns? Be mindful of your *Outward Behaviors*, your words, and your body language, which all affect whether your tide is high or low. We can't govern the ocean tides, but we can raise the tide in our conversation, so it feels safe, and the other person is open and not concerned with the dangers of getting hurt. All members of *Dynamic Positive Cultures* are intentionally aware and continuously improving their speaking and listening to *Practice Positive Communication*.

Practice Positive Communication
Anchor Planning

<u>Questions for Self and/or for the FTO as a group:</u>

Think of occasions when someone you were confiding in listened distractedly or only enough to reply. How did it make you feel?

_____

_____

Now think of an occasion when someone listened to you *Wholeheartedly*. How did you feel then?

_____

_____

Now think of situations when you listened to others distractedly or only enough to reply. Contrast that with times when you listened *Wholeheartedly*. Were the results or byproducts of the situations different? How?

_____

_____

How can you incorporate *High Tide Safe Talk* with your *family, team, or organization?* List some specific examples.

_____

_____

Download all the _IOU Anchor Planning_ pages
Free at: www.iouanchors.com

OUTWARD LIVING
LIFE ANCHOR 9

CREATE COMMON LANGUAGE
The Principle of Outward Effectiveness

Everyone hears only what he understands.

—Johann Wolfgang von Goethe

Common Language keeps everyone on the same course. Language provides a common framework for understanding the purpose and norms of the organization. It defines the way people behave toward each other and lends a feeling of camaraderie. *Common Language* is a shorthand for the organization's Life Vision and Daily Mission and is, therefore, a meaningful way to keep them in the forefront. *Create Common Language* is based on the *Principle of Outward Effectiveness*, which will accelerate communication and alignment of your *FTO's* Life Vision, Daily Mission, and Life Goals.

Creating unique *Common Language* for your *family, team, or organization* creates a sense of culture, togetherness, and unity. When *Common Language* is used, all members have a shared understanding. Your message is clear and consistent. *Common Language* helps create efficient and effective communication that builds teamwork and bonding. It helps maintain positive morale. *Common Language* also helps you promote your *FTO* to the *Outward World* because it sends a consistent message about who you are and what you believe.

When there is a concerted effort to use *Common Language* based around the Life Vision, Life Principles, and Life Values consistent with the Daily Mission, it creates alignment in the culture. Even though individuals have their own perspectives and opinions, using *Common Language* will keep everyone moving in the same direction toward your Life Goals. Regarding school communities but applicable to other types of organizations, Peter Senge stated that alignment starts with respect for each other and establishing common mental models. A critical component of that is the use of *Common Language* among all stakeholders.

> *As great minds have the faculty of saying a great deal in a few words, so lesser minds have a talent of talking much and saying nothing.*
>
> —François de La Rochefoucauld

BIG MEANING - FEWER WORDS

Using *Common Language* promotes *positive and effective* results by increasing the speed of communication and providing greater meaning using fewer words. Using *Common Language* helps to get your point across and reduces the time necessary to explain complex concepts. *Create Common Language* is based on the *Principle of Outward Effectiveness.*

Use and model the language of your Life Vision, Daily Mission, Life Principles, and Life Values every day. Involve the *FTO* in the development of these *Inward Anchors* so they will readily adopt, hear, and repeat them. The *Common Language* will take on a life of its own because everyone will feel the connectedness and camaraderie that comes through the use of *Common Language.*

Why is Common Language So Effective?

Perhaps the greatest benefit of *Common Language* is that it builds a sense of belonging, camaraderie, and identity. It builds culture and bonds people together because everyone understands the phrases used. In fact, misunderstandings are minimized. *Common Language* also helps all members understand expectations.

Common Language exists when *FTO* members use words or phrases that hold significant meaning. It's like using shorthand or showing a picture. You've heard the saying that a picture is worth a thousand words. Well, *Common Language* is worth a thousand words related to the *FTO's* culture.

One day, my daughter came home frustrated and tearing up. She was confronted by one of her teachers for talking in class out of turn and given an extra assignment for her poor behavior. My daughter told us what she did. She was upset and felt she let her teacher and us down. My wife and I listened to her and sensed she was remorseful; therefore, there was no need to rehash the situation. We simply told her that it appeared she knew what she did wrong and that it was up to her to change her behavior in class moving forward. As she walked away with tears in her eyes, I told her, "No matter what." This short phrase is an example of meaningful *Common Language* my family uses, which grew from discussions of the love we have for each other—no matter what happens. It does not matter what action was done; it does not matter how wrong an action might have been. Our children know we still and always will love them, no matter what. They also know, however, there will be consequences for inappropriate or negative actions. The consequence might be significant, but the message is, "we still love you." The phrase "no matter what" is *Common Language* in our family, which has tremendous meaning for all of us.

On a soccer team I coach, there are many short phrases that carry a lot of meaning. We have created *Common Language* we use during a game to give directions to players quickly. A few words carry a lot of meaning, such as when we need the team to return to their defensive positions, we say, "get your shapes." When the team hears this, they know exactly what to do. Ten players simultaneously move to positions to defend the ball.

Great nautical examples of *Common Language* with tremendous meaning include:

Batten down the hatches: These four words carry specific orders for several tasks. Instead of ordering each task, the crew knows exactly what to do in preparation for a coming storm or rough seas.

All hands-on desk: This is used to get the entire crew to their stations and prepare for action.

As the crow flies: These words carry a lot of meaning to a captain of a ship needing to find a direct route to the nearest land. Before there were modern navigational systems, vessels carried a cage of crows onboard. To find the nearest land, the crew released a crow that would always fly in a direct route to the nearest land, thereby giving the direction and route for the captain to steer the ship "as the crow flies."

I was driving home from my son's early Sunday morning soccer game. He sat next to me in the front seat, and his twin sister was in the back. He wanted to stop for some snacks on the way home. Because it was a tough game, I was willing to make the stop. On the way, I reminded my children that when we got home, we need to get ready to go to church. My son said that he did not want to go and would not be going. My daughter listened quietly in the back while my son and I traded reasons for attending or not. My patience waned, and I decided to rescind my offer to stop for the snacks.

Before I did, my daughter said, "If you stop for him, and he goes to church, it's a win-win."

My son said, "No, it's a win-lose because I don't want to go to church. You win, and I lose." I asked why he didn't want to go, and he replied he was tired.

"Then, we'll go straight home, and I'll take your phone so you won't be bothered and therefore you can just rest."

"That's a lose-lose," he said.

We continued the drive in silence. To break the tension, my daughter connected via Bluetooth to the car radio and played the song, "The Sound of Silence," and then the song "Help."

We were getting closer to the store, and my daughter asked her brother to Think Win-Win. I asked him what his final decision was, and he said he would go to church.

The *Common Language* of "Think Win-Win" from the book, *The 7 Habits of Highly Effective People* led to the speedy resolution of our disagreement. As the situation with my son illustrates, *Common Language* helps when emotions are high. When emotions are calmer, *Common Language* helps us strengthen our language, so when emotions rise, we can make our points with fewer, meaningful words.

Creating Common Language

What *Common Language* do you want to introduce to your *FTO*? Write the words and phrases down, then discuss or introduce them by modeling the language. Begin to *Create Common Language* for your *family, team, or organization*. Start with your family. Are there unique phrases your family has used to make a point, support each other, or convey information? You may be using *Common Language* and not even be aware of it. Identify the *Common Language*, then discuss, document, and celebrate it. If there is no *Common Language*, listen for *Common Language* themes and create a phase together or by yourself and begin to use it.

In the workplace, there are ample opportunities to *Create Common Language*. You may already have technical language common to everyone; however, *Create Common Language* around the team or organization's Life Vision, Daily Mission, Life Principles, and Life Values. It will build a framework for understanding the purpose and norms of the organization while at the same time, developing camaraderie. *Create Common Language* for stressful situations, so others don't need an explanation of every detail. "I'm up the ladder right now" is a phrase my organization commonly uses based on the Ladder of Inference thinking process developed by Chris Argyris. When you jump to the top of a ladder without thinking, you are usually in a state of high emotions and high stress. If you walk into the room and the other person says, "I'm up the ladder right now," you immediately understand the person's state and how to communicate.

The social dynamic of teenagers can be a great example of *Common Language* and its effects on a group. Think back to when you were a teenager. Were there unique phases you and your friends used? *Common Language* used today functions in the same way. Teenagers take pride in "their" *Common Language* and don't want adults to understand or use it. Recently, I tried to use my teenage children's *Common Language,* and they let me know immediately that I should stop. It was clear it was their *Common Language,* not mine!

The Common Language Model

The Principle of Outward Effectiveness

The model of *Create Common Language* emphasizes the idea that everyone in a *family, team, or organization* has *Common Language* that builds culture. It brings a sense of identity and community and is a unique shorthand for the group. It can be a fun and powerful way to build relationships and effectiveness among an entire group.

Create Common Language
Anchor Planning

Questions for Self and/or for the FTO as a group:

Write down some examples of *Common Language* that you share with your *family, team, or organization.*

_____

_____

Think of and write down one or two examples where having *Common Language* would have helped a difficult situation with your *family, team, or organization.*

_____

_____

How can you involve your *family, team, or organization* in the creation of *Common Language?*

_____

_____

Download all the _IOU Anchor Planning_ pages

Free at: www.iouanchors.com

OUTWARD LIVING
LIFE ANCHOR 10

CONSTRUCT A COHESIVE
ENVIRONMENT

The Principle of Outward Connectedness

Alone, we can do so little; together, we can do so much.

—Helen Keller

The *Outward Principle* is acting out; the doing. Once we define who we are in the *Inward Principle*, we must act and begin creating a culture of safety, character, and competence. This does not happen alone but can only occur with the entire team or family members working together fulfilling the Life Vision. *Construct a Cohesive Environment* is based on the *Principle of Outward Connectedness*. It's about the overall sense of who you are or what your *family, team, or organization* is about. It is expressed both physically and relationally. Other people will look at you or your *FTO* and know what you stand for and what you represent.

Construct a Cohesive Environment has two dimensions: the physical environment and the relational environment. The physical environment consists of what you see and how you feel when you walk into a home, office, lobby, or classroom. For example, what's hanging on the walls, what are the colors, and what type of furniture is present. The relational environment is about the interactions between members of the group. Do you sense an interconnectedness between *the family, team,* and *members of the organization*? Is there a high level of teamwork practiced?

Construct a Cohesive Environment brings *Life Anchors 1-9* under one umbrella. Cohesive is defined as sticking together. In science, it's a force that holds a piece of matter together. In *IOU Life Leadership*, it's the glue that connects *Life Anchors 1-9* and creates an attitude of "We-ness!"

When you walk into the environment, words are not needed to sense the *family's, team's, or organization's* Life Vision, Daily Mission, and culture. It is evident through unspoken and symbolic items that the environment is a well-connected and supportive *Cohesive Environment.*

A *Cohesive Environment* within the *family, team, and organization* creates a Super Team where each individual understands their role and importance. Working together cohesively, the team becomes stronger than any one person in the group. Steven Covey describes synergy as creative cooperation where two or more people produce significantly better results than any one of them could individually. *Construct a Cohesive Environment* results from synergy.

The first step to *Construct* a *Cohesive Environment* is to make sure you have intentionally developed Life Anchor 7, IOU Trust. When trust is high, family members, team members, and organization members will feel comfortable being open, taking risks, and unconcerned about failing. When there is a high trust environment, you will feel the cohesiveness among all stakeholders.

Individual commitment to a group effort - that is what makes a team work, a company work, a society work, a civilization work.

—Vince Lombardi

Cohesive Family Environment

Do you have a cohesive family environment? If not, create it! First, look at the physical environment. Are there positive messages hanging on the wall? Do the material things in the home represent the family values? You don't have to redecorate the entire house, but by adding even one small item, you can change the feel of a home. A quick and easy way is to put up a positive message that resonates with the family.

The second dimension is the relational environment. How are the family members treating each other? Have you had a meeting to discuss the family's Life Values? Get the family together and discuss how everyone should treat each other to start *Constructing a Cohesive Environment*. This should be done when everyone is calm and rational; it will be a powerful guide when a family member is stressed and irrational. You will not have to point out appropriate behavior since it was already discussed and agreed upon. The previously established *Cohesive Family Environment* will be self-evident to everyone involved.

Cohesive Organization Environment

Does your organization environment reflect its shared Life Vision, Daily Mission, and Life Values? As you walk into the environment, the purpose of the organization should be visually clear. Additionally, it should be clear that the culture is aligned to a common Life Vision with individuals that are committed, connected, and supportive of each other. Is the organization's brand visible as soon as you walk in, and is it evident throughout the entire environment? If it's only present in the entranceway with no sign of the organizational brand or theme anywhere else, it will be apparent to outsiders that the Life Vision is not systemic and is only a facade. Attend to the details when creating the physical environment of your organization. The staff will notice, and when people enter your environment, they will feel it and know they are in a place that is committed to its Life Vision and Life Values.

> *The heart that gives thanks is a happy one,*
> *for we cannot feel thankful and unhappy at the same time.*

—Douglas Wood

Construct a Cohesive Thankful Environment

Construct a positive and thankful environment. Name what you are grateful for, and let your *family, team, or organization* know. "I'm really thankful for having you on my team." "I am so thankful to have you as a mother." "I am thankful for our home, a place I know is always here and safe." It does not cost anything, so just do it! Being thankful creates a mentally *Cohesive Environment* for everyone in the group. You should sense thankfulness throughout the environment. Be mindful of what is hung on the walls and the room layouts, and other physical factors. Are these items connected to the *family's, team's, or organization's* Life Vision and Life Values?

Constructing a Cohesive Environment as a Daily Mission

As a leader of an educational organization and a home, I remind myself that both environments need to be places of safety, character, and competence. Each morning when I get up,

I repeat three words I use as one of my Daily Missions—Safe, Happy, Learning. These three words provide a clear, practical guide as I begin my day.

- Is my organization/home safe? What can I do today to improve the safety of my organization/home?
- Are my staff/students/family members happy? What can I do today to improve their feelings and emotions?
- Is authentic learning occurring? What can I do today to improve learning in my organization/school/home?

Safety, character, and competence encompass the entire culture of an organization or home. Start by thinking about your home. Everything will fall into one of these three categories.

Safe (Safety)
- Heat
- Air conditioning
- Smoke detectors
- Door locks
- Security measures
- CO detectors

Happy (Character)
- Loving environment
- Caring environment
- Supportive environment
- Relationships

- Be cheerful
- Be optimistic
- Project positive energy
- Be a peacemaker

Learning (Competence)
- Importance of team
- Chores
- Skills
- Problem-solving
- Creativity
- Health Education
- Hygiene

Inward and Outward Cohesive Environments

When *Constructing a Cohesive Environment*, we need to make sure we have *I* and *O Living* places in our environment. David Thornburg discusses the ultimate school environment to promote rich learning experiences for students. It includes "campfires" (home of the lecture), "watering holes" (home to conversations with peers), and "caves" (a quiet place of reflection). Do you have campfires, watering holes, and caves in your environments for storytelling, conversations, and self-reflection? A campfire is a wonderful analogy for a storytelling environment. I remember as a young child sitting around my neighbor's campfires and listening to the adults telling stories. Vincent was the ultimate storyteller.

You didn't need a fire to create the "campfire" atmosphere, only a quiet place with no *Outward* distractions to engage and get drawn into Vincent's stories and messages.

Watering holes are places in your environment that invite conversions and group discussion. Areas that lend themselves to *Outward* group discussions or gatherings are considered watering holes. At home, it can be at the kitchen or dining room table, or in a den or living room. At work, it can be a meeting room or a clustered group of chairs, either indoors or outdoors.

The ultimate *Inward* environment is a cave, a place where you can be alone to reflect, read, think, or meditate. Both home and work environments should have caves where individuals can be alone to think *Inwardly*.

How'd You Make Out?

One person alone can make a huge difference in *Constructing a Cohesive Environment*. In my family, that person was my father.

He did a plethora of things to *Construct a Cohesive Family Environment*, but I'd like to share one simple thing that any of us can do—always show concern and compassion toward others. A Common Language question he always asked was, "How'd you make out?" That simple question carried so much meaning to all of us. Whatever we were working on, troubled with, challenged by, or presented with, we would always get a call showing my father's concern and giving his compassionate support. He would always begin the conversation with, "How'd you make out?" When you heard those four simple words, you immediately knew you were going to be heard. You felt like you were in a *High Tide Safe Talk Environment* with him *WholeHeartedly Listening*. Even after his passing, we still hear him asking his question and use it ourselves. My father *Constructed* a positive, caring, and *Cohesive Environment* where you could express yourself and know he would stick with you no matter what. His strong impact is shown in the "How'd you make out?" banner hanging in our home and flag on our boat. He still affects our *Family Environment*. Begin to think about your environments at home, work, and on teams. Think about ways to make them more cohesive. Start small and simple, and send me an email at ***howdyoumakeout@iouliving.com*** and tell me, "How'd you make out?"

The Cohesive Environment Model

The Principle of Outward Connectedness

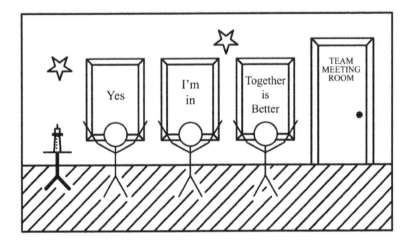

The *Cohesive Environment* Model emphasizes the two necessary dimensions - the physical environment and the relational environment. The physical environment consists of what you see and how you feel when you walk into the environment; the relational environment is about the interactions between members of the group. Each environment should create a feeling of *Outward Connectedness* for all members of the *FTO. Construct a Cohesive Environment* is an *Essential Life Anchor* which can help create a *Dynamic Positive Culture* where your *PH2E* can thrive.

Construct a Cohesive Environment
Anchor Planning

Questions for Self and/or for the FTO as a group:

Think about the physical environment of your *family, team, and/ or organization.*

How does it make you feel?

_____

_____

What are its strengths?

_____

_____

How can you improve upon it?

_____

_____

Now think about the relational environment.

How does it make you feel? _____

Do you have *IOU Trust?* _____

What are its strengths? _____

How can you improve it? _____

Write a *Daily Mission* about *Constructing a Cohesive Environment.*

_____

_____

_____

_____

Download all the _IOU Anchor Planning_ pages
Free at: www.iouanchors.com

OUTWARD LIVING
LIFE ANCHOR 11

ESTABLISH EVERLASTING
TRADITIONS

The Principle of Life History

Cultures grow on the vine of tradition.

—Jonah Goldberg

Establish Everlasting Traditions reinforces *Life Anchors 1-10* and means we should strive to create fun, loving, team-building traditions that everyone anticipates. The tradition could be in the form of a celebration, gathering, event, or a special occasion. *Establish Everlasting Traditions* is based on the *Principle of Life History.* Continually establish new traditions with your *family, team, and/or organization.* These traditions will create *Life History* leading to *Upward Living* and raise the spirit and culture for all stakeholders.

It is essential that people in your *family, team, and/or organization* have *Everlasting Traditions.* Traditions bring people together. In a team or organization, it's a great way to learn more about each other apart from the team or organization. It will build trust, a sense of teamwork, and support, in a similar yet different way than Life Anchor 10 (Construct a Cohesive Environment).

The word tradition comes from the Latin word *tradere,* which means to hand over or to give for safekeeping. Traditions can be passed down from generation to generation for each group member to feel a special connection to the past and the present. *Everlasting Traditions* can begin with you or can be inherited. It's a specific way of *Inward Thinking* and *Outward Action* by a group of people in your *family, team, or organization.* Traditions provide numerous benefits. They bond people together, creating everlasting memories, and providing a sense of identity for everyone involved. Traditions pass on values, morals, customs, and culture for future generations or groups. Traditions in our *family, teams, or organizations* ground us and preserve history.

In the song, "Tradition" from *Fiddler on the Roof*, Tevye, the wise father, says that without our traditions, we would lose our grounding. He sings, "Because of our traditions, we've kept our balance for many, many years . . . and without our traditions, our lives would be as shaky as . . . a fiddler on the roof."

There are many family traditions that bond everyone and help move them toward a *Dynamic Positive Culture*. Family meals can be a wonderful time to create traditions that will positively influence all involved. Each family member can share something about their day that was fun, exciting, or challenging. In my family, we share about our day at the dinner table. Another tradition that can be established is for each family member to share something for which they are grateful. Other family traditions include bedtime stories, Saturday morning walks, movie nights during the year, yearly holiday movies, birthday celebrations, holiday celebrations, family picnics, and sing-a-longs. Within each tradition, you should add your special little twist to make it your unique family tradition that can be passed on from generation to generation. My favorite *Everlasting Tradition* when I was a child was Mom's Sunday meatballs!

As previously mentioned, an *Everlasting Tradition* my wife and I have practiced with our children is developing a Family Life Vision statement. For the past twenty years on Christmas Eve, we've sat with our three children and asked questions like, "How do we want to treat each other?" "How do we want people to feel when they enter our home?" "How can we help when someone is frustrated?" The questions create conversations that then lead to concrete *Outward Actions*. My wife and I jot down all of the comments and, at a later date, form the responses into a statement. In some years, we've completed this step together, and sometimes I've finished it and then asked everyone to edit it. Once completed and agreed to, we hang it in a prominent place in the home. It is a powerful *Everlasting Tradition* that helps guide everyone's behaviors.

The Everlasting Traditions Model
The Principle of Life History

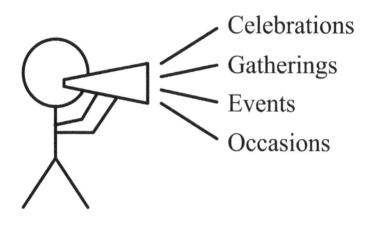

Celebrations
Gatherings
Events
Occasions

The *Everlasting Traditions* model reminds us of the importance of maintaining and establishing traditions for your *family, team, and/or organization*. Celebrations, gatherings, special events, and occasions tell a story about everyone involved. Traditions strengthen the bond among everyone, offer comfort and security, form lasting memories, and create a *Life History*. Think about your *family, team, or organization* and the traditions you practice. Begin to build on them and establish new traditions that will be everlasting for everyone involved.

Establish Everlasting Traditions
Anchor Planning

Questions for Self and/or for the FTO as a group:

Think of *Everlasting Traditions* you have with your *family, team, and/or organization* or have heard of in others. How do they help build a sense of togetherness and fun?

_____

_____

Write down specific celebrations, gatherings, events, and/or occasions that you can develop with your *family, team, and/or organization.* How can you make these *Everlasting Traditions?*

_____

_____

Download all the _IOU Anchor Planning_ pages
Free at: iouanchors.com

OUTWARD LIVING

LIFE ANCHOR 12

MODEL A MINDSET OF PROPELLING *PH2E*

The Principle of Life Gifts

Happiness is the meaning and the purpose of life, the whole aim and end of human existence.

—Aristotle

The turning of a ship's propeller propels everyone forward. Before a journey, the captain must inspect and make sure that each propeller blade is in top working order. When the propeller is balanced and full, it turns in a smooth and even manner at great speed, pushing the captain and entire crew on their journey. Similarly, if your *PH2E Life Propeller* is full and balanced, you will move forward on your *Life Journey* in a *positive and effective* manner. If it's unbalanced, chipped, or broken, you will be exhausted from the excessive work put on your engine. The ineffectiveness of the turning of the broken blades results in little or no progress on your journey.

I submit that the greatest gifts in life are your *PH2E!* The *Upward Life Gifts of Peacefulness, Happiness, Healthiness, and Excellence* are the most important things we all strive for in life. Every relationship, event, and action comes with a byproduct or result. Our hope is for a byproduct that can be placed in one of the *PH2E* areas.

Your *PH2E Life Propeller* is represented by four key life dimensions—the *Life Gifts of Peacefulness, Happiness, Healthiness, and Excellence.* That's why you must keep your *PH2E Life Propeller* in good working order. It is essential for receiving the *Upward Living Life Gifts.* To keep your *Peacefulness* and *Happiness* blades balanced and full, you need to take time to reflect and rediscover your *Inward* and *Outward Life Anchors.* You can only receive *PH2E* by living the *Life Anchors* in a *positive and effective* manner. To keep your *Healthiness* blade balanced and full, you need to keep yourself physically fit, eat healthily, exercise regularly, and give yourself the proper rest to recover and recharge. Lastly, to keep your *Excellence* blade balanced and full, you need to read regularly, keep your mind sharp, learn new skills, write, and stay away from excessive time wasters.

Propelling your PH2E is a mindset of continuously improving your *Inward* and *Outward Living* to lead to ever greater *Peacefulness, Happiness, Healthiness, and Excellence.* You want to propel each *Life Gift* to a higher level by *Inward Thinking* and *Outward Actions,* which results in the *Upward Living* byproducts. These four key life dimensions are critical for living life in a *positive and effective* manner.

Peace is the result of retraining your mind to process life as it is, rather than as you think it should be.

—Wayne W. Dyer

Propel Your *PH2E* Today

You can't just reach out and grab any of the *PH2E's.* They come to you by living in a *positive and effective* intentional manner, both *Inwardly* and *Outwardly. The 12 Essential Life Anchors* give you the framework to begin to live in a *positive and effective* manner by your design. It's all up to you to stay focused and implement the *Anchors* into your daily life. The key is not to be overwhelmed by the practice of *The 12 Essential Life Anchors.* You don't have to practice them in order. Pick one and focus on it for a period, as long or short as you wish. Many self-help books give specific instructions with a timeline for how to proceed. When you go off track, you feel like a failure and permanently give up because you feel unsuccessful.

I want to emphasize that there is no order or timeline you need to follow with *The 12 Essential Life Anchors*. This is a process for a lifetime. As you focus on an *Anchor*, you will immediately begin to feel an *Upward Lift*, since you are taking control of your one and only precious life.

> *Peace is a day-to-day problem,*
> *the product of a multitude of events and judgments.*
> *Peace is not an "is," it is a "becoming."*

—Haile Selassie

PH2E Propeller Maintenance

It is crucial to perform regular maintenance to keep your *PH2E Life Propeller* in good working order. If you don't intentionally make time for each blade, they will become broken and unbalanced. You want to take the time to attend to each one, so you receive the highest levels of *PH2E*.

Here's how.

- **Peacefulness** - Reflect on your Life Vision and Daily Mission. Understanding yourself leads to a peaceful feeling. Meditating, praying, or reflecting on your *Inward Life Anchors* are all ways of maintaining your *Peacefulness*.
- **Happiness** - One of the most potent ways to increase happiness is by practicing gratitude. Moving toward the Life Goals within your reach produces a happy feeling. Feeling successful also contributes to happiness. As

mentioned previously, having enriched *Outward* social relationships is strongly related to happiness.

- **Healthiness** - You must move your body, eat better, and get the necessary amount of sleep. Make little changes that you can maintain over time rather than attempting large changes that are too drastic. Lasting changes will result.

- **Excellence** - Reading, learning about things you are interested in, and practicing skills are ways to maintain and increase your levels of *Excellence*. You are attending to *Excellence* right now by reading this book.

Peace is a daily, a weekly, a monthly process, gradually changing opinions, slowly eroding old barriers, quietly building new structures.

—John F. Kennedy

Propelling vs. Restraining

Do you have a *Propelling Mindset* or a restraining mindset? To attain the *Upward Living Life Gifts,* you need to have a positive view of things. If you have negative thoughts more often than not, you will be *Downward Living* and receiving the *Downward Life Drains of Anxiety, Unhappiness, Unhealthiness, and Ineffectiveness.*

Cramer and Wasiak discussed asset-based thinkers and deficit-based thinkers and how each views the world. An asset-based thinker propels into the positive aspects of life while the deficit-based negatively restrains their outlook on life.

Propelling Mindset	**vs.**	**Restraining Mindset**

- What you want
- What you have
- What is possible
- What you can do
- What is working
- Who is with you
- What is propelling you forward
- What you stand to gain
- Your achievements

- What you don't want
- What you need
- What is problematic
- What you can't do
- What isn't working
- Who is against you
- What is holding you back
- What you stand to lose
- Your setbacks

Don't ever be satisfied with mediocrity. You shouldn't ever say or feel you've reached your limits. You need to be ok with failing. A task may seem impossible, but if you can see it and have a clear vision of what you are trying to achieve, you will get there with an efficient plan.

Kaizen is a Japanese term based on the philosophical belief that everything can be improved. It's having the mindset of continuous improvement, meaning there is always room for improvement, even if it's small. Small incremental improvements can add up to substantial positive change. Adopt a kaizen mentality to increase your *PH2E*.

We all set goals or have big ideas, but we fall short when acting on them. Continuous improvement is the mindset of all successful people; it is a stepping stone to success.

Better to fail at doing the right thing than to succeed
at doing the wrong thing.

—Guy Kawasaki

"Take it apart," my father said.

"Again?" I replied.

I had the great fortune to witness continuous improvement hundreds of times as I was growing up. My father was a self-taught design thinker. He read every book and manual on electronics, mechanics, and many other topics. I can clearly visualize him sitting at the end of the couch, next to the lamp, reading a technical book every night. He fixed everything in our home—TVs, cars, radios, appliances, and lawnmowers. You name it, and he could fix it. He always wanted it done right and could never accept "good enough." For example, we would take apart a motor and fix it. It would start, and I would think we were finished, but if he heard something that might be a little off, he would tell me to take it apart again. That could happen several times until it was 100% right. My father taught me patience and steadfastness in continually improving until it's 100% correct. He would tell me that 100% correct does not mean perfect; it means you gave it your all and have not settled for less than your best. The truth is that when he would tell me to take something apart, I would think, *Again?* I would never have dared to say it aloud. After giving it our all and experiencing the improvement when fixing whatever we were working on, the byproduct was always *Peacefulness* and *Happiness*. My father lived that way his whole life, and his SelfCulture projected an abundance of *Peacefulness*. It was a great life lesson I try to model for others and my children.

> *Life is changing all the time, and if we fail to change with it, we get left behind.*

—Brian Colbert

Continuous Improvement Means Change

You must change. We all must change. If you don't change regularly, you are not improving. Think about this—if you don't think you need to change, you are saying you are perfect, you have figured out life, all your opinions are correct, and your mental *Life Maps* are all correct. Do you really think that is true? Probably not. Therefore, we must all change—and change regularly. Each week identify something about yourself that has changed. It can be something small or large. It could be a belief you've held for years and are now looking at differently. It can be a small part of a viewpoint you have modified. My point is, there is always a need for some change. No one is perfect. Therefore, *Propelling your PH2E* is an *Anchor* that is critical for success and navigating toward a *Dynamic Positive Culture* for *yourself, your family, your team, and/or your organization.*

Scientific evidence has suggested that experiencing positive emotions can make your life longer and healthier. This is all the more reason to strive for *Upward Living* and receiving the *Upward Life Gifts of PH2E*. As reported in a Harvard Medical School publication, you can lower your stress levels and reduce your risk of health problems with an intentional, sustained, and positive outlook and relaxation techniques. First, you must have the mindset that you can increase the levels of *Peacefulness, Happiness, Healthiness, and Excellence.* Living a *positive and effective* intentional life begins with your thoughts. Say aloud to yourself right now, "Yes, I can live a *positive and effective intentional* life. Yes, I will live a *positive and effective intentional* life. Yes, I am living a *positive and effective intentional* life."

Begin today to have a *Mindset of Propelling your PH2E!*

Propelling *PH2E* Model

The Principle of Life Gifts

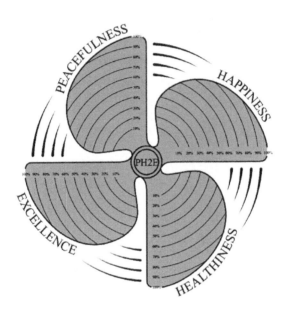

The *Propelling Your PH2E* model represents *Upward Living* and the *4 Life Gifts of Peacefulness, Happiness, Healthiness, and Excellence*. The goal is to propel each of the blades, so your propeller is balanced and continually increased.

As suggested in Chapter 4, take the *PH2E* Assessment at: www.PH2E.com. You will get a personalized score for *Peacefulness, Happiness, Healthiness, and Excellence* based on your perceptions. You will receive a personalized *"PH2E Life Propeller,"* which will show you areas of strength and those that need improvement.

After assessing your *PH2E Life Propeller*, take the lowest blade or *Life Gift*, and create a plan to increase it to the level of your other, higher, *Life Gifts*. Remember, we are first striving for balance. Once each blade is balanced, then we will work on increasing all the blades to their highest levels. By increasing your *PH2E*, you will become a *Life Leader*, leading yourself and others as you strive for a *Dynamic Positive Culture of Peacefulness, Happiness, Healthiness, and Excellence*.

Life Anchor 12 provides you with life's greatest gifts. These *Life Gifts* are universal principles and timeless. Begin *Propelling your PH2E* today!

Model A Mindset of Propelling PH2E
Anchor Planning

<u>Questions for Self and/or for the FTO as a group:</u>

Write down specific steps you can take to continuously improve and receive higher levels of:

Peacefulness _____

Happiness _____

Healthiness _____

Excellence _____

How are you living your *Life Vision* and *Daily Mission*? How can you take time to think and understand through meditation or reflecting on your *Inward Life Anchors*?

_____

_____

What is something you are grateful for?

_____

_____

How can you practice gratitude on a regular basis?

_____

_____

Make a commitment to yourself to improve upon your healthy habits. Write it down here:

_____

_____

Write down one or two ways you are committed to practicing self-improvement (e.g. reading, learning, etc.).

_____

_____

Download all the _IOU Anchor Planning_ pages
Free at: www.iouanchors.com

Captain's Log for Chapter 12

The 6 Outward Life Anchors

Captain's Log:

Point 1   *Inspire IO Trust* is the foundational *Life Anchor* for all of the other *Outward Life Anchors*. Without trust, there is no loyalty or commitment. When you *Inspire IO Trust*, you are leading with authenticity from your heart and mind.

Point 2   When there is trust, there is connection and consistency between what we *Inwardly* believe and how we *Outwardly* act. We trust what others tell us and act *Outwardly* based on their words and commitment. We can *Inspire, Influence,* and have *Alignment on our Life Principles* with others.

Point 3   There are five levels of trust: *IOU Trust, IO Trust, Trust, Low Trust,* and *No Trust.* You should always strive for the highest levels of trust.

Point 4   *Practice Positive Communication* is a mindset that will enhance all of your relationships. Strive for *WholeHearted Listening* instead of *Distracted, Reply,* or *HalfHearted Listening.* In *WholeHearted Listening,* you neither agree nor disagree, but you try to understand their perspective from their words and nonverbal communication.

Point 5   Use *High Tide Safe Talk* instead of *Low Tide Unsafe Talk*. Make sure your words communicate respect and positivity. Communicate openness and vulnerability, so people feel safe sharing and being their authentic selves with you.

Point 6   When you *Create Common Language*, you build a sense of belonging and identity around your *Life Vision*, *Life Principles*, and *Life Values*. It will keep everyone moving in the same direction toward the same destination. You can use fewer words to convey bigger meaning.

Point 7   *Construct a Cohesive* physical and relational *Environment* to facilitate an overall sense of who you are or what your *family, team, or organization* is about. Create a positive culture through building safety, character, and competence.

Point 8   *Establishing Everlasting Traditions* brings people together, bonds them through common experiences, creates lasting memories, and provides a sense of identity for everyone involved.

Point 9   When we *Model a Mindset of Propelling our PH2E*, we focus on continuous improvement. We want to increase our *PH2E* to the highest levels and maintain a balanced propeller. To do that, stay focused and implement the *Inward* and *Outward Anchors*, picking one at a time to practice. Don't get overwhelmed—strive for a little improvement each day.

Teach to Learn

The best way to deepen your understanding and, at the same time, share and stimulate new conversations with others is to teach. Share what you have learned with a friend, family member, coworker, or anyone else who will listen. Teaching is, by far, the best way to deepen one's understanding of new insights and concepts. Take any of the Points in the Captain's Log or this chapter for thought-provoking discussions.

New Daily Voyage:

Activity:

Pick one *Outward Anchor* to work on. Reflect on what it means, how you are currently using it (if at all), and how you can improve.

Ask yourself:

Are my *Outward Anchors* propelling me forward?

PART IV

The Benefits of IOU Life Leadership

Your Life Ship Reaches Its Destination

Chapter 13

Principle "U"

UPWARD LIVING LIFE GIFTS

Receiving *PH2E*

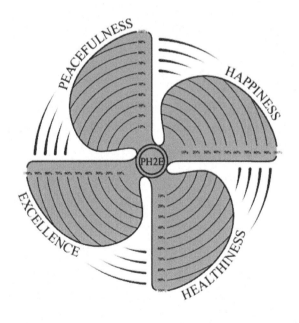

Happiness is not a goal; it is a by-product.

—Eleanor Roosevelt

Vincent always worked hard. He kept himself in top physical shape his entire life, even well into his 90's. He often said you need to be always physically prepared for the intensity of life. However, as a sharp 92-year-old, the leader of his family, he also knew his limitations and always modeled integrity for his entire family. One day, he was driving along Brookside Avenue in his hometown and didn't stop for a stop sign. A police officer pulled him over. When he handed over his license and registration, the officer saw his last name and mentioned that three brothers with that name owned the car service station down the block.

Vincent replied, "Yes, they are my sons."

The officer said, "Did you know you passed through a stop sign?"

Vincent said he hadn't seen it and apologized for his error. He then told the officer, "I'm done driving. Call my son and tell him to get the car. If I missed the stop sign, I could have hurt somebody. I'm done driving."

The police officer was stunned but complied. Soon, Vincent's son came and drove him home. The next day, Vincent gave the car to his daughter because he knew his reflexes weren't what they used to be, and he might be a danger to others. Vincent was at peace with his *Inward Decisions* and *Outward Actions* and didn't second guess himself. He didn't miss a beat; he was at peace and was just as happy the next day as he was his entire life. Once he reached a conclusion, he executed it immediately. Vincent modeled these types of *Outward Actions* his whole life. After he decided something, he didn't waffle. He just did it and accepted the natural consequences. It was obvious to his family that Vincent continually propelled his *PH2E*, received the *Upward Living Life Gifts* throughout his life, and was an inspiration to everyone.

Peacefulness, Happiness, Healthiness, *and* ***Excellence*** **(*PH2E*)** are the greatest gifts in our lives. These gifts operate on every level of our *Inward Being* – our physical, emotional, mental, and spiritual dimensions. Our *PH2E* does not solve all our problems in life; instead, our *PH2E* helps us push through challenges as we travel on our journey, just as a propeller pushes a ship through waters, whether calm or stormy. We

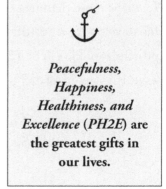

Peacefulness, Happiness, Healthiness, and Excellence (*PH2E*) are the greatest gifts in our lives.

must take care of our *PH2E Life Propeller* and keep it balanced and full. *PH2E* comes to our *Inward World* and is not in any of our physical possessions, such as cars, boats, or houses. It's deep inside us, and only we can ultimately balance and expand these *Life Gifts*. We have 100% control of our *Inward Thinking* and *Outward Actions*. By beginning to live the *Life Anchors* intentionally, we will feel the natural expansion of our *PH2E* as we receive the *Upward Living Life Gifts*.

Upward Living and receiving *PH2E* are the greatest *Life Gifts* one can obtain. If you want to gain more *PH2E* in your life, don't just focus on your feelings. Remember, you can't directly increase your *PH2E*. They are gifts that come to you and are due to your *Inward Thinking* and *Outward Actions*. When you focus and improve on your *I* and *O*, you will feel the byproduct of the *Upward* lift.

Becoming an *IOU Life Leader* involves intentionally practicing *The 12 Essential Life Anchors*. It's training your brain to scan the world for *positive and effective* solutions instead of focusing on the *negative and ineffective*. *IOU Living* will pull you up out of *IOD* and *IOW Living*, where things are *Negative* and *Neutral*. *IOU Living* is more than just trying to change a behavior or feeling. It's developing a sturdy foundation using timeless, universal principles of life—*The 12 Essential Life Anchors*, over which you have 100% control.

> *Happiness is when what you think, what you say,*
> *and what you do are in harmony.*
>
> —Mahatma Gandhi

Distractions

How many things can you think of at one time? Try it right now. See how many items you can think about concurrently. The answer is, few. So, when you find yourself in an *IOD* or *IOW Mode*, try distracting yourself by getting up and moving around. This won't make the problem go away, but it will prime the pump to start thinking about what you have control over. I have found that getting up, taking a walk, or doing some large muscle activity helps get

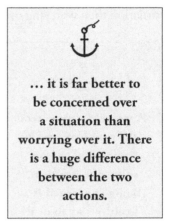

... it is far better to be concerned over a situation than worrying over it. There is a huge difference between the two actions.

my mind into a more controlled environment. When you are upset, is it easier to read a book or work on a complex thinking assignment or to involve yourself in a physical activity such as cleaning? Next time you are upset, get involved in something physical. You have control over your physical actions, which will spread to the other parts of your being. Soon, you will see that your *Inward Thinking* will begin to clear, and you will be able to make sound, reasonable *Inward* decisions. They will be followed by *Outward Actions* that start to move you in an *Upward* and more *positive and effective* manner.

A good question to ask yourself when you are in an *IOD* or *IOW Mode* is, what would an *IOU Living* person do to address this situation? Another way to phrase this would be, what *Life Anchor* can guide me and begin to move me along on my journey to *Upward Living*?

When I was growing up, my mother always said, "Worrying never helps." We all worry, but what I learned from her is that there is a difference between "worrying" and "being concerned." My mother modeled that it is far better to be concerned over a situation than worrying over it. There is a huge difference between the two actions. Many studies demonstrate that when we worry, hormones such as adrenaline and cortisol are released into the bloodstream. These chemicals equip our bodies for action. Our heart rate increases, our breathing becomes deeper, and our bodies prepare to fight or flight. This all happens unconsciously and is an essential and potentially lifesaving response in a dangerous situation, but not when you are only worrying. This is *IOD Living*, which is negative and toxic to your body's glands, nervous system, and heart. Worrying not only affects your body but also affects your brain. It moves you far away from *Peacefulness*, making it harder to concentrate on a particular task. It may impact your sleep, which in itself then leads to a whole other set of physical and mental stresses. I rarely witnessed my mother in a worried state; instead, she modeled concern.

A worried person sees the problem, and a concerned person solves the problem. Being concerned is a healthy way to deal with a problem.

Winfred Rhoades stated, "Worrying is a waste of energy and utterly useless. It saps vitality and reduces efficiency. It accomplishes nothing constructive, but it results in a preoccupation, which makes it more difficult to do the things that are needed. It produces irritability and the habit of complaining."

A quote often attributed to Winston Churchill is, "When I look back on all these worries, I remember the story of the old man who said on his deathbed that he had a lot of trouble in his life, most of which had never happened."

A worried person sees the problem, and a concerned person solves the problem. Being concerned is a healthy way to deal with a problem.

IOU Living Concerned	vs.	IOD Living Worried
• Creates a goal to help		• Has no goal
• Builds relationships		• Weakens relationships
• Receives *Peacefulness*		• Receives *Anxiety*
• Moves toward *Happiness*		• Moves toward *Unhappiness*
• Healthy		• Unhealthy
• Solves the problem		• Perseverates on the problem

The concerned person lives *Inwardly* in the moment, understands the realities of the situation, sees the problem and challenges, and acts *Outwardly*. The worried person sees the problem and challenges and perseverates on them without taking *Outward Action*.

We have control! The research of Lyubomirsky, Sheldon, and Schkade argues that we can increase our happiness because 50% of our happiness is accounted for by our genetics, and 10% is accounted for by our circumstances. Still, the remaining 40% is based on our intentional activities. Therefore, changing our intentional *Inward Thinking* and *Outward Actions* can propel our happiness by a significant amount.

Visualize this thing that you want, see it, feel it, believe in it.
Make your mental blueprint and begin to build.

—Robert Collier

Mindful Visualization

Mindful Visualization can physically impact your *Inward* brain. It's an empowering tool for enhancing self-awareness and focus. *Inwardly* visualizing your thoughts of the outcome of an *Outward Action* before you act will help you to better prepare you

Inwardly visualizing your thoughts of the outcome of an Outward Action before you act will help you to better prepare you for the action you are taking.

for the action you are taking. You should also visualize the result you are anticipating and the feeling(s) you may receive. Your mind has an enormous impact on your body and how you feel. In the so-called "Piano Study," neuroscientist Alvaro Pascual-Leone instructed one group of volunteers to play a piano scale for two hours each day for five consecutive days. Another group of volunteers was instructed to imagine playing the notes in their minds. Every day all the volunteers' brains were scanned in the region connected to the finger muscles. The changes in the brain in those who imagined playing the piano were the same as in those who actually played piano.

The stress response has evolved in humans to give us the ability to fight or flee when faced with danger. Chemicals, including cortisol and adrenaline, help kick start the body, pushing blood toward the major muscles to give you strength. However, the same stress response kicks in when you imagine danger, producing cortisol and adrenaline and pushing blood around the body. The same chemistry is produced regardless of whether the threat is real or imagined. What does all this mean in real life? It means that what you imagine to be happening is actually happening as far as your brain is concerned.

Ed Diener is known as "Dr. Happiness" based on the volumes of research he has conducted relating to the subject. One of his studies concluded that happiness can be significantly increased through positive social relationships. Dr. Happiness also concluded that there is no strong relationship between higher income and happiness; instead, positive relationships and enjoyment at work were necessary for well-being.

The *6 Outward Life Anchors* are based on relationships with others and building a *positive and effective* culture in the *family, team, or organization*. When this *positive and effective* culture occurs, the *Upward Living Life Gifts* will come to you beginning with *Happiness*. Diener also purports that well-being leads to good social relationships and does not just follow them. Therefore, as you increase your *PH2E*, your relationships will improve as well.

In Benjamin Franklin's autobiography, he wrote that to receive intense happiness, one needs to practice truth, sincerity, and integrity when *Outwardly* interacting with another person.

Buddha was asked, "What have you gained from meditation?" He replied, "Nothing! Let me tell you what I've lost—anger, anxiety, depression, insecurity, fear of old age, and death."

Thirty million people meditate daily. Mindful Visualization is a form of meditation. Meditation will help you get into your *Inward Being* and gain access to your deepest inner thoughts and feelings. There is no right way to meditate. If it works for you, then that is the right way for you. However, some common guidelines can help you get started and help you to receive the benefits of meditation.

Don't rush. Go slowly. Be present.

—Leo Babauta

Breathing

The word "mantra' comes from "*manas*," which means mind and "*tra*," which means tool. So, you need a "mind tool" to exercise your *Inward Living*. Use each word of the *PH2E* for a mantra. For example, you might think, *The lake is so peaceful, Happiness is seeing my daughter smiling, I feel healthy when I'm on the treadmill,* or *I feel I reached excellence when I'm working with the team.*

Next, close your eyes and form a mental image. Feel the moment, don't just think it; see it in your mind. Use all your senses to immerse yourself back to that moment. Sink deep into the feeling. Keep breathing, and when you feel your mind drifting, say the mantra.

Then, take deep breaths in and out. As you breathe in, feel your body relax. As you exhale, release whatever tension or negative thoughts you may have. Keep inhaling and exhaling, feeling your *Inner Being* becoming relaxed and peaceful.

Next, see yourself in the place that gave you that peaceful feeling. Say your soothing mantra in your mind. See in your mind and feel the details of your image using all your senses.

Breathe in and out. If your mind drifts and you begin to think of other things, say the mantra and keep repeating it. You feel the peacefulness of that moment and feel the relaxation of it.

When you are ready, open your eyes slowly and continue to feel the peacefulness of that moment. Notice how you feel and continue your day. Be mindful of a new moment in your day of peacefulness so that you can use it for your next Mindful Visualization exercise.

As we've seen again and again, what you do with your mind changes your body, including the brain.

—Daniel J. Siegel

The IOU 90-SECOND SECRET

Two leading experts, Jill Bolte Taylor, a Harvard-trained neuroanatomist, and Dr. Daniel Siegel, a clinical professor of psychiatry at the UCLA School of Medicine, discuss the brief, approximate 90-second long lifespan of emotions. They argue that if you just sit quietly and allow yourself to feel your feelings without fighting them, the unimpeded emotion will begin to transform and dissipate on its own in only 90-seconds. Just 90-seconds! This finding profoundly resonates with me. It takes no time at all to shift out of a mood caused by some *Outward Action* pressing on a person. The science behind the theory is that there is a 90-second chemical process in the body that occurs when some *Outward* stimuli causes a person to feel anger, fear, or another negative emotion. After the 90-seconds, it's on you. The continued feeling is now in your *Inward Thinking.* If you are still feeling the emotion, you are re-stimulating the circuitry in your body, thereby having the physiological response over and over again. You are choosing to stay in this emotional loop. It sounds easier said than done, but it works!

When something happens in the *Outward World* and chemicals are pulsing through your body, it puts your *Inward Being* on high alert. The good news is, for those chemicals to dissipate completely, it takes fewer than 90-seconds.

If you stop and try this, during the 90-seconds, you can feel the process happening, and the emotion fading and going away.

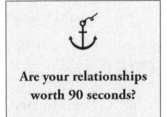

Are your relationships worth 90 seconds?

You will have broken that thought cycle. After that, it's on you if you choose to continue to have that high emotion. If you continue to have those high emotional feelings, you need to examine your *Inward Thoughts* and examine what is stoking your *Inward* fire. This is an excellent tool as a parent. Your child, especially a teenage child,

414

can often hit your emotional buttons, putting you in a high emotional state. Take 90-seconds before responding. Let the chemicals in your body flush out so you can choose a calmer response for your child. The 90-seconds can also help your child to flush out their *Inward* high emotions. By giving your child 90-seconds, you will see a difference in their actions and responses, too. It may seem like such a long time to wait to continue the conversation, but think about it, it's only a minute and a half! Are your relationships worth 90-seconds? Discuss this technique when things are calm and agree to use it at a future time if and when it is needed. Give it a try!

Another game-changer is using this tool with your relationships. Do we enjoy having negative high emotional events with the people we love the most? Of course not! Unfortunately, sometimes when we are in those interactions, we say things we regret. We say them because our *Inward* body is flowing with chemicals spurring on our emotions resulting in a poor *Outward* response.

When things in the *Outward World,* such as a report on social media or in a newspaper, trigger your emotions to a high level, taking 90-seconds will be very effective to reset your thinking.

On the next page is a model that will help you remember and internalize the *IOU 90-Second Secret* technique in your daily life.

The IOU 90-SECOND SECRET

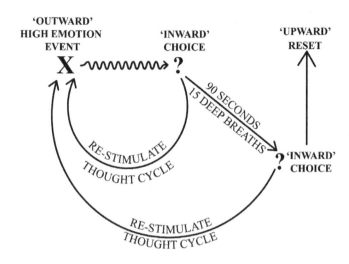

Outward High Emotion Event. When an *Outward* high emotion event occurs, you physically feel your body and thoughts at an intense emotional level. When this happens, some chemicals rush through your body and put you in a fight or flight state of mind. During *Outward* high emotional events, your nervous system sends a signal to your adrenal medulla to release epinephrine (adrenaline) and norepinephrine (noradrenaline), as well as other hormones and neurotransmitters into your bloodstream. This increases your heart rate and blood pressure, thus putting you in a high emotional state.

Inward Choice. Take the "90-second choice" rather than the "re-stimulating the emotion thought cycle choice." The 90-second choice gives you the space to reset your thoughts. Take 15 deep

Inward breaths and then exhale. Five breaths should be about 30 seconds. Practice this right now with a timer on your phone. Ok, I know you didn't try it, but try it later. As you are taking your breaths, name the emotion you are striving for (e.g., peace, calm, etc.) which will then activate your prefrontal cortex. Your prefrontal cortex contains your executive functioning and controls behaviors such as planning, decision-making, problem-solving, and self-control. During the 90-seconds, name your feelings. For example, repeat, "I am angry but getting calmer." Keep repeating this, and as you feel the anger fade away, change your *Inward* mantra to, "I am getting calmer." Finally, near the end of the 90-seconds, repeat to yourself, "I am calm."

Upward Reset. After the 90-seconds are up, you have another choice. You can choose to allow the *Upward* reset of your emotion or re-stimulate the negative event and start the cycle all over again.

Now, I know what you're thinking—this can't be! Well, you're right. Not all the time. However, it will work sometimes, and sometimes is better than zero times! It's another strategy to break the cycle of anger, frustration, annoyance, etc. For me, it works more often than not. You have more control of your *Inward Living* than you are aware. This technique is just another tool to help you move from *IOW* and *IOD Living* to *IOU Living*, which will move you closer to the *Upward Life Gifts of PH2E*. Start living intentionally by your design, not the design of others. Remember, you have 100% control of your *Inward Living*. Start using it!

Take the *PH2E* Challenge
"Realign Your Daily Journey"

We all have experienced the *PH2E Upward Life Gifts* in our lives but tend to forget those moments. Alternately, life obstacles, and life currents pull us away from those special moments and take us off-course of our daily journeys. The *PH2E Challenge* is a moment of Mindful Visualization to realign our voyage in life and get us back on track when we feel we may have been experiencing *Downward Life Drains.*

PH2E are the *Upward Life Gifts* we can receive in life that are universally always good and the result of positive *Inward Thoughts* and positive *Outward Actions.*

PH2E are the *Upward Life Gifts* we can receive in life that are universally always good and the result of positive *Inward Thoughts* and positive *Outward Actions.* They are the byproduct of *Living Inwardly* and *Outwardly* around universal *Life Anchors.*

Set the intention to seek at least one of the *PH2E* each day for five days out of the next seven. Each day when you are attempting the challenge, we will consider that you have reached your goal for that day, even if you get interrupted by a phone call, a needy human, or any other interruption. Don't be stressed that you were interrupted; you are rewarded because of the effort. Too often, we stop something new because we *Inwardly* think we can't do it, or we failed. As Elbert Hubbard is quoted, "There is no failure except in no longer trying."

PH2E Challenge Setup

Think of a moment when you have reached the highest level of each of the *PH2E*'s in your life.

Peacefulness. In your mind's eye, see that moment when you reached the highest form of *Peacefulness*. (e.g., it may be at the beach, in a room, in nature, or after successfully reaching a goal).

Happiness. In your mind's eye, see that moment when you reached the highest form of *Happiness* (anything that produced the byproduct of *Happiness*).

Healthiness. In your mind's eye, think of yourself doing something that adds to your health, whether it's exercising or seeing something you are eating that is healthy for you.

Excellence. In your mind's eye, think of something you feel you are excellent at, and that shows the best of you, whether it is a social action, a skill, or a quality. When you have established the moment when you have reached the highest form for each of the *PH2E*, you are ready to take the challenge.

PH2E Mindful Visualization for Peacefulness

Say the word *Peacefulness* aloud or silently and think of that past moment when you have reached the highest form of *Peacefulness*. Keep seeing that moment in your mind's eye while you take a deep breath in from your nose. Hold it for a second, then exhale through your mouth. At the very end of your exhale, hold and feel the *Peacefulness* of that moment for another second. Repeat four times.

Here's the Challenge:

Follow the *PH2E* Mindful Visualization for each of the *Upward Life Gifts.*

4X *PH2E* Mindful Visualization for **Peacefulness**
4X *PH2E* Mindful Visualization for **Happiness**
4X *PH2E* Mindful Visualization for **Healthiness**
4X *PH2E* Mindful Visualization for **Excellence**

This can be completed throughout the day or all at once. Once you have finished all of the Mindful Visualizations for all *Upward Life Gifts of PH2E,* you have completed the challenge.

The benefits:

- You will realize that you have experienced the *Upward Life Gifts* and how they made or make you feel.
- It will remind you of the byproducts of your *Life Vision* and *Daily Miss*ion.
- You will feel that you have realigned your course for your daily journey. It helps you to get back on track.
- You will *Inwardly* feel each of the *PH2E's,* which will give you energy and clear your mind of unwanted distractions. It gives you focus and clarity as you continue your daily journey.

Journal writing is a voyage to the interior.

—Christina Baldwin

The *PH2E* Journal

Another good exercise is to create a *PH2E* Journal. Write down moments when you have reached the highest form of each of the *Upward Life Gifts*. From this moment on, start recording when you have felt *Peacefulness* in a day.

For example, write the word *Peacefulness* in your journal, then write examples of when you felt peacefulness.

Examples:

- Walking in the park observing nature
- When I sit down to read
- After organizing my desk
- Today when I was driving and listening to music

Similarly, record moments for *Happiness, Healthiness, and Excellence* in your *PH2E* Journal.

How many *PH2E* moments can you think of that were at the highest level? Are the moments recent or from months or years ago?

Living the *IOU Principle* will create new moments for your *PH2E* Journal. They can be used when you take the *PH2E Challenge* each day. If you miss a day or two or three, it's ok. Just don't stop completely because you think you are not doing it correctly. You will receive the benefits of taking the *PH2E Challenge* whenever you can complete it, even if it's once per week. Do it when you can, and don't ever stop completely. We all get off-course and need to take time to realign our course and feel the great *Upward Life Gifts* that are here for all of us to receive and enjoy!

What Does Propelling Your *PH2E* Look Like?

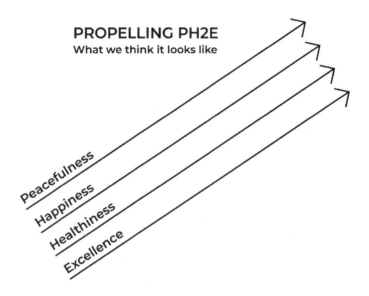

PROPELLING PH2E
What we think it looks like

Peacefulness
Happiness
Healthiness
Excellence

When you get your *I*'s and *O*'s in order, you will feel an *Upward Peacefulness* which contains the ultimate joy and happiness in life.

If your *Inward* and *Outward* (*I* and *O*) *Modes* are coordinated, then you should feel an *Upward* (*U*) *Lift of Peacefulness*. Isn't that what we want in life, to be at peace? When someone dies, it is usually said they are at peace. Let's not wait until we die to be at peace. Let's live in peace right now at this very moment. When you get your *I*'s and *O*'s in order, you will feel an *Upward Peacefulness,* which contains the ultimate joy and happiness in life. With your *I* and *O* in order, when adversity comes, it will be easier to deal with because you proactively have a set of principles that will help guide you through.

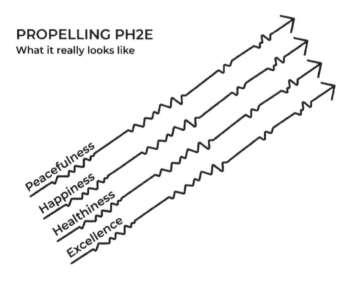

PROPELLING PH2E
What it really looks like

Peacefulness

Happiness

Healthiness

Excellence

I want to emphasize that you shouldn't give up. Simply take any area of this book that resonates with you and try it. You can focus on just one of *The 12 Essential Life Anchors* and begin to incorporate it into your life. Expect that it won't always work and expect it to be difficult at first. However, if you stay the course and don't give up, in a very short time, you will begin to feel your *PH2E* move to a higher level. The upper diagrams demonstrate the steady overall upward progress that will come to you during your *Upward Living.* There will be ups and downs, but overall, the goal is to propel *Upward.*

Become an *IOU Life Leader* and practice *The 12 Essential Life Anchors*. Your intentional *Inward* and *Outward* efforts will be rewarded by *Upward Living* and thereby propel your *PH2E* as you navigate on your one and only precious *Life Journey*.

Captain's Log for Chapter 13

Principle "U"

UPWARD LIVING LIFE GIFTS

Receiving PH2E

Captain's Log:

Point 1   Becoming an *IOU Life Leader* involves intentionally practicing *The 12 Essential Life Anchors*. It is how you train yourself to scan the world for *positive and effective* solutions instead of focusing on the *negative and ineffective*.

Point 2   When you find yourself in an *IOW* or *IOD Mode*, try distracting yourself. Ask yourself, What would an *IOU Life Leader* do to address this situation?

Point 3   Be concerned instead of worried. A worried person sees the problem; a concerned person solves it. Being concerned is a healthy way to deal with a problem.

Point 4   You can increase your *Happiness* by changing your *Inward Thinking* and *Outward Actions*. It can be significantly increased through positive social relationships.

Point 5   The *IOU 90-Second Secret* is a tool to help you live your life by design. Stay out of the *Downward* cycle whenever there is an *Outward High Emotion* event. Make the *Inward* choice not to re-stimulate the emotion, but give yourself 90-seconds and watch it dissipate.

Point 6   Use Mindful Visualization to impact your *Inward Thinking* physically.

Point 7   Set the intention to seek at least one of the *PH2E* each day for five out of seven days. Make an effort, and don't be frustrated if you are interrupted.

Point 8   Practice *PH2E* Mindful Visualization and keep a *PH2E* Journal to help you live the *IOU Principle* and be a *Life Leader*.

Teach to Learn

The best way to deepen your understanding and, at the same time, share and stimulate new conversations with others is to teach. Share what you have learned with a friend, family member, coworker, or anyone else who will listen. Teaching is, by far, the best way to deepen one's understanding of new insights and concepts. Take any of the Points in the Captain's Log or this chapter for thought-provoking discussions.

New Daily Voyage:

Activity:

Take the *PH2E Assessment* and record the results in your *PH2E* Journal.

Go to www.PH2E.com to take the Assessment.

Ask yourself:

How can I change from worrying to being concerned?

Chapter 14

Living the IOU Life Leadership Principle

IOU Living

Grant me the serenity to accept the things I cannot change,
the courage to change the things I can, and the wisdom
to know the difference.

—Serenity Prayer

"Torpedo, stern, starboard," Vincent yelled to the bridge. "I was on the deck of the USS *President Grant* and saw the bubble-track of the torpedo along the top of the water off the starboard side of the vessel," he later shared with me. His communication was quickly relayed to the bridge where the captain gave the order, "Full steam, hard port!" The ship turned hard and violently to the left to avoid the impact and explosion of the torpedo. The torpedo had been launched by a submarine.

During World War I, most torpedoes could be seen traveling above-water with a maximum speed of 35 knots and a range of only 2000 yards. Also, they could only travel straight, so if spotted immediately, they could be avoided with evasive maneuvers. That's why Vincent's keen observation was so important. The captain honored Vincent for his quick actions and especially for his clear and precise description of the location of the torpedo, telling him, "Vincent, you are a first-rate Navy Man." Because the captain knew exactly where and from what direction the torpedo was coming, he knew immediately what orders to give and how to maneuver the ship. It's split-second decisions that often make the difference between safety or devastation.

This captain's order was carried out quickly due to the efficient, *Dynamic Positive Culture* established on his ship, where there was *Outward Common Language* and *IOU Trust*. Vincent also explained that when the captain gives the order, Full Ahead, it takes a team to put the ship into this mode. There is an Engine Order Telegraph (EOT) on the bridge that looks like a round brass circle with a lever on one side of the unit. It has different commands on it, such as Full Ahead, Half Ahead, Slow Ahead,

Full Astern, Half Astern, Slow Astern, and Stop. When the lever is moved to any of these commands, a bell sounds in the engine room, where there is a second EOT. The engineer officer in the engine room moves the handle on his EOT to the same position as the bridge. When the commands match, the bell stops ringing, which indicates that the engine room understands and acknowledges the command of the captain. The team in the engine room then executes the command.

Vincent also explained how many people it takes to complete just one command and how much involvement it takes. There are many people working on each engine in the engine room. The engineering officer keeps the EOT in proper order and relays the command to the team in the engine room; a chief engineer oversees the engine department and is responsible for the engine operation and maintenance; the water tender makes sure the boilers have enough water, are at the right pressure, and do not have too much steam or too little; the fireman makes sure the fire is maintained properly, which provides steam to the engines; and the coal trimmers load the coal into the furnace.

"My actions were only one step in avoiding the torpedo. I could not have done it by myself." Vincent always stressed the importance of leadership and teamwork. He often referred to all of his teams as family. Today, like Vincent, we need to live a life building our teams and families with high *IOU Trust*, incorporating *The 12 Essential Life Anchors*. When this happens, we move toward a *Dynamic Positive Culture* that can meet and exceed all challenges in life.

Vincent lived a full life of leadership serving his country, his family, and his community. He had his internal compass set to true north and achieved greatness both professionally and personally. He clearly identified his purpose and shared his wisdom with others throughout his life. His greatest life lessons were delivered simply by his modeling. He lived his *Live Values* and *Life Principles* every day and made them so clear to others that you learned by experiencing it with him. He lived a life of high integrity, which impacted everyone around him. He never let his circumstances dictate his life and would rise above his conditions and always design a new path. He was a *Life Leader* governed by timeless, universal principles, both *Inwardly* and *Outwardly* serving his family, friends, church, coworkers, and country. Vincent truly lived *IOU Life Leadership*!

You must be the change you wish to see in the world.

—Mahatma Gandhi

IOU Living is a Choice

Living the *IOU Principle* is having the wisdom to live intentionally in the areas you can control while at the same time continuously developing the mental calmness for those things you cannot control. *IOU Living* is a foundational framework for *positive and effective* intentional living based on universal principles that will propel you to your highest level of *PH2E*.

IOU Living is about choice. You have the choice right now to start living your life by design. As you navigate your journey, there will be obstacles you will not be able to avoid, but you will have 100% control over how you interact with them. The principle of choice seems simple, but when you are confronted with deciding, there are many *Outward* forces trying to take you off your course. Those choices will determine if you are living your life according to your *Life Vision* or instead based on a feeling of regret.

Living the *IOU Principle* is having the wisdom to live intentionally in the areas you can control while at the same time continuously developing the mental calmness for those things you cannot control.

Choice is the greatest gift we have in life. *The 12 Essential Life Anchors* give us the ability to choose our journey in life. If you are living *IOD* and *IOW* more times than not, you have the ability to change and act differently. You are free to choose to live in a *positive and effective* intentional manner.

To live an *IOU Life*, you must remove negativity from around you. If you are acting negatively, you will attract negative people. If you act positively, you will attract both positive and negative people. Rid the negative from your life who are constantly trying to bring you down. Remember, you have chosen *IOU Living*. You are ready to receive *Upward Living* and the *Upward Life Gifts of Peacefulness, Happiness, Healthiness, and Excellence.*

Love is freedom.

—Mother Teresa

Inward Outward Upward (IOU) Love

Vincent always referred to himself as a sailor or captain, and later in life, as an "old seadog." The love for his country, community, faith, and family was clear. Every story or life lesson was always connected to ships and the sea. He would say the world is like the sea—unpredictable—yet if studied, you can navigate and connect with it to reach your destination. The sea is also beautiful and filled with amazing creatures and provides you the freedom to explore. When I listened to him, I would think of it as the *Outward World* filled with obstacles and beauty. He also would refer to himself and how he interacted and took action by knowing the winds, waves, currents, and the dangers of the waters. That was all learned first by *Inward Living*. He was definitely a thinking person. The byproduct of his *positive and effective IO Living* was *Upward Living* and a wonderful long life lived into his 90's. Until his last moments, Vincent created a wonderful, loving environment that everyone gravitated toward in his home, his businesses, and at his sons' service station. His *Upward Living* produced *PH2E* for himself and everyone around him. I learned from Vincent that a loving relationship should include mutual *PH2E*. Vincent was also a dynamic person who always spoke positively and offered important life lessons. He was the essence of a *Dynamic Positive Culture* and practiced and modeled *Life Leadership* throughout his life. I now understand that his stories about leadership were also stories about love—the many levels of love you have with others. Love is the ultimate *Outward Living* as you exercise the *Life Anchors* with others and the world.

434

Lead from the Captain's Wheel

To navigate your *Life Journey*, you need to see the big picture, all your *Outward* surroundings with unobstructed views. As the captain of your ship, you see the horizon while steering the captain's wheel. You have all the navigation equipment at your fingertips that will keep you on course in an effective manner. You know the ship better than everyone else and have thought about and developed your *12 Essential Life Anchors*. You are now on your way after a careful review of the weather and sea conditions. The heading is set. You have your closest *Inward Relation-Ships* with you on your *Life Journey*.

As you leave port, you get asked a question from below deck about a setting on a gauge. Rather than offer advice, you leave the bridge and go below deck. After all, you know every aspect of this ship. You easily fix the issue and then start to make your way back to the bridge. Before you can return, you are asked another question about a small oil leak in the engine room. Instead of asking some questions to get more information, you head right to the area of the leak. After all, the engine room is where you spend most of your time when the ship is at port,

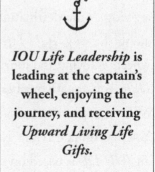

IOU Life Leadership **is leading at the captain's wheel, enjoying the journey, and receiving** *Upward Living Life Gifts.*

and you've rebuilt every component many times over. It takes much longer than you thought, but once you figure it out, you simply turn a small screw, and the issue is resolved. You start to head back to the bridge when someone asks you about your next journey. You love discussing and sharing all the planning, details, and well-thought-out preparations, so you share about your upcoming journey. By the time you finally return to the bridge, you have nearly arrived at your first port-of-call. Your journey is almost over, and you have spent the whole-time below deck. This was your journey, and you are the captain, but your first officers navigated the ship. You navigate the ship into port and review your plans for the next journey.

It's important to have the mindset that you do not need to do everything. You must trust others to tend to tasks that support your journey. Share the responsibilities and support and develop leadership for others. Being a leader is trusting others and staying above deck as much as possible to navigate and enjoy your *Life Journey.*

Your life is filled with many small journeys that will comprise your *Life Journey.* Don't spend it below deck. It's not just about arriving at the destination, but it's about enjoying the journey along the way. *IOU Life Leadership* is leading at the captain's wheel, enjoying the journey, and receiving *Upward Living Life Gifts.* You are at your best when you are at the captain's wheel, making important decisions that will benefit everyone involved. You may think it's easier to do everything yourself; however, living an *IOU Life* is based on the interactions of yourself and others, centered around *The 12 Essential Life Anchors.* The *Relation-Ships* are based on *IOU Trust* and propelling everyone's *PH2E.*

As you live the *IOU Life Principle*, your journey will continually uncover life lessons to learn from, which will help you when you leave for the next port of call. The journey will present numerous variations of the same challenge. It will always seem like a new situation has arisen, but the skilled captain makes connections to past experiences to deal with the issue at hand. That will be the norm. Expect the challenges with the mindset that you have 100% control of your actions and reactions to the situation. This attribute will keep you in *E2 (Environment 2)* and on course.

> *Life is what happens to you while you're busy making other plans.*
>
> —Allen Saunders

You don't want to wait your whole life for something to happen to you. You need to *make* it happen to you! Your *Life Vision* is *your Purpose, your Potential, and your Passion* that will bring *PH2E* to you and the loved ones around you. As John Lennon said, many people are just making plans, talking a good game, and life is flying by. You want to make a meaningful difference in life. Whether it is

Your *Inward Thinking* contains your rules about how the world works.

making an impact on society or on your family, the results are the same—making the world a better place.

Your *Inward Thinking* contains your rules about how the world works. As you examine your *Inward Thinking* and *Inward Life Anchors*, you get a better understanding of nature's rules and universal laws that are always true. You will continually fine-tune, adjust your *Inward Thinking,* and get closer to the way things genuinely are—the natural life laws. The *IOU Life Leader* makes upgrades to their *Inward Thinking* and refines their *Life Maps.* That is a never-ending process, and at each level, you may think it is complete until you let go and enjoy the shifts to greater awareness of the way things actually are.

An excellent example of an organization that demonstrated *IOU Life Leadership* and employed *The 12 Essential Life Anchors* is the town of Pasadena, California. In the late 1800s, after a series of bad winters, some professionals from Indiana decided to relocate to southern California. They settled in Indiana Colony. To receive mail, they had to incorporate as a city and come up with a name. They chose Pasadena because it was a Chippewa American Indian name, which reminded them of their Midwestern roots.

At the same time, their region was undergoing an economic and real estate downturn, and the new city founders decided to come up with a way to address these issues. The manner in which they did so demonstrated *IOU Life Leadership.* The city founders had a *Life Vision,* a big picture of how they wanted their city to be—vibrant and growing. They also had a *Daily Mission* and *REBEL Goals,* the steps they would take to realize this vision.

The first step they took was to create and then raise awareness of their brand (*SelfCulture*). Pasadena's warm climate made it a great place to live. To raise awareness of that, they organized a track and field event that would take place in mid-winter and decided to invite the Midwestern newspaper writers to be the judges. While they were judging the different events, the writers would presumably be attracted to the wonderful weather and view Pasadena as a great place to live. Further, to cement their brand, the city founders chose a name for the track and field event that highlighted the many blooming flowers in the area—The Tournament of Roses.

The event was a huge success, and it was decided to continue it the following year. To build on their *SelfCulture*, they decorated carriages and cars with flowers to drive to the tournament grounds, thus beginning the *Everlasting Tradition* of the Rose Parade. A football game was added to the annual event after a few years, eventually turning into a competition between college teams from the Big 10 (the old) versus teams from the Pac 12 (the new). The genius of those first city founders was finding ways to attract Midwestern people to their area by highlighting the desirable climate and all of its advantages. Today, the Tournament of Roses is synonymous with Pasadena and with New Year's traditions. Both the game and the parade are attended by thousands, with millions more watching on television. Clearly, the *Life Vision* of the founding settlers of Pasadena has been realized as the city is a highly desirable place to live.

By failing to prepare, you are preparing to fail.

—Benjamin Franklin

Do the Prep

The prep is everything!

How many times do we jump right into something new, sometimes even with no preparation? What usually happens? It becomes hard, and we fail. We try again, it becomes hard again, we fail again, and we quit, feeling like we're not good at it, don't have the skills, or it wasn't meant to be. And we move on, never trying it again. Well, how many times did you take the time to prepare for that thing before trying it? Did you do the prep work?

You see, most of the time, the actual task is just a number of sub-tasks or skills. If we don't practice and do the prep, we won't be successful at the main task. For example, one summer on a family vacation, I was on the beach watching beginner kite and windsurfers being taught by highly skilled teachers.

You might think you learn those skills by getting on the surfboard or the ski and trying. Not at all. The teachers worked with just the sail with the students in one foot of water for over two hours. The skis and surfboards were nowhere in sight. Knowing how to control the sail and use the winds for the journey was the most important and challenging skill needed. They were doing the prep work before actually trying the windsurfing or kite surfing.

This is classic *IOU Living*. You have 100% control of your *Inward Thinking* and *Outward Actions* and no control over the wind. When living *Outwardly*, you have 100% control over your actions and reactions, and can only interact by following the lead of the *OI Actions* that come to you and use the wind to your benefit to move successfully where you want to go.

As I observed the experienced kite surfers and windsurfers, their joy and happiness were evident. That was the byproduct of successful and effective *IOU Living*. The *Upward Life Living Gifts of PH2E* they received was clearly evident.

Doing the prep will improve your *Inward Living* over which you have 100% control. This will help you when you interact with the *Outward World* over which you have no control and result in receiving the *Upward Life Gifts of your PH2E*.

Take the Inward Mirror Test

Take the *Inward Mirror Test* before you are about to act *Outwardly*. When you are about to do something that you may be unsure of, you should consider if there could be negative consequences for your *Outward Action*. By imagining yourself looking in a mirror and scrutinizing what you're about to do before you do it, you will have one last opportunity to make sure your actions are the "right thing to do." Use the *Life Map Cycle* as a tool to clarify your actions. Remember to *Evaluate* the situation first by taking in the raw data. Do not short circuit the cycle by jumping to conclusions

> By imagining yourself looking in a mirror and scrutinizing what you're about to do before you do it, you will have one last opportunity to make sure your actions are the "right thing to do."

and implementing a plan! After you take in the data, *Calculate* the data by organizing it in a way that makes sense. See how it fits in with what you already know, your *Life Vision*, your *Daily Mission*, your *Life Principles*, and your *Life Values*. Once you have sufficiently taken in and organized the data, you *Formulate* an opinion and a plan. Finally, take action and *Navigate* it, and then start the cycle again by taking in data on the results.

There are many scenarios in which it is appropriate to take the *Inward Mirror Test*:

- There may be times when you believe there is no issue with proceeding forward. Before proceeding, take the *Inward Mirror Test*!
- You are responding to an email or text that upset you. Before hitting send, take the *Inward Mirror Test*!
- You are offered something for free and about to take it. Before accepting it, take the *Inward Mirror Test*!
- You are given permission to do something that may have unintended consequences. Before acting, take the *Inward Mirror Test*!

My teenage daughter was having a sleepover with a good friend. It was October, a few weeks from Halloween, so they decided to watch a scary movie. They had a craving for candy corn, but there was none in the house, and all the stores were closed. The girls remembered a friend who had some, so they instant-messaged her and asked if they could stop by to get some. Their friend agreed but told them she was away with her family. She proceeded to tell my daughter where her parents kept a hidden key to the house. My daughter asked if it was OK with her parents, and her friend said that it was. What should have screamed in my daughter's mind? Alert! Alert! Alert! Take the *Inward Mirror Test*!

This was a classic example of getting permission for something that, on the surface, seemed fine and even sounded like fun. They decided to go, and the outcome was neither fine, fun, nor OK. The mother had not been asked, the alarm went off, and the police came.

By taking the *Inward Mirror Test*, it would have given my daughter a moment to think of the unintended consequences and may have given her the wisdom to change her course of action. By pausing and taking the *Inward Mirror Test*, she may have arrived at a different outcome and hopefully concluded that it wasn't a good idea to go into a house when no one was home. In fact, she could have concluded that she could live without satisfying her craving for candy corn!

There are too many times when we react and don't take the time to think things through. As we previously discussed, Victor Frankl stated that between a stimulus and response, there is a space, and in that space is our freedom to choose. Make a choice and choose *IOU Living*. Live the *IOU Life Principle* so you can enjoy the highest levels of *PH2E*.

> *Life is a mirror and will reflect back to the thinker what he thinks into it.*
>
> —Ernest Holmes

Diana Nyad is known throughout the world as the first person to swim from Cuba to Florida. This historic feat of 110 miles in treacherous open waters took over 50 hours to complete. Diana achieved this milestone, a lifelong goal, at the age of 64! Her journey to realize this dream was filled with seemingly insurmountable obstacles and challenges throughout her life. In persevering and meeting each challenge, Diana embodied *IOU Life Leadership*. She showed high levels of *Inward Thinking* and *Outward Actions* and received high levels of *PH2E* throughout the long journey toward her goal.

By the age of 10, she was committed to swimming, showing extreme discipline and perseverance by getting up at 4:30 a.m. daily for practice and exercise. She never missed a day. She possessed a strong *Inward SelfCulture* and knew her *Life Vison*, *Daily Mission*, *Life Principles*, *Life Values*, and *Life Goals* were 100% within her control.

During her junior year of high school, Diana contracted endocarditis and was placed on bed rest for three months. She could have reacted to this in a negative fashion by focusing on all that she had lost (e.g., months of training, and her standing on the swimming team), but instead decided to use the time to study her academic subjects. She had her sister go to the library to get her books so she could read and learn. In other words, Diana did not dwell on what she could not control—the fact she was sick and on bed rest—but used her strong *Inward SelfCulture* to set a new goal about learning and based her *Daily Mission* on that short-term goal.

Diana believed her competitive swimming days were over when, as her high school years drew to a close, she failed to make the Olympic Trials for the Mexico City games. However, years later, a friend mentioned that open water marathon swimming was a sport, and Diana was intrigued. Thus, she began her new life challenge. In her mid-20's, she decided to swim around the island of Manhattan, a feat that hadn't been completed since 1927 and never by a woman. Her first attempt was thwarted more than halfway through because of strong, outgoing tide speeds. Diana didn't deem it a failure and knew the circumstances were *Outward* and out of her control. Fewer than two weeks later, Diana attempted the swim again with success and became the first woman to swim around Manhattan and did so at record speed.

After this feat, Diana set a new goal to swim a world record—100 nonstop miles in open water. She eventually decided that her goal was to swim from Cuba to Key West, the southernmost tip of the United States, considered the "Mount Everest" for open-water ocean swimmers.

Diana made her first attempt at the Cuba to Florida swim at the age of 28. The preparations for this swim were intense and began a year before the actual attempt. Eight-hour swims in pools and open water were the norm. She moved to Miami to continue her training. Her *Inward* resolve and *SelfCulture* propelled her *Outward Actions* to guide the pursuit of this goal.

Although open-water swimming might seem like a solitary sport, it actually involves a team of people to support the swimmer. Diana literally has a *Life Relation-Ship* of helpers near her at all times while she is completing a marathon swim. She needs people to navigate, monitor weather and tide positions, monitor her ongoing status, and provide her nourishment and encouragement. Diana demonstrates high *IOU Trust* with her team, and they demonstrate it with her as well. In preparing for the Cuba to Florida swim, Diana had to use her well-developed *Inward Thinking* to plan and set her *Daily Mission* according to her *Life Principles*, *Life Values*, *Life Goals*, and *Life Vision*. She also had to develop the *Outward Anchors* of *Practice Positive Communication*, *Create Common Language*, and *Construct a Cohesive Environment* to create the strong team necessary to succeed.

There were many challenges to address proactively, including the dangers of both hypo- and hyperthermia, sharks and jellyfish, navigational complications such as how to negotiate the Gulf Stream that would push her east instead of north, and arranging for the necessary permits and permissions given the strained relationship and embargo in effect between the United States and Cuba. Diana prepared thoroughly and trusted the team around her. Once in Cuba, the weather was entirely outside of her control in the days and hours leading up to the swim. The wind conditions were a challenge that delayed the start, but she and her team finally decided to go forward after getting pressure from Cuban officials. The waters were exceptionally rough with surging waves causing seasickness, jellyfish stings necessitating medical treatment, and strong winds. After nearly 42 hours and 79 miles, the swim ended when Diana's team informed her that they had been blown off-course into the Gulf of Mexico with no hope of making any landfall.

Almost immediately, Diana thought ahead toward making another attempt the following year. Exemplifying *IOU Life Leadership*, she used everything she learned from her first attempt to make adjustments and modifications to plan better for the possible *Outward* occurrences that were out of her control. After almost another year of training, the team was disappointed when they were denied entry to Cuba. Although her dream swim would not be possible, Diana refused to give up and let her and her team's many months of preparation and training go to waste. They quickly regrouped and determined that she would attempt a Bahamas to Florida swim, which was almost as long but not as challenging. This was a great example of Diana's strong *Life Leadership* in deciding to continue to pursue a goal and to be flexible because of circumstances outside of her control. If she had spent any amount of time being upset about the denied entry to Cuba, she would have lost the window to complete a long-distance ocean swim that year. Because of the well-established *Cohesive Environment*, *Positive Communication*, and *Common Language*, Diana's team was united behind her in this effort. After 27 hours of swimming and traversing over 102 miles, Diana achieved her *Daily Mission* and set a world record. Although still disappointed she didn't achieve her true dream, she put the Cuba swim aside and said goodbye to swimming.

At age 60, Diana was inspired to evaluate her life, thinking of the famous poet, Mary Oliver's quote, "What is it you plan to do with your one wild and precious life?" She set her mind toward finally achieving her original goal of completing the Cuba to Florida swim. That this goal was even a possibility was due to the high levels of *PH2E* Diana had received over her lifetime by living the *IOU Life Leadership* principle and using *The 12 Essential Life Anchors*. In particular, she was in excellent physical health and had maintained a very high level of physical fitness. She reassembled her team and began training in earnest. In fact, Diana would do that four more times over the next few years. She encountered difficult obstacles, nearly died from lethal box jellyfish stings, and had to keep leading her team in staying true to the journey and not giving up. In fact, her motto for the entire effort was "*Onward.*"

It was always important to Diana that the journey was a valuable way to spend her time. In other words, did it align with her *Inward Beliefs* and *SelfCulture*? Each time she decided that, it did. Diana was finally successful in achieving her goal. On September 2, 2013, after swimming for nearly 53 hours and traversing 110 miles, Diana Nyad, at the age of 64, walked onto the shores of Key West.

The joy and happiness Diana felt when accomplishing her lifelong goal was obvious, but what is more inspiring is the joy and happiness she exhibited throughout her whole *Life Journey*. When there is a clear goal, the value of the journey—rather than the goal attainment—will propel your *PH2E*. Creating *Life Goals* throughout your life enriches the present since you know where you are heading. If you don't know

When there is a clear goal, the value of the journey—rather than the goal attainment—will propel your PH2E.

where you are heading with a *Life Goal*, you are always focusing on which way to go and evaluating every action to give it purpose and meaning before moving on. This constant evaluation can cause stress and anxiety because life is lived reacting to unknowns rather than living proactively by design like Diana.

> *And in the end, it's not the years in your life that count. It's the life in your years.*
>
> —Abraham Lincoln

Upward Living Each Day for The Life Gifts

Approximately 90,000 people who go to sleep tonight will not wake up tomorrow morning. So, if we are lucky enough to wake up tomorrow morning, isn't that a wonderful thing? Shouldn't we wake up and say thank you and think how awesome it is and how grateful we are to begin another day? We don't usually do that because we don't think about our mortality. We know we are mortal, but we don't think about our lives ending. We may go through each day as if we will live forever. If we are conscious of mortality, would

If we remind ourselves that we have finite moments in our lives, we would only do what is good for our mind, body, and heart. We would continuously look for opportunities to increase our *PH2E*.

we have time to waste on negative things? Do we want to waste our precious time around others that are negative? Do we want to waste our time arguing with others? Do we want to waste

449

our precious time living in *Environment 4* (Chapter 2) staring excessively at our phone or computer? If we remind ourselves that we have finite moments in our lives, we would only do what is good for our mind, body, and heart. We would continuously look for opportunities to increase our *PH2E*.

We would also look for ways to increase *PH2E* in others. I am not saying to live in fear of death; instead, let it give value to our lives. We have 100% control of our *Inward Living* and our *Outward Actions*. That's a lot of control! Don't give away your control, but rather, understand it and unleash it from this moment forward. Living *IOU Life Leadership* and practicing *The 12 Essential Life Anchors* will help us to begin to design our lives with purpose and meaning and add value to our one and only precious life.

A ship is not meant to stay at port; it is designed to sail the seas, just as you are meant to interact with others and the world and live your life dreams. When the *Life Matrix* (Chapter 2) was discussed, *E3 (Environment 3)* was described as when everyone's pressing issues are thrust onto you. It may be *Urgent and Important* to others but not for you. You have a choice to say no or move their issue to *E2 (Environment 2)* and help them if it's important for you to build your relationship with them. However, if you never say no, you will never get sailing on your journey. You will be stuck at port. If your *Life Ship* stays at port too long, barnacles attach to your hull and your propeller. The longer you are stuck at port, the more barnacles latch on and grow into bumpy masses, which will slow down your boat and can cause vibrations that can cause damage throughout your ship.

Be aware of others' urgent issues pressing on you. You must say no (politely), cut the lines of others holding you back, and start navigating your *Life Journey*.

Captain's Log for Chapter 14

Living the IOU Life Leadership Principle

IOU LIVING

Captain's Log:

Point 1   Living the *IOU Principle* is having the wisdom to live intentionally in the areas that you can control while continuously developing the mental calmness for things that you cannot control.

Point 2   *The 12 Essential Life Anchors* give us the ability to choose our *Life Journey.* Surround yourself with positive thoughts, actions, and relationships, and you will receive the *Upward Living Life Gifts of PH2E.*

Point 3   Lead from the captain's wheel. Do all the preparations and look at the big picture. Use *The 12 Essential Life Anchors* to aid you on your journey.

Point 4   Live your life "above deck" and enjoy the journey. Collaborate with others and share the responsibilities. Develop the leadership talent in others.

Point 5   Don't just jump into a new journey or *Daily Mission.* Do the Prep work necessary for success. Make sure that you have all the *Inward* and *Outward* skills that will assist you.

452

Point 6   The *Inward Mirror Test* is a tool you can use before *Outward Action* to scrutinize your planned actions for any possible negative consequences. The *Life Map Cycle* tool will help clarify your actions and make sure that you are not short-circuiting important steps.

Point 7   Continuously look for opportunities to increase your *PH2E* and to increase *PH2E* in others. Live each day to the fullest. Strive for an attitude of gratefulness.

Teach to Learn

The best way to deepen your understanding and, at the same time, share and stimulate new conversations with others is to teach. Share what you have learned with a friend, family member, coworker, or anyone else who will listen. Teaching is, by far, the best way to deepen one's understanding of new insights and concepts. Take any of the Points in the Captain's Log or this chapter for thought-provoking discussions.

New Daily Voyage:

Activity:

Think of a situation when you were trying to complete a task but kept getting distracted by *Outward Actions* from others. This kept you from leading from the caption's wheel. Could you have avoided the distractions? Be conscious of your next task, try to avoid those distractions, and keep reminding yourself to stay on course and lead from the captain's wheel.

Ask yourself:

What can I do, right now, to intentionally improve my *IOU Living*? How can I take steps to improve my *Inward Self* and my *Outward Actions*?

Chapter 15

Become a Life Leader - Be a Life Changer

I Wanted To Change The World

When I was a young man, I wanted to change the world.
I found it was difficult to change the world,
so, I tried to change my nation.
When I found I couldn't change the nation,
I began to focus on my town.
I couldn't change the town, and as an older man,
I tried to change my family.

Now, as an old man, I realize the only thing
I can change is myself,
and suddenly I realize that if long ago I had changed myself,
I could have made an impact on my family.
My family and I could have made an impact on our town.
Their impact could have changed the nation, and
I could indeed have changed the world.

—Unknown 12th-Century Monk

Your goal should be to become a *Life Leader*, which will automatically make you a *Life Changer*. I define a *Life Leader* as someone who profoundly augments their *Inward* and *Outward Living* centered around *Life Principles*. They then take action to help and inspire others to find their unique *Inward* and *Outward Life Principles*, which gives them the *Upward Living Life Gifts of Peacefulness, Happiness, Healthiness, and Excellence*, along with the hope that they ultimately will do the same for others. When this occurs, all involved will thrive as the culture grows *Dynamic and Positive,* receiving the *Upward Living Life Gifts of PH2E.*

I define a *Life Leader* as someone who profoundly augments their *Inward* and *Outward Living* centered around *Life Principles.*

When you become a *Life Leader*, you will be a *Life Changer* for yourself and others. You will be a lighthouse that is solid, stable, and immovable because of the natural laws of life that guide your life as well as the lives of others. As a *Life Leader* and a *Life Changer,* you are in control of your voyage and have the necessary tools and skills to use on elements in your life as they come to you, and will be able to adapt and adjust course to reach your destination.

As I was researching material for this chapter, I came across a book written in 1914 called, *Technique of Success.* I was struck by a section discussing concentration, which is referred to as focusing all one's energies and abilities on a single point—a single point that represents your whole world for that moment in time. Concentration is the seed of character sown that will subtly influence *Inward* bodily processes

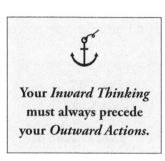

Your *Inward Thinking* must always precede your *Outward Actions.*

and *Outward* conduct. It's focusing on intentional living. We must take time out and think and concentrate on our *Inward* and *Outward Anchors.* Think about the most important asset you have—yourself. *The 12 Essential Life Anchors* provide you with a framework for *positive and effective Inward Thinking* and *Outward Actions* to become a *Life Leader.* This process will help you reach down into your infinite *Inward* reservoir and bring forward your *Purpose, Potential,* and *Passion,* your *Life Vision* that will change those around you in an extraordinary way and build a *Dynamic Positive Culture* for *yourself, your family, team, and organization.*

Your *Inward Thinking* must always precede your *Outward Actions.* Take the time and act now, meditating over your *Inward Life Anchors.* Practice the exercises at the end of each chapter often.

Simplicity boils down to two steps:
Identify the essential. Eliminate the rest.

—Leo Babauta

IOU Living in Simplicity

When notable philosopher Henry Thoreau was 27 years old, he left his hometown to live alone in the woods of Walden Pond on a 14-acre parcel of land owned by his friend, Ralph Waldo Emerson. Thoreau wrote in his journal about observing nature and the importance and benefits of simplifying your life. He was a critic of the materialistic culture in 1845. What do you think he would say about the materialistic culture of today? Thoreau's thoughts give insight into the destructive nature of living a life consumed with the pursuit of having material things. His writings focused on

The 12 Essential Life Anchors are foundational, universal, timeless principles for *Inward* and *Outward Living* to aid in simplifying, clarifying, and navigating your *Life Journey.*

Inwardly and *Outwardly* simplifying one's life. A mathematician approaches a difficult problem by eliminating all complications and reducing it to its simplest terms. Thoreau's goal was to simplify his life to only the necessary and to understand his main roots and purpose.

IOU Living is precisely that. It is simplifying your life into two modes—*Inward Living* and *Outward Living*. When that occurs, you will receive *Upward Living* and the *Life Gifts of PH2E*. Remember, you cannot just go out and grab *PH2E*. As adapted from Thoreau's quote about happiness, *PH2E* is like a butterfly. The more you chase it, the more it eludes you. If you turn your attention to your *Inward* and *Outward Living*, the butterfly will come and sit softly on your shoulder. *The 12 Essential Life Anchors* are foundational, universal, timeless principles for *Inward* and *Outward Living* to aid in simplifying, clarifying, and navigating your *Life Journey*. As Thoreau suggested in his book *Walden: Life in The Woods*, live the life you've imagined. As you simplify your life, the laws of the universe will be simpler—solitude will not be solitude, and poverty will not be poverty nor weakness.

In the book, *Lead Yourself First*, Ray Kethledge and Mike Erwin argue that solitude is necessary for leadership. During the development of Microsoft, Bill Gates took what he called "think weeks" to reflect on his goals. George Washington would ride his horse alone around Mount Vernon for hours to think. Dwight D. Eisenhower considered writing as the best way to think about issues. He made a practice to journal often and made time to be alone to think and write his priorities.

Whether it's taking a walk, playing an instrument, writing, or painting, find the activities that help you think and reflect in solitude. You need to spend time daydreaming and thinking freely to generate ideas and purpose. As the saying, which has been widely attributed to Einstein, goes, "If I had one hour to solve a problem, I would spend 55 minutes defining the problem and five minutes solving the problem,"

Like Eisenhower, try thinking by writing. When was the last time you wrote down your thoughts? It's a wonderful way to look *Inward* and truly understand who you are. No therapist or psychologist needed, just a pen and a piece of paper. Try it!

> *I felt my lungs inflate with the onrush of scenery—*
> *air, mountains, trees, people.*
> *I thought, This is what it is to be happy.*

—Sylvia Plath

Nature Moments by Dr. Joe

I have always enjoyed the *Outward Living* of being outside in nature and, in the past few years, have taken up nature photography. Instead of merely enjoying a hike in the woods, I am now much more attentive to the surroundings. The lives of birds and animals are inspiring, and it's peaceful to observe them in their natural world. Being in nature can lead to significant health benefits. Several studies have shown being in nature can reduce stress, improve blood pressure, and boost mental health. A study conducted by Berman, Jonides, and Kaplan showed people's performance on a test improved by 20% after taking a nature walk among trees compared to those who walked a busy street.

Check out my photographs capturing nature moments from my forest baths.
Go to my Instagram @naturemomentsbydrjoe.

Try "forest bathing," a practice in Japan which means bathing in the forest atmosphere. It's taking in nature through all your senses. Using your sight, hearing, taste, smell, and touch, you open your senses to the natural world. At least once a week, I take a hike and photograph the nature moments I experience. Such *Outward Living* leads to the *Upward Living Life Gifts of Peacefulness and Happiness*, and as studies have shown, even leads to greater *Healthiness and Excellence*

Check out my photographs capturing nature moments from my forest baths. Go to my Instagram **@naturemomentsbydrjoe.**

Your inner knowing is your only true compass.

—Joy Page

THE LIFE GUIDING HANDLE

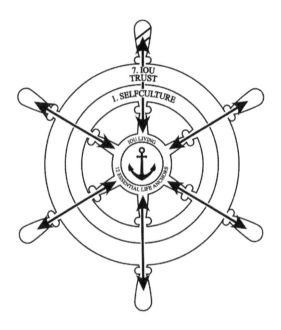

The captain's wheel is a significant symbol for *IOU Life Leadership*. Have you noticed the hash marks on the handle for both *Inward Life Anchor 1 (SelfCulture) and Outward Life Anchor 7 (IOU Trust)*? These hash marks have been on every captain's wheel in this book, and they represent the texture purposely placed on only one handle of an actual captain's wheel. This ingenious tool was and is still used by every captain as an important guide. The texture makes the top handle feel different from the other handles and is extremely important to a captain when steering a ship. I refer to it as the *Life Guiding Handle*. When a captain is in a storm or disoriented because of the darkness of night or other elements and needs to navigate the boat dead straight immediately, this will be easily accomplished because of the textured handle. When the captain grabs the textured *Life Guiding Handle* and moves it to the top or north position, it moves the rudder perfectly straight in line with the hull. In the dark or a storm, the captain can simply feel for the *Life Guiding Handle* and keep focused on the journey ahead. Without that ability, the captain has to guess which handle will move the rudder dead straight. In rough seas, not knowing the exact position of the rudder could result in danger or even capsizing the boat.

Reach for your *Life Guiding Handle* and reflect on your *SelfCulture* and *IOU Trust* for stability regarding who you are, what you believe *Inwardly*, and your closest *Outward* supportive relationships.

The most critical and foundational *Inward* and *Outward Life Anchors* are represented by this *Life Guiding Handle*. In *IOU Living*, your two most important guiding *Life Anchors* are aligned to your *Life Guiding Handle*—an *Inward Anchor* and an *Outward Anchor*. They are *Inward Life Anchor 1* (*SelfCulture*) and *Outward Life Anchor 7* (*IOU Trust*). These two anchors are your go-to *Anchors* when you are in the dark or the midst of a life storm. Whenever you are disoriented, confused, and need help, find the handle with the etches and turn it straight up on top. Reach for your *Life Guiding Handle* and reflect on your *SelfCulture* and *IOU Trust* for stability regarding who you are, what you believe *Inwardly*, and your closest *Outward* supportive relationships.

There will be many times when you will be faced with a major decision, and you are pondering the right course of action to take. By finding your *Life Guiding Handle* and putting it on top, front, and center, it will ground and remind you of who you are and your beliefs. It will point you back to your *Life Vision, Life Principles, Life Values,* and *Life Goals,* which is your *SelfCulture.* This will help clear your mind and help you easily find the correct heading or direction and get you back on course.

It especially helps to weed out all the *Outward* forces trying to influence your course of action. When you are under pressure,

IOU Trust is the foundation for all of our closest relationships.

your *Life Guiding Handle* is about clarity of mind. Our mind is usually weighed down by many options, usually influenced by *Environment 3,* which are urgent items for others but not important to us. When you think in accordance with your *SelfCulture,* which you have developed your whole life, and act according to the highest form of trustworthiness to others, the decision or course of action will be obvious.

IOU Trust is the foundation for all of our closest relationships. In times of difficulty, put your *Life Guiding Handle* to the top and lean on your *IOU Trust* relationships. These are the most important relationships in your life. There is a special two-way connection with your *Inward Living* to another person. This *IO* special relationship leads to you both receiving *Upward Living* and the *Life Gifts of PH2E.* When you have *IOU Trust,* you know you have someone to help overcome any problem. In those relationships, you can be vulnerable, let your guard down and share secrets and fears. You have someone who will provide *WholeHearted Listening* for you, giving you the freedom to be authentic and know you will not be judged.

The next time you have a difficult challenge and need support, grab your *Life Guiding Handle* on your personal captain's wheel and put it straight up to align your rudder. Remember who you are with your *SelfCulture* and your important *IOU Trust* relationships. This will help your well-being and create stability for your ship and get you back on course for your *Life Journey.*

> *Yesterday I was clever, so I wanted to change the world.*
> *Today I am wise, so I am changing myself.*
>
> —Mevlana Rumi

Change Always Starts Inwardly First

Too many times, we focus *Outwardly*. We focus on how we look to others, how our body looks, how we speak, and all the things we have that the *Outward World* sees. We should be focusing on how we *Inwardly* feel first, not how we look *Outwardly*. How does our *Inward* heart and mind feel? Time and time again, we neglect our *Inward Being* and expect to see an *Outward* change. It is a requirement to change *Inwardly* first before we are able to make a real *Outward* change. Doug Conant, the former president and CEO of the Campbell Soup Company, said, "Leadership is an inside-out process. You need to be fortified within before you can lead people around you." If we just focus on changing our *Outward Living*, it may look good, but changing *Inwardly* first will feel better and will lead to lasting change. Changing *Inwardly* will change our *Outward Living*. Then, we will not only feel good inside, but others will notice our genuine *Inward* positive culture, and it will inspire them to be positive as well.

We need to take care of our *Outward* appearance but, at the same time, develop our *Inward Living*, our *Inward Life Anchors* that are foundational for *positive and effective* living. In today's

We have 100% control to begin right now to develop our *Inward Life Anchors* and rediscover our *Life Vision* and our purpose in this one wild life that we all have.

society, we are bombarded with social media showing us how we should look, what things we should have, and how happy everyone is. It's an illusion since the pictures are highly edited and, therefore, unreal. Too many times, we compare ourselves with fake social media pictures and events. If we are continuously trying to achieve that level, we will fail and be disappointed. There is so much more to life than what we see on the outside. There are endless, timeless, and everlasting *Inward* rewards just waiting for us to tap into. We have 100% control to begin right now to develop our *Inward Life Anchors* and rediscover our *Life Vision* and purpose in this one wild life that we all have.

We are all two people. One is of the past journeys that led us to the now, and we cannot change that person. The second is the person we are from this moment forward toward the future with untapped potential for our journey ahead.

As you Live Outwardly, don't perseverate on the doors that close or you will miss the doors that are opening right next to you with new opportunities, new challenges, and new relationships.

—Dr. Joe Famularo

New Thoughts—New You

Filling your mind with fresh creative thoughts can move us to the next highest level. Sometimes we need to fill our minds with new ideas, new approaches, and new *Life Journeys* because we think we have figured out life. We have our opinions, our views, our routines. We repeat them over and over daily, reinforcing them. It's easy, too; we are almost on automatic pilot when a particular topic arises. We go right into our script, and we feel good because we can articulate it and make it sound

To be a *Life Leader* you must get comfortable with being a *Life Changer*— starting with yourself.

like it's been well thought out. What if our opinions or *Life Maps* are wrong? Maybe not wholly wrong, but if any small part is wrong, are we ok with that? We need to have new thoughts to update and possibly replace our old thoughts. The world we live in is not determined by our *Outward* conditions or our *Outward* circumstances. It's determined by our *Inward Living*, our being, and our thoughts.

To be a *Life Leader*, you must get comfortable with being a *Life Changer*—starting with yourself. That is and will be a continuous process for the rest of your life, but how beautiful it is to change for the better continuously! How marvelous to change toward a higher level of *PH2E* continuously, to change so others continually feel your trustworthiness exponentially increasing right in front of them. Living in a *positive and effective* manner develops positive outcomes, just as living *negatively and ineffectively* develops negative outcomes. To change your circumstances, you must start *Inwardly* thinking differently.

Analyze Both Your Success and Failures

Analyze your successes and failures based on *The 12 Essential Life Anchors*. Use them as a measuring tool, and you will clearly see connections in usage and omission. You can always benefit from analyzing things that have gone wrong personally, in a relationship, in the family, on the team, in the workplace, and in the organization.

Looking at the root cause and not superficial reasons requires having a tool to analyze the failure. *The 12 Essential Life Anchors* can provide the tools to detect the root cause of the problem for yourself and *FTO* by asking questions such as:

- **Anchor 1—SelfCulture.** Does the culture have a clear identity?

- **Anchor 2—Life Vision.** Was there a clear vision developed for the task at hand?
- **Anchor 3—Daily Mission.** Was there a day to day mission that all stakeholders understood that drove the implementation of the task?
- **Anchor 4—Life Principles.** Were there principles clearly agreed upon by all stakeholders that echoed the vision and mission of the *FTO*?
- **Anchor 5—Life Values.** Were there shared core values guiding the behavior of all stakeholders?
- **Anchor 6—Life Goals.** Were the task goals clearly defined?
- **Anchor 7—Inspire IOU Trust.** Is it a high trust culture?
- **Anchor 8—Practice Positive Communication.** Is positive communication practiced in the culture?
- **Anchor 9—Create Common Language.** Is a common language used throughout the culture?
- **Anchor 10—Construct a Cohesive Environment.** Is it a cohesive environment?
- **Anchor 11—Establish Everlasting Traditions.** Are there everlasting traditions embedded in the culture?
- **Anchor 12—Model a Mindset of Propelling *PH2E*.** Is there a sense that everyone is working hard to propel their *PH2E*?

Life Leaders continually change and update their *Life Maps*. They understand that failure is part of life and are always looking for it, correcting it, and learning from it before others do. *Life Leaders* don't wallow in failure. They don't blame others. They understand it's a necessary part of life, analyze it, step back, create a new plan, and then move forward.

The journey of a thousand miles begins with one step.

—Lao Tzu

Be a Trim Tab Life Leader and Life Changer

In 2019, Symphony of the Seas was the world's largest cruise ship measuring 1,188 feet long, 238 feet tall, and weighing 228,081 tons. It is so large it cannot navigate the English Channel or the Panama Canal. Imagine this massive ship creating huge waves with 10-foot swells as it passes by you. As this giant ship continues to move, you look up at the stern of the boat and notice this tiny piece of metal gently turning at the edge of the rudder. This miniature rudder is called the trim tab. When this trim tab turns, it creates low pressure in the water that moves the large rudder, which then turns the gigantic ship that houses two malls, several swimming pools, dining halls, theaters, basketball courts, 2788 guest rooms, and much more.

By focusing on the small things, we will begin to see the ship turn ever so slightly in the direction of our *Life Journey* for ourselves, family, team, and/or organization.

The "Trim Tab" principle, coined by Buckminster Fuller, suggests that we can do more with less. In other words, small things can create big results. Relating this to *IOU Living*, we must start with ourselves and focus on our

Inward Thinking and our *Outward Actions*, which we have the power to change. By focusing on the small things within ourselves, we may have a significant influence on others and may have a much larger effect on society. However, we often find ourselves trying to change others and change the big things with big ideas and techniques. By focusing on the small stuff, we will begin to see the ship turn ever so slightly in the direction of our *Life Journey* for *ourselves, family, team, and/or organization*. Be a *Trim Tab Life Leader*!

Vincent, who was a major theme mentioned throughout this book, changed my life and the lives of generations. By concentrating on his life, he modeled living a principle-centered life, focused on what was in his control, and did not try to change others or the world. He modeled *The 12 Essential Life Anchors*, lived a life of integrity, and made clear the importance of family. It was obvious he spent a great deal of time on *Inward Thinking* and clearly defined his *Inward Living (SelfCulture)*. Through stories and actions, he shared *Outwardly* that doing the right thing was always the goal (*IOU Trust*). He and his wife Maria enjoyed *Upward Living* and received the *Upward Living Life Gifts*, and they had four children—three sons and one daughter.

Vincent created a *Dynamic Positive Culture* for himself, his family, his teams at work, and the organizations he was a part of—the US Navy and the Brooklyn Navy Yard. This *Dynamic Positive Culture* was infused into his three sons, who also served in the United States military. His children all married, blessing him with 14 grandchildren, who all married and had children. This youngest generation is now also having children of their own, so the family is still growing and carrying on Vincent's traditions and wisdom.

There were also countless friends, coworkers, and community members whom Vincent influenced. The small trim tab actions that Vincent lived in his life truly changed his family, friends, community, and even the nation, when you look at all the accomplishments of the people he affected. His stories and lessons continue, and perhaps he may have also changed the world. We all have the opportunity to be a *Life Leader* and thereby be a *Life Changer*, just like Vincent.

I can see and hear him now, raising his glass and saying, "Centi Anni," wishing everyone to live happily for a hundred years. I am proud to have known this *Great American Sailor*, son, husband, father, captain, seadog, service member, friend, community member, and an inspiring man. He was known by his full name, Vincent Famularo, but I had the privilege and honor to call him *Grandpa*.

Grandpa—A Wise Leader

Grandpa once told me a story that he heard about an old, wise leader with magical powers who gave all humans super extraordinary life gifts. Over time, when people abused these special gifts, the wise leader decided to take them away and hide them so they would never be found.

Where to hide these special life gifts was the question, so the wise leader called a meeting of his special council to help him decide.

"Let's bury them deep in the earth," said one of the council members.

But the wise leader said, "No, that will not do because humans will dig into the earth and find them."

Then another council member said, "Let's sink them into the deepest ocean."

But the wise leader said, "No, not there, for they will learn to dive into the ocean and will surely find them."

Then another council member said, "Let's take the life gifts to the top of the highest mountain and hide them there."

Once again, the wise leader said, "No, that will not do, either, because they will eventually climb every mountain and once again take the special life gifts."

The council members said, "We do not know where to hide them because there is no place on earth or in the sea that human beings will not eventually reach."

The wise leader thought for a long time and then said, "Here is what we will do. We will hide these super extraordinary life gifts deep in the center of their being, for humans will never think to look for them there."

The entire council agreed that this was the perfect hiding place, and the deed was done. And since that time, all humans have been going up and down the earth, digging, diving, climbing, and exploring, searching for something already within themselves.

The *Life Gifts* are all within us just waiting for us to use to the fullest, and to guide us on our one and only precious *Life Journey!*

We all have within us greatness, talents, and the super extraordinary *Life Gifts of PH2E* waiting to expand *Upward* to great heights. If we could only take the time to think *Inwardly, Evaluate, Calculate, Formulate, and then Navigate* our *Life Plan Outwardly*, our lives would have greater purpose, success, and meaning.

With the aid of *The 12 Essential Life Anchors,* you can rediscover yourself, propel your *Upward Living Life Gifts*, and begin to navigate toward a *Dynamic Positive Culture* for *yourself, family, team, and/or organization.* The *Life Gifts* are all within you just waiting for you to use to the fullest, and guide you on your one and only precious *Life Journey!* Practice *IOU Living* and become a *Life Leader. IOU Life Leaders*hip begins now. Remember, "*You Owe it to Yourself and Others!*"

Captain's Log for Chapter 15

Become a Life Leader - Be a Life Changer

Captain's Log:

Point 1   Your goal should be to be a *Life Leader*, someone who profoundly augments their *Inward* and *Outward Living* centered around *Life Principles* and who takes *Outward Action* to help and inspire others to find their unique *Inward* and *Outward Life Principles* that lead to the *Upward Living Life Gifts of PH2E*.

Point 2   *IOU Living* is about simplifying your life into *Inward* and *Outward Modes*, which lead to receiving *Upward Living* and the *Life Gifts of PH2E*.

Point 3   The most critical and foundational *Inward* and *Outward Life Anchors* are found on your *Life Guiding Handle*. They are *Inward Anchor 1* (*SelfCulture*) and *Outward Anchor 7* (*IOU Trust*). They are the go-to true north *Anchors* that will get you back on course and guide you through the darkness. Using both of them will help give you clarity of mind.

Point 4   Focus *Inward* before acting *Outward* on your appearance. You need to concentrate on your thinking, using the *Inward Life Anchors* to rediscover your *Life Vision* and purpose in your life. Fill your mind with new and creative thoughts to update and replace your old *Life Maps*. Be a *Life Changer*, starting with yourself.

475

Point 5	It is important to analyze both your successes and failures based on *The 12 Essential Life Anchors*. Reflecting on your failures helps us to determine their root cause and make changes. Consider failure a productive struggle.
Point 6	You can always benefit from analyzing things that have gone wrong personally, in a relationship, in the family, on the team, in the workplace, and in the organization. Use *The 12 Essential Life Anchors* to look at the root cause and not superficial reasons. You can ask yourself questions based on those *Anchors* to analyze the failure and move forward.
Point 7	By focusing on the small things within yourself, you may have a major influence on others and an even larger effect on society. Work to change yourself, not others. This is the *Trim Tab* principle.

Teach to Learn

The best way to deepen your understanding and, at the same time, share and stimulate new conversations with others is to teach. Share what you have learned with a friend, family member, coworker, or anyone else who will listen. Teaching is, by far, the best way to deepen one's understanding of new insights and concepts. Take any of the Points in the Captain's Log or this chapter for thought-provoking discussions.

New Daily Voyage:

Activity:

Make a list of some recent successes and failures based on *The 12 Essential Life Anchors.* Try to identify the root cause of each success and failure.

Ask yourself:

How can I be a *Trim Tab Leader*? What small changes can I make in myself that will ripple out to others and the world?

IOU FOUNDATIONAL CONCEPTS

Part I—Why IOU Life Leadership?

Chapter 1

IOU LIVING—IOU LEADERSHIP

"You Owe it to Yourself and Others."

- A foundational framework for intentional living and **Life Leadership** based on life principles.
- **Life Leadership** is about leading yourself, leading with others, leading others, and inspiring others to do the same.
- **IOU Living** will assist you in navigating toward a *Dynamic Positive Culture* for *yourself, family, team, and organization.*
- **IOU Living** is **Inward-Outward-Upward Living**
- **Inward Living** is your thinking, **Outward Living** is your actions with others and the world, and **Upward Living** is when we receive *Life's Gifts.*
- **Life Leadership Age** is the present, the world in which we must all be leaders of *ourselves, our families, teams, and organizations.*

Chapter 2

LIFE MAP

- Your opinions, beliefs, and judgments about the world and beliefs about *Life Principles*
- The result of all of your experiences and thoughts
- Must constantly be examined for accuracy

OI (OUTWARD INWARD) ACTIONS

- You have no control over what acts on you
- You have 100% control over how you react to it

LIFE LEADERSHIP MATRIX—
The 4 Life Living Environments

E1: Important & Urgent—Your Ship is Sinking—Must do Now

E2: Important & Not Urgent—Your Ship is On Course—Plan and Schedule

E3: Not Important & Urgent —Your Ship is Stuck at Port—Say NO, Delegate, or Move to E2

E4: Not Important & Not Urgent—Your Ship is Drifting— Eliminate, or Move to E2

HIDDEN OUTWARD LIVING DIMENSION

- Nonverbal communication
- Produces a positive or negative environment when interacting with others

- Be conscious about how you communicate to others through this dimension
- Design it—don't live it by default

Chapter 3

LIFE MAP CYCLE—SELF

A systems thinking tool to examine our patterns of thinking and make our *Life Maps* more accurate. This tool helps us to understand or make sense of situations so that our *Inward Life Maps* become closer to reality.

- **Evaluate (Inward)**—Take in the data without judgment
- **Calculate (Inward)**—Think about and organize the data
- **Formulate (Inward)**—Make conclusions based on the data
- **Navigate (Outward)**—Share your opinion and act out a plan based on the three previous steps

LIFE MAP CYCLE SHORT CIRCUITED

- When we short circuit the steps of the cycle
- We make automatic responses to a situation based on our bias and ignore the data in front of us
- We move from *Evaluating* something to *Navigating* and ignore the stages of *Calculating* and *Formulating*.

Chapter 4

UPWARD LIVING LIFE GIFTS

- The byproducts that come to you based on your *positive and effective Inward* and *Outward Living*
- The byproducts of your *Upward Living are your **PH2E***
  - *Peacefulness*
  - *Happiness*
  - *Healthiness*
  - *Excellence*

PH2E LIFE PROPELLER

- A four-blade propeller where each blade represents one of the *Upward Living Life Gifts—your PH2E*
- The goal is to have the propeller balanced and full—which means you have high amounts of each of the *PH2E's*

Chapter 5

DYNAMIC POSITIVE CULTURE

- A positive and growing culture for *self, family, team, and organization*
- Characterized by common and aligned beliefs, behaviors, values, and symbols
- *Inward Intentions* match *Outward Actions*

The 4 LIFE CULTURES

A culture is a way of life and is symbolic communication. The individuals' beliefs, behaviors, values, and symbols are common to a set of ideals. *The 4 Life Cultures* are:

- *SelfCulture*
- *Family Culture*
- *Team Culture*
- *Organization Culture*

LIFE MAP CYCLE—FAMILY, TEAM, ORGANIZATION (FTO)

- *Evaluate—Inward/Outward*
- *Calculate—Inward/Outward*
- *Formulate—Outward*
- *Communicate—Outward*
- *Navigate—Outward*

Part II—What is IOU Life Leadership?

Chapter 6

IO LIVING CULTURE CONTINUUM

IOU LIVING PRINCIPLE—UPWARD
IOU LIFE LEADERSHIP

Your *IO Living* is **Positive and Effective**

- The byproduct will be **Upward Living**
- You will receive the **Upward Life Gifts** *of PH2E:*
  - *Peacefulness*
  - *Happiness*
  - *Healthiness*
  - *Excellence*

IOU Living creates a **Dynamic Positive Culture**

IOW LIVING PRINCIPLE—WAYWARD
IOW LIFE DRIFTING

Your *IO Living* is **Neutral and Mediocre**

- The byproduct will be **Wayward Living**
- You will receive the **Wayward Life Impassivities** of:
  - *Apathy*
  - *Indifference*
  - *Unfitness*
  - *Mediocrity*

IOW Living creates a **Static Neutral Culture**

IOD LIVING PRINCIPLE—DOWNWARD
IOD LIFE SINKING

Your IO Living is *Negative and Ineffective*
- The byproduct will be *Downward Living*
- You will receive the *Downward Life Drains* of:
  - *Anxiety*
  - *Unhappiness*
  - *Unhealthiness*
  - *Ineffectiveness*

IOD Living creates a *Toxic Negative Culture*

THE 3 LIFE PRESERVING DIMENSIONS

Three dimensions that can change or reverse course when your *PH2E* is draining downward.

- **"Inward Self" Dimension**: Your go-to Life Saver because you always have it on hand. You have all the tools to receive positive *Upward Life Gifts* by reviewing your *Inward Life Anchors*.
- **"Outward Others" Dimension:** This *Life Preserver* is *Outward Others*, which may be a family member or a friend who supports you. Although they may not always be there, there will be opportunities in your life that your *Outward Relationships* will be there to support you.
- **"Inward-Outward Spiritual" Dimension:** The spiritual dimension is an *Inward-Outward Relationship* through meditation, prayer, nature, or music and is unique for each person. Spiritual support can come in many forms;

485

however, it can have a major *Inward* impact on your confidence and motivation to solve a problem.

Chapter 7

INWARD LIVING LIFE PRINCIPLE

- Thinking - Opinions - *Life Maps*
- The life inside of you
- Your thinking while alone
- Your *Inward Life Maps* of how you see others and the world

YOUR "YOU" WORLD

- **Y**our **O**wn **U**nderstanding of the world
- Your paradigm
- Not 100% accurate
- Use the *Life Map Cycle* to adjust

Chapter 8

INWARD LIVING LIFE ANCHORS

Solid, grounded, immovable, timeless, and universal *Life Principles* included in all effective life plans for intentional living

- Thinking - Opinion - *Life Maps*
- *I Now*—In the moment
- *I Later*—In the future
- *I Past*—In the past
- *I Gratitude, I To Do's and Tasks, I Relationships, I Learning, I Triggers, I Create, I Self-Trust, I Health, I Service, I Entertainment/Hobby, I Spirit, I Questions, I Problem-Solving, I Body*

RELATIONSHIP MAP

A *Relationship Map* contains all of the relationships and roles that you have in your life. Writing down your role and the name of the person associated with the role will clarify all the important relationships on both your *Inward* and *Inward* and *Outward Relation-Ships*. Frequently update your *Relationship Map* and use it to create a plan to connect more frequently with the people in your life that are most important to you.

10-YEAR EXERCISE

- Use your past thinking to help your current situation

- Think about a difficult situation from 10 years ago and how the stress and anxiety you experienced was unnecessary
- Think about a current difficult situation and visualize yourself handling it with little to no stress or anxiety
- When you think back on the situation 10 years from now, how will you wish you handled it?

Chapter 9

OUTWARD LIFE LIVING PRINCIPLE

- Actions - Relationships - Trust
- Interactions with people
- Interactions with nature—non-human and living
- Interactions with the environment—the geological world, the physical non-living world

IO ACTIONS

- You have 100% control of your *Inward Intentions* (I) *and Outward Actions* (O)
- Action through:
  - Facial Expressions
  - Words, Tone
  - Body Language
  - Physical Acts

The 3 LIFE RELATION-SHIPS

SHIP 1: Inward Relation-Ship
- Self-Relationship (I)
- Spiritual Relationship (IO)
- Family Relationships (IO)
- Friendship Relationships (IO) or (OI)

SHIP 2: Inward-Outward Relation-Ship
- Mentor Relationship (OI) of (IO)
- Collegial Relationship (OI)
- Acquaintance Relationships (OI)

SHIP 3: Outward Relation-Ship
- Stranger Relationships (O)

THE DINGHY
- People who are negative and acting against your *Life Vision*
- Get them off your *Relation-Ship*, have them Walk the Plank and move them to your dinghy
- You can move them back to your ship when you decide they will support your *Life Vision*

Chapter 10

OUTWARD LEADER RELATIONSHIP (OI)

This is positional leadership you may have, such as a parent to a child, a teacher to a student, a manager to a staff. You have 100% control of your actions but no control over the other person.

The 3 LEVELS OF OUTWARD RELATIONSHIPS

You do not have *Outward* control over anyone or anything, but you do have influence. The amount of influence depends on the closeness of your relationship. You either have *High, Moderate,* or *Low* to *No Influence.* Here are some examples to illustrate the difference:

1. **High Influence.** Your health, your close family members, friends, and colleagues.
2. **Moderate Influence.** Acquaintances, some laws, some businesses with whom you have dealings.
3. **Low to No Influence.** The rotation of the earth, the sun, moon, galaxy, the weather, natural disasters, the past, or strangers.

The 3 LEADER RELATIONSHIP ACTIONS

1. **Inspire.** To motivate with the heart
2. **Influence.** To reason with the mind
3. **Consequence.** The cause and effect of an action

IO INACTIONS

- *Outward Living*
- By not acting when you should, it can cause an *Outward* effect on others and the world.

OI INACTIONS

- *Outward Living*
- When you don't get the call, invitation, opportunity, response to a question or communication that you sent to someone, or when you get ignored
- You have no control over the *Inactions* toward you, but you have 100% control over how you react to it

Part III—Executing IOU Life Leadership

IOU LIFE LIVING WHEEL

The *IOU Life Living Wheel* embodies and synergizes *The 12 Essential Life Anchors* and is a powerful tool which will help you on your *Life Journey.*

1. *SelfCulture*, based on the *Principle of Self-Identity*
2. *Life Vision*, based on the *Principle of Life Living*
3. *Daily Mission*, based on the *Principle of Intentional Actions*
4. *Life Principles*, based on the *Principle of Life Realities*
5. *Life Values*, based on the *Principle of Life Character*
6. *Life Goals*, based on the *Principle of Life Aspirations*
7. *Inspire IOU Trust*, based on the *Principle of Life Relationships*
8. *Practice Positive Communication*, based on the *Principle of Outward Understanding*
9. *Create Common Language*, based on the *Principle of Outward Effectiveness*
10. *Construct a Cohesive Environment*, based on the *Principle of Outward Connectedness*
11. *Establish Everlasting Traditions* based on the *Principle of Life History*
12. *Model a Mindset of Propelling PH2E*, based on the *Principle of Life Gifts*

Chapter 11

The 6 ESSENTIAL INWARD LIFE ANCHORS

1. **SelfCulture.** It's who you are and the culture that you project to others. It's made up of *Life Anchors* 2-6.
2. **Life Vision.** It's your big picture life destination made up of your *Purpose, Potential, and Passion.*
3. **Daily Mission.** It's your daily actions, the things you do. You should think of who, what, and the *PH2E* byproduct you aim to receive each day.
4. **Life Principles.** They are universal, timeless, natural foundational life laws true in any society. We all have opinions, points of view, perceptions, and beliefs, of *Life Principles* called *Life Maps.* Our *Life Maps* define and guide our *Inward Thoughts* and *Outward Actions* based on how we interpret *Life Principles.*
5. **Life Values.** It's the way you behave *Inwardly and Outwardly.*
6. **Life Goals.** They are your short-term destinations. REBEL Goals is a tool that keeps you on course to your goal. There are three types of goals: Stretch goals, Comfort goals, and Delusional Goals.

The 6 ESSENTIAL INWARD LIFE ANCHORS MODELS

The SelfCulture Model projects who you are and identifies:

- Your *Life Vision*, which is your *Purpose, Potential, and Passion* in life
- Your *Daily Mission*, which guides your daily actions
- Your *Life Principles*, which are your beliefs, opinions, and *Life Map*s
- Your *Life Values*, which are how you behave toward yourself and others
- Your *Life Goals*, which set your daily directions and destination

The Life Vision Model

- The intersection of
    - Your life *Purpose*
    - Your unique talents and *Potential*
    - Your life *Passion*

The Daily Mission Model

- The intersection of
    - Who you want to affect
    - What you will do
    - What byproducts you hope to produce for the other person and yourself

The Life Principle Model

- A representation of your *Life Maps*
- It drives your *Inward Thoughts* and *Outward Actions* toward all things in the world
- The *Life Principle* is a natural law, 100% correct
- *Life Map* is how a person defines and acts on the principle

The Life Values Model

- Represents your *Outward Behavior* and how you treat others when you are in an *Outward Mode*
- *Inwardly* by determining the *Life Values* you want to live by
- *Outwardly* by how you behave as you travel on your *Life Journey*

The Life Goals Model

- A tool for setting meaningful and purposeful goals aligned to your *Life Vision*
- Set goals for *yourself, family, team, and organization*
- Goals should be *Stretch*—you need to reach for them; not *Delusional* (out of reach) or *Comfort* (too easy)

REBEL Goals

Helps you set and meet *Stretch Goals* in five steps.

1. **Rudder** - Set your *Rudder* to your destination or *Life Goal*.
2. **Engine** - The *Engine* is the system that will move you toward your destination.
3. **Buoys** - The *Buoys* are your checkpoints. They will help you with direction and progress toward meeting your goal.
4. **Evaluate** - *Evaluate* your progress and make necessary adjustments.
5. **Lifeline** - Have an accountability partner who can encourage you and give honest feedback to help you complete your goal. Find someone whom you trust to talk with about your challenges and progress.

Chapter 12

THE 6 ESSENTIAL OUTWARD LIFE ANCHORS

1. **Inspire IOU Trust.** It is made up of *Life Anchors* 7-12. *IOU Trust* is when two or more people inspire, influence, and their *Life Principles* are aligned.
2. **Practice Positive Communication.** It occurs when there is *Wholehearted Listening* and *High Tide Safe Talk*.
3. **Create Common Language.** The language that is developed by the group that bonds and defines the culture.
4. **Construct a Cohesive Environment**. Create an environment focusing on the physical aspects aligned to

the vision and promote collaboration and teamwork in a positive manner. The environment feels Safe, Happy, and promotes Learning.

5. **Establish Everlasting Traditions**. The *FTO* promotes celebrations, gatherings, events, and occasions that are fun, team building, and connect to the history of the *FTO*.

6. **Develop a Mindset of Propelling *PH2E***. To have a mindset to continuously improve your *Peacefulness, Happiness, Healthiness, and Excellence*. The mindset is to propel your *PH2E* to the highest level by living *The 12 Essential Life Anchors*.

THE 6 ESSENTIAL OUTWARD LIFE ANCHORS MODELS

The IOU Trust Model

- Represents the highest form of trust that you can share with other people and within groups, teams, and organizations

- When you are experiencing *IOU Trust*, there is a two-way reciprocal *Inspiration, Influence,* and *Alignment of Life Principles*

- You and the others receive *Upward Living,* and one of the *PH2E's* consistently

The Positive Communication Model

- Practice *Wholehearted Listening*—listen with your whole heart and mind, neither agreeing nor disagreeing with what is being said, but rather try to understand from the speaker's point of view. Create a *High Tide Safe Talk Environment*
- When speaking to another person, be aware of the environment you are creating and make it safe for others to communicate their deepest joys and concerns and be vulnerable with you

The Common Language Model

- Emphasizes the idea that everyone in a *family, team, and/ or organization* should share a *Common Language* that builds culture
- Brings a sense of identity that everyone belongs to the same community
- Shorthand unique to the group
- A fun and powerful way to build relationships and efficiency among an entire group

The Cohesive Environment Model

- Emphasizes the physical environment and the relational environment
- Physical environment—what you see and how you feel when you walk around the environment

- Relational environment—the interactions between members of the group
- In a *Dynamic Positive Culture*, you sense a positive interconnectedness between members in the environment from the positive messages displayed and places where groups, lectures, individuals can go to *Outwardly* and *Inwardly* live

The Everlasting Traditions Model

- Reminds us of the importance of maintaining and establishing traditions for our *family, team, and organization*
- Celebrations, gatherings, special events, and occasions tell a story about everyone involved
- Traditions strengthen the bond among everyone, offer comfort and security, and create lasting memories

The Propelling Your *PH2E* Model

- Represents *Upward Living* and the *4 Upward Life Gifts of Peacefulness, Happiness, Healthiness, and Excellence*
- The goal is to propel each of the blades, so your *Life Gifts* are balanced and are continually increasing

THE 5 LEVELS OF TRUST

1. **IOU Trust** - Your closest relationships—The highest form of trust where you *Inspire, Influence,* and have *Alignment on Life Principles.* This person is on your *Inward Life Relation-Ship.*

2. **IO Trust** - Close relationships—A high form of trust where you *Inspire* and *Influence* each other. *Alignment on most Life Principles,* some may be unclear. This person is on your *Inward or IO Relation-Ship.*

3. **Trust** - A relationship where you believe that the other person has high character and high competence. This person is on your *IO Life Relation-Ship.*

4. **Low Trust** - The relationships that you're developing and building. This person is on your *IO or Outward Relation-Ship.*

5. **No Trust** - The relationships that are taking advantage of you, have not kept their commitment to you, are manipulative, are not respectful toward you. This person is on the "Dinghy!"

THE 4 LISTENING STAGES

1. **WholeHearted Listening**—At this level, your whole heart and mind are trying to understand the other person. You neither agree nor disagree with what is being said, but rather try to understand from the speaker's point of view.

2. **HalfHearted Listening**—Instead of deep listening, you are evaluating, judging, and drawing conclusions in your mind based on what the person is saying.

3. **Reply Listening**—This is when you are listening to a reply.

4. **Distracted Listening**—You are only pretending to listen while thinking of something unrelated to what the other person is saying.

THE 2 LEVELS OF OUTWARD TALK

1. **High Tide Safe Talk**—It occurs when you create an *IOU Trust* environment where the other person feels safe to communicate their deepest joys and concerns.

2. **Low Tide Unsafe Talk**—It is when you create an environment where the other person feels unsafe and shares minimal information and feelings. This occurs when your speaking is negative, unsafe, and/or judgmental.

Part IV—The Benefits of IOU Life Leadership

Chapter 13

THE IOU 90-SECOND SECRET

- A powerful tool that will help you break the cycle of negative emotions, including anger, frustration, and annoyance
- It can help you move from *IOW* and *IOD Living* to *IOU Living*, closer to the *Upward Life Gifts of the PH2E*
- The secret is that the negative emotions dissipate on their own within about 90 seconds
- When you or someone with whom you are interacting is faced with these kinds of emotions, build in a pause, give yourself 90 seconds before reacting
- You will feel the negative emotions lessen and leave, and the peacefulness return so that you can return to productivity

PH2E MINDFUL VISUALIZATION AND THE PH2E CHALLENGE

- Realign your *Life Journey*
- Set aside a regular time to practice *PH2E Mindful Visualization* for each of the *Upward Life Gifts*

- A technique to help you picture moments when you have realized the highest levels of *Peacefulness, Happiness, Healthiness, and Excellence*
- Helps to give energy, focus, and clarity

Chapter 14

INWARD OUTWARD UPWARD (IOU) LOVE

- Loving relationships should include mutual *PH2E*
- Love is the ultimate *Outward Living*

INWARD MIRROR TEST

- A tool to help you to *Inwardly* scrutinize what you're about to do before you do it
- Imagine yourself looking into a mirror before you act
- Give yourself one last opportunity to make sure your actions are the "right thing to do"
- Use the *Life Map* Cycle as a tool to clarify your actions

Chapter 15

LIFE GUIDING HANDLE

- A symbolic representation of your foundational *Life Anchors - Inward Anchor 1 SelfCulture* and *Outward Anchor 7 Inspire IOU Trust*
- On a real captain's wheel, there is one handle that is textured so that in the dark or a storm, the captain can feel for the guiding handle and move the rudder straight in line with the hull to navigate the ship safely
- When you are faced with adversity or a major decision, find your *Life Guiding Handle* and use your *SelfCulture* and *IOU Trust* to help guide and get you back on track to your *Life Journey*

TRIM TAB LEADER

- A trim tab is a tiny piece of metal that turns all ships, even large ones, suggesting that you can do more with less
- Small turns or changes can create big results
- Start with yourself and focus on your *Inward Thinking* and *Outward Actions*
- The small things within us that we can change may have a major influence on others and a much larger effect on society

IOU Definitions

What is IOU Life Leadership?—Chapter 1

A foundational framework for intentional *Inward* and *Outward Living* based on timeless, universal principles leading to a *Dynamic Positive Culture* that embodies the *Upward Living Life Gifts of Peacefulness, Happiness, Healthiness, and Excellence (PH2E)*. In short, it is a foundational framework for intentional living based on timeless, universal principles leading to *Peacefulness, Happiness, Healthiness, and Excellence (PH2E)*.

1. Life Leadership is the Vision—*Living Inwardly* and *Outwardly* in a *positive and effective* intentional manner, to receive *Upward Living* and the *Life Gifts of Peacefulness, Happiness, Healthiness, and Excellence (PH2E)*, which will assist you in navigating toward a *Dynamic Positive Culture* for *yourself, family, team, and organization*.

2. IOU Living is your Daily Mission—Intentional awareness of one's *Inward* and *Outward Living*, designing a life plan using *The 12 Essential Life Anchors* leading to *Upward Living* embodying *Peacefulness, Happiness, Healthiness, and Excellence (PH2E)*, which will assist you in navigating toward a *Dynamic Positive Culture* for *yourself, family, team, and/or organization*.

3. Life Anchors are the Principles—Solid, grounded, immovable, and timeless, universal *Life Principles* that are included in all *positive and effective* life plans for intentional living.

What does IOU stand for?—Chapter 1

IOU stands for *Inward, Outward, Upward,* which refers to the three states of living. At any given moment, you are either living *Inwardly* (interacting only with yourself) or *Outwardly* (interacting with others or with the environment). *Upward Living* occurs when you enjoy the *Life Gifts of PH2E* based on your *positive and effective* intentional *Inward* and *Outward Living.*

What is an IOU Life Coach?—Chapter 1

An *IOU Life Coach* is <u>YOU!</u> It's how you help yourself on your journey to *Life Leadership.* As a Life Coach, you have all the capabilities for assessing your current levels of *PH2E* and formulating a plan for intentional *positive and effective* life living.

What is the Life Leadership Age?—Chapter 1

The *Life Leadership Age* is the current time we are living in when everyone is called to be a leader in their actions and behaviors. In this age, leadership is no longer defined by position, but by intentional actions and behaviors and how each person lives their life by design.

What is a Life Plan?—Chapter 1

A *Life Plan* is a framework for intentional living. It includes a deep reflection of the *6 Essential Inward Life Anchors* - one's *SelfCulture, Life Vision, Daily Mission, Life Principles, Life Values, and Life Goals.*

What do you have 100% control over?—Chapter 1

You have 100% control over your *Inward Thinking* and your *Outward Actions.*

What does it mean to be a Life Leader?— Chapters 1 & 15

A *Life Leader* is a person who lives a *positive and effective Inward* and *Outward Life* resulting in *Upward Living* and receiving the highest levels of *PH2E*. *IOU Life Leadership* leads to a *Dynamic Positive Culture* for *self, family, team, and organization.*

What does it mean to live a life by design?— Chapter 2

To live a life by design means to live intentionally through *Inward* and *Outward Living* of *The 12 Life Anchors*, designing a *Life Plan*, ultimately leading to the highest levels of *PH2E*. Living a life by design keeps you on course toward your destination (goal).

What is a Dynamic Positive Culture?— Chapters 2 & 5

A *Dynamic Positive Culture* is one of the results of intentional *positive and effective Inward and Outward Life Living*. When you achieve a *Dynamic Positive Culture* for *yourself, family, team, and organization*, you are living your *Life Plan* by design. You will be on course toward your *Life Vision*, living out your *Daily Mission* and moving closer to achieving your *Life Goals*. Everyone will experience high levels of *Peacefulness, Happiness, Healthiness, and Excellence*. When you are immersed in a *Dynamic Positive Culture*, there is high trust, and all stakeholders' actions are heading in the same direction in a safe, enjoyable, and effective manner. The culture is guided by the universal principles of *The 12 Essential Life Anchors*, where everyone has a *Mindset of Propelling* their *PH2E*.

What is the Life Leadership Matrix?—Chapter 2

The *Life Leadership Matrix* is a systems thinking tool that divides tasks into four different quadrants based on two dimensions. Tasks are ether "Important" or "Not Important." You can be either "On Course" to your destination or "Off-course" away from your destination. Similarly, tasks are either "Urgent and Stressful" or "Not Urgent and Peaceful." This results in four unique quadrants or environments. The goal is to spend your time in *Environment 2 (E2)*—"Not Urgent and Important", "On Course" activities to achieve your highest level of intentional life living.

What does it mean to be living life by default?— Chapter 2

It means living the same day after day. You may want to improve and try something new, but you don't persist and return to the same behaviors that you have always been doing.

What is a Hidden Outward Living Dimension?— Chapter 2

This includes nonverbal communication, such as facial expressions, body language, tone, and physical movements.

What are psychological biases?—Chapter 3

These are biases that may distort your *Life Maps*, and that may have developed over your whole life from experiences and interactions with others.

What is *PH2E*?—Chapter 4

PH2E stands for *Peacefulness, Happiness, Healthiness, and Excellence.* These are the *Upward Living Life Gifts*, which are the desirable byproducts of *positive and effective Inward* and *Outward Living.*

What does "How's your Propeller" mean?— Chapter 4

"How's Your Propeller" refers to the results of the *PH2E* Assessment. Are you aware of your current levels of *Peacefulness, Happiness, Healthiness, and Excellence*? Are they high on the 0-100% scale? Are they balanced (at similar levels)? Knowing how your propeller is will help you know which area(s) to concentrate on in your growth efforts.

Why assess your *PH2E* Propeller?—Chapter 4

We should assess our *PH2E* Propeller to think about and determine the levels of our *Peacefulness, Happiness, Healthiness, and Excellence* so we can then begin to balance and then enlarge our *PH2E* Propellers.

What does it mean to balance your *PH2E* Propeller?—Chapter 4

After assessing your *PH2E* levels, it means increasing your lowest *Life Gifts*, so all of your gifts are at the same level or balanced. Each *Life Gift* of our *PH2E* is represented by a blade on a four-blade propeller.

What is the *PH2E* Challenge?—Chapter 4

The *PH2E Challenge* is a weekly challenge that will assist you in achieving the highest level of your *PH2E*.

What is the *PH2E* Assessment?—Chapter 4

It's a self-assessment that will show you your self-reported current levels of *Peacefulness, Happiness, Healthiness, and Excellence*. To take the assessment, go to www.PH2E.com

What is a Culture?—Chapter 5

A culture is the aura or feeling one gets when in the presence of a person or an organized group of people. It is unspoken and symbolic communication that is felt instantly without thinking or analyzing the specifics of the environment.

What is SelfCulture?—Chapter 5 & 11

SelfCulture is your personal culture, which is the feeling people get when in your presence. Perhaps you have never reflected on your *SelfCulture*, but reflecting on it provides an opportunity to define how you want to be and how you want to be perceived by others. It's your personal brand and the lifestyle you live by design. It is who you are in every way—your authentic self! *SelfCulture* focuses on the *Principle of Self-Identity*; it's your *Inward Being*, who you are at the deepest level. If you don't create your *SelfCulture*, the *Outward World* will create it for you. Your *SelfCulture* can either bring others toward you or drive them away from you.

What are the 4 Life Cultures?—Chapter 5

The *4 Life Cultures* are *SelfCulture, Family Culture, Team Culture*, and *Organization Culture*. These cultures are defined by the *IO Living* of a member or members within the group. Everyone has a *SelfCulture*, which is based on one's *IO Living*. The *4 Life Cultures* encompass the four important groups that a person can be part of in life.

What is the IO Living Culture Continuum?—Chapter 6

The *IO Living Culture Continuum* displays the byproducts of your *Inward* and *Outward Living*. If you are living a *positive and effective* life based on *The 12 Essential Life Anchors*, then you are *Upward Living* and will receive the *Life Gifts of Peacefulness*,

Happiness, Healthiness, and Excellence. If you are not living by design, but just drifting, then you are *Wayward Living* and will receive *Life Impassivities of Apathy, Indifference, Unfitness, and Mediocrity.* If you are living off-course in a downward spiral, then you are *Downward Living* and will receive the *Life Drains* of *Anxiety, Unhappiness, Unhealthiness, and Ineffectiveness.*

What are the 3 Life Preserving Dimensions?— Chapter 6

You can depend on each of the *3 Life Preserving Dimensions* to help you when you experience difficulty. Specifically, you can look to your *Inward Self,* to your trusted *Outward Others,* or to your *IO Spiritual* supports when faced with a difficult situation. Any of these dimensions will support you when you encounter difficulty on your journey. They can reverse the course of downward draining of your *PH2E* and move you in a better direction to receive *Upward Life Gifts.*

What is Inward Living?—Chapters 7 & 8

Inward Living is the state when you are thinking and not interacting with anyone else. You are focused on your thoughts, your purpose, *Life Maps,* and passion. It is your total *Inward Being.*

What does "Examine Your *I*'s" mean?—Chapter 8

It's thinking, and examining your *Inward Being, Inward Anchors,* and *Inward Living.*

What is Outward Living?—Chapters 9 & 10

Outward Living is when you are interacting with a person, groups of people, or the world. You are *Outward Living* as soon as you speak to someone, send an email, or perform any action that can affect a person or the world.

What are the 3 Life Relation-Ships?—Chapter 9

The *3 Life Relation-Ships* are a tool for understanding the different relationships that we encounter in our lives. Closest to us are the people on our *Inward Relation-Ship*. These are our relations with self, family, friends, and spirituality. The second ship is our *IO Life Relation-Ship*, which encompasses our colleagues, mentors, and acquaintances. Finally, our most distant ship is our *Outward Life Relation-Ship*, which includes strangers and those individuals you may see, briefly interact with, walk by, but do not know.

Who's on your Dinghy?—Chapter 9

These are the people that may be negative and working against your *Life Vision*. They need to get off your ship. Ask them to walk the plank and move them to the dinghy. The dinghy is a small boat next to your ship, which is a holding place until you decide they will support your *Life Vision* and *Life Journey*. At that point, you move them back onto your ship.

What does "Examine your *O's*" mean?—Chapter 10

It means to examine your *Outward Actions*, *Outward Anchors*, and *Outward Living*.

What is a Life Anchor?—Chapters 11 &12

Life Anchors are solid, grounded, and immovable, timeless, universal *Life Principles* included in all effective *Life Plans* for intentional living.

Why Life Anchors?—Chapters 11 & 12

Anchors are strong and stable, whether or not you have sea legs. The anchor is a symbol of security, stability, and being grounded—a symbol of steadfastness. The raising of the anchor on a ship is a metaphor for leaving port and living *Outwardly*.

We may be leaving one phase of our life to begin a new *Life Journey* heading to our next port-of-call. When you reach your destination, you drop your anchor. When the anchor locks into the ocean floor, you become moored to that location. This is a good time to think *Inwardly*. You are secured and stabilized from the elements of the waves, tides, and storms as you think *Inwardly* and plan for your next journey.

Take time to reflect on the things that are anchors in your life. Are they a person, a place, a thing? Do you intentionally choose for them to anchor you? *The 12 Essential Life Anchors* are foundational principles for intentional living that can help navigate your *Life Journey*.

What is Upward Living?—Chapter 13

Upward Living refers to when you are receiving the *Life Gifts of Peacefulness, Happiness, Healthiness, and Excellence* based on living *Inwardly* and *Outwardly* in a *positive and effective* intentional manner. *Upward Living* cannot be sought out in its own right but instead can only come to you based on your *IO Living*.

What is a Life Changer?—Chapter 15

A *Life Changer* is a person who can make significant positive contributions to society and the world by focusing *Inwardly* and acting *Outwardly*. A *Life Changer* focuses on *Propelling one's PH2E* each day, making small positive changes within and without, based on universal principles. As the captain thinks and then turns the captain's wheel, moving only a very small trim tab on a rudder, which, in turn, slowly changes the course of an enormous ship, we must focus *Inwardly* on the small things within us that we can change. Then we make changes we can *Outwardly* control that may ultimately have a major positive impact on the *Outward World*.

What is a Trim Tab Life Leader?—Chapter 15

A trim tab is a tiny piece of metal gently turning at the edge of a ship's rudder. When this miniature trim tab is moved, ships, even large ones, are turned, suggesting that you can do more with less. Small turns or changes can create big results. Relating this to *IOU Living*, we must start with ourselves and first focus on our *Inward Thinking* and *Outward Actions*, which we have the power to change. A *Trim Tab Leader* focuses on the small things within us that may have a major influence on others and may have a much larger effect on society.

References and Further Reading

Chapter 1

HR4.0: Shaping People Strategies in the Fourth Industrial Revolution. World Economic Forum, December 2019. https://michaelserwa.com/ Accessed December 5, 2019.

Covey, S.R. (1989). *The 7 habits of highly effective people.* London, United Kingdom: Simon & Schuster.

Frankl, V.E. (2006). *Man's search for meaning: An introduction to logotherapy.* Boston, MA: Beacon Press.

Hatfield, E., Cacioppo, J. T. & Rapson, R. L. (1992). Primitive emotional contagion. In M. S. Clark (Ed.), *Review of personality and social psychology,* Vol. 14: Emotion and social behavior (p. 151–177). Sage Publications, Inc.

Chapter 2

Warrell, M. (2017). *The hidden cost of operating on auto pilot.* Forbes. https://www.forbes.com/sites/margiewarrell/2017/06/15/living-on-autopilot-why-your-default-mode-is-derailing-your-decisions-and-how-to-stop-it/?sh=4baa0e8f0e45 Accessed January 13, 2020.

Massey, R. (2015). *Why do more than 800,000 people a year run out of fuel despite the Warning light coming on? (and why are most of them men?).* Daily Mail. https://www.dailymail.co.uk/news/article-3212222/More-800-000-drivers-year-run-fuel.html Accessed March 4, 2020.

Bloom, Noelle. (2018). *10 signs you're living on autopilot.* Success Magazine, March 28, 2018. https://www.success.com/10-signs-youre-living-on-autopilot/ Accessed December 20, 2019.

Cherry, Kendra. (2019). *How many neurons are in the brain?* Very Well Mind. https://www.verywellmind.com/how-many-neurons-are-in-the-brain-2794889 Accessed December 20, 2019.

What is the Eisenhower matrix? How to use it to be more productive. (n.d.). https://www.ntaskmanager.com/blog/eisenhower-matrix/ Accessed December 20, 2019.

Hannam, P. & Shelby, J. (2006). *Take charge of your mind: Core skills to enhance your performance, well-being, and integrity at work.* Charlottesville, VA: Hampton Roads Publishing.

Mehrabian, A. Some referents and measures of nonverbal behavior. *Behav. Res. Meth. & Instru.* (1968) 1: 203. https://doi.org/10.3758/BF03208096.

Brugoon, J.K., Guerrero, L.K. & Floyd, K. (2010). *Nonverbal communication.* Boston, MA: Allyn & Bacon.

Are facial expressions universal? (n.d.). *Paul Ekman Group.* https://www.paulekman.com/resources/universal-facial-expressions/ Accessed December 30, 2019.

Hatfield, E., Rapson, R. L. & Le, Y.-C. L. (2009). Emotional contagion and empathy. In J. Decety & W. Ickes (Eds.), *Social neuroscience. The social neuroscience of empathy* (p. 19–30). MIT Press. https://doi.org/10.7551/mitpress/9780262012973.003.0003

Sustained enjoyment of life and mortality at older ages: analysis of the English Longitudinal Study of Ageing. BMJ 2016;355: i6267 (Published December 13, 2016). Accessed December 30, 2019.

Ohio State University. (n.d.). Body posture affects confidence in your own thoughts, study finds. *ScienceDaily*. <www.sciencedaily.com/releases/2009/10/0910051 Accessed July 12, 2020.

Hall, E.T. (1966). *The hidden dimension*. Garden City, NY: Doubleday. https://westsidetoastmasters.com/resources/book_of_body_language/chap6.html) Accessed February 12, 2020.

Trager, G. (1961). The typology of paralanguage. *Anthropological Linguistics, 3*(1), 17-21. Retrieved from www.jstor.org/stable/30022290

Reiman, T. (2008). *The power of body language: How to succeed in every business and social encounter*. New York, NY: Pocket Books.

Babauta, L. (2016). *Focus: A simplicity manifesto in the age of distraction*. Danville, IL: Founders House Publishing.

Razzetti., G. (n.d.). *How to stop living life on autopilot. It's time to turn it off*. Psychology Today. https://www.psychologytoday.com/us/blog/the-adaptive-mind/201811/how-stop-living-life-autopilot Accessed January 15, 2020.

Chapter 3

Tversky, A. & Kahneman, D. (1974). Judgment under uncertainty: Heuristics and biases, *Science*, 185, 1124-1131.

Slocum, J., Fogarty, T. & Varian, G. (1969). *Sailing alone around the world*. New York, NY: Dover Publications.

Wason, P. C. (1960). On the failure to eliminate hypotheses in a conceptual task. *Quarterly Journal of Experimental Psychology*, 12, 129-140.

Felt, H. (2013). *Soundings: The story of the remarkable woman who mapped the ocean floor.* New York, NY: Picador.

Korzybski, A. & Pula, R.P. (2005). *Science and sanity: An introduction to non-Aristotelian systems and general semantics.* Forest Hills, NY: Institute of General Semantics.

Chapter 4

Spanish Flu: The deadliest pandemic in history, (n.d.). *Live Science,* https://www.livescience.com/spanish-flu.html Accessed August 14, 2020.

Brickman, P. & Campbell, D. T. (1971). Hedonic relativism and planning the good society. In N. H. Apply (Ed.), *Adaptation-level theory* (pp. 287-305). New York: Academic Press.

Pennock. S.F. (n.d.). *The hedonic treadmill – Are we forever chasing rainbows?*

Positive Psychology._https://positivepsychology.com/hedonic treadmill/ Accessed April 20, 2020.

Seneca. (2018). *On the happy life.* Stewart, A. Trans. London, United Kingdom: Vigeo Press.

Prusak, L. (2010). *What can't be measured.* Harvard Business Review. https://hbr.org/2010/10/what-cant-be-measured Accessed December 30, 2019.

Lavinsky, D. (n.d.). *The two most important quotes in business.* Growthink. https://.www.growthink.com/content/two-most-important-quotes-business Accessed November 20, 2020.

Martin, K.L. (2019). Medscape Physician Lifestyle & Happiness Report 2019. https://www.medscape.com/slideshow/2019-lifestyle-happiness-6011057 Accessed December 30, 2019.

Brickman, P., Coates, D. & Janoff-Bulman, R. (1978). Lottery winners and accident victims: Is happiness relative? *Journal of Personality and Social Psychology,* 36(8), 917–927. https://doi.org/10.1037/0022-3514.36.8.917

Chapter 5

Gendlin, E.T. (1982). *Focusing.* New York, NY: Bantam Books.

Gendlin, E.T. (1997). *Experiencing and the creation of meaning: A philosophical and psychological approach to the subjective.* Evanston, IL: Northwestern University Press.

Lansing, A. (2015). *Endurance: Shackleton's incredible voyage.* Basic Books.

Schien, E.H. (2017). *Organizational culture and leadership – fifth edition.* Hoboken, New Jersay: Wiley.

Spencer-Oatey, H. (n.d.). *What is culture?* Global People. https://warwick.ac.uk/fac/cross_fac/globalpeople2/knowledgeexchange/gp_cc_what_is_culture_final_181204.pdf Accessed November 23, 2019.

Chapter 6

Fredrickson, B.L. (n.d.). *Leading with positive emotions.* Center for Positive Organizations. https://positiveorgs.bus.umich.edu/wp-content/uploads/CPOSweb-TryingTimes-Fredrickson-PositiveEmotions.pdf Accessed December 31, 2019.

Fredrickson B. L. (2001). The role of positive emotions in positive psychology. The broaden-and-build theory of positive emotions. *The American Psychologist,* 56(3), 218–226. doi:10.1037//0003-066x.56.3.218

Horowitz, A. (2011). *15 people who got fired before they became filthy rich.* Business Insider. https://www.businessinsider.

com/15-people-who-were-fired-before-they-became-filthy-rich-2011-4 Accessed December 20, 2019.

Dyer, F.L. & Martin, T.C. (1910). *Edison: His life and inventions.* New York, NY: Harper & Brothers.

Chapter 7

How many thoughts do we have per minute? (n.d.). *Reference.* https://www.reference.com/world-view/many-thoughts-per-minute-cb7fcf22ebbf8466 Accessed December 23, 2019.

Pescitelli, D. *An analysis of Carl Rogers' theory of personality.* Retrieved from: http://pandc.ca/?cat=carl_rogers&page=rogerian_theory Accessed December 31, 2019.

Crisp, R.J. & Turner, R.N. (2014). *Essential social psychology.* Los Angeles, CA : Sage Publishing.

Korzybski, A. & Pula, R.P. (2005). *Science and sanity: An introduction to non-Aristotelian systems and general semantics.* Forest Hills, NY: Institute of General Semantics.

Rogers, C.R. (1962). Toward becoming a fully functioning person. in Freidberg, H.J. (Ed.) *Perceiving, behaving, becoming: A new focus for education.* http://www.ascd.org/publications/books/199031/chapters/Toward-Becoming-a-Fully-Functioning-Person.aspx Accessed January 15, 2020.

Olsen. A. (2013). *The theory of self-actualization: Mental illness, creativity, and art.* Psychology Today. https://www.psychologytoday.com/us/blog/theory-and-psychopathology/201308/the-theory-self-actualization Accessed January 15, 2020.

Chapter 8

Leaf, C. (2013). *Switch on your brain: The key to peak happiness, thinking, and health.* Grand Rapids, MI: Baker Books.

Ackerman, C. (n.d.). *What is neuroplasticity? A psychologist explains.* Positive Psychology. https://positivepsychology. com/neuroplasticity/ Accessed December 31, 2019.

How mindfulness can change your brain and improve your health. (n.d.). *Harvard Health.* https://hms.harvard.edu/sites/ default/files/assets/Harvard%20Now%20and%20Zen%20 Reading%20Materials.pdf. Accessed December 10, 2019.

Types of meditation—an overview of 23 meditation techniques. (n.d.). *Live & Dare.* https://liveanddare.com/types-of- meditation/#4_CHRISTIAN_MEDITATION Accessed December 31, 2019.

In praise of gratitude. (n.d.). *Harvard Health Publishing.* https:// www.health.harvard.edu/mind-and-mood/in-praise-of- gratitude Accessed December 10, 2019.

Emmons, R. A. & McCullough, M. E. (2003). Counting blessings versus burdens: an experimental investigation of gratitude and subjective well-being in daily life. *Journal of Personality and Social Psychology, 84*(2), 377-389.

Joseph, S. (2012). *Unconditional positive regard: If you think it's about smiling and nodding, you are doing it wrong.* Psychology Today. https://www.psychologytoday.com/us/blog/what- doesnt-kill-us/201210/unconditional-positive-regard Accessed December 27, 2019.

Crash landing on the moon. (n.d.). *NASA Science.* https:// science.nasa.gov/science-news/science-at-nasa/2006/28jul_ crashlanding Accessed December 27, 2019.

Chapter 9

Feltman, C., Hammond, S.A., Hammond, R., Marshall, A. & Bendis, K. (2009). *The thin book of trust: An essential primer for building trust at work.* Bend, OR: Thin Book Publishing.

Bryk, A.S. & Schneider, B. (2004). *Trust in schools: A core resource for improvement.* New York, NY: Russell Sage Foundation.

Maxwell, J. (2015). *Culture vs. vision; is it really either-or?* John Maxwell. https://www.johnmaxwell.com/blog/culture-vs-vision-is-it-really-either-or/ Accessed January 2, 2020.

Covey, S.M.R. (2008). *The SPEED of trust: The one thing that changes everything.* New York, NY: Free Press.

Chapter 10

Brown, B. (2018). *Dare to lead: Brave work. Tough conversations. Whole hearts.* New York: NY: Random House.

Bryk, A.S. & Schneider, B. (2004). *Trust in schools: A core resource for improvement.* New York, NY: Russell Sage Foundation.

Chapter 11

Pike, K. L. (1954). *Language in relation to a unified theory of the structure of human behavior.* Glendale, CA: Summer Institute of Linguistics.

Covey, S.R. (1989). *The 7 habits of highly effective people.* London, United Kingdom: Simon & Schuster.

Woodenisms.(n.d.) *The Wooden Effect.* https://www.thewoodeneffect.com/motivational-quotes/ Accessed December 30, 2019.

Vygotsky, L.S. (2012). *Thought and language.* Cambridge, MA: The MIT Press.

Dyer, F.L. & Martin, T.C. (1910). *Edison: His life and inventions.* New York, NY: Harper & Brothers.

Seligman, M. E. P. (2012). *Flourish: A visionary new understanding of happiness and well-being.* New York, NY: Free Press.

McChesney, C., Covey, S., & Huling, J. (2016). *The 4 disciplines of execution: Achieving your wildly important goals.* New York, NY: Free Press.

Yale Law School. (2008). I have a dream by Martin Luther King, Jr; August 28, 1963 [Speech transcript]. https://avalon.law.yale.edu/20th_century/mlk01.asp Accessed September 15, 2020.

Gilruth, R. (n.d.). *I believe we should go to the moon.* NASA History Division. https://history.nasa.gov/SP-350/ch-2-1.html#:~:text=Speaking%20to%20Congress%20and%20the,returning%20him%20safely%20to%20Earth. Accessed November 17, 2020.

Chapter 12

Adande, J.A. (2010) *Life lessons learned from Wooden.* ESPN. https://www.espn.com/los-angeles/ncb/columns/story?id=5255041 Accessed December 31, 2019.

Johnson, K. (2020). *Reaching for the moon: The autobiography of NASA mathematician Katherine Johnson.* New York, NY: Atheneum Books for Young Readers.

Shetterly, M.L. (2016). *Hidden Figures.* New York, NY: William Morrow.

Covey, S.M.R. (2008). *The SPEED of trust: The one thing that changes everything.* New York, NY: Free Press.

Prayers for Peace. (n.d.). *General Order of Franciscan Missionaries*. https://franciscanmissionassoc.org/prayers_for_peace/?gclid =EAIaIQobChMIlpCgiuDf5gIVhcDACh0UBgpgEAAYAS AAEgLTMvD_BwE. Accessed December 31, 2019.

Begley, S. (2007, January 19). The Brain: How the brain rewires itself. *Time Magazine*. http://content.time.com/time/ magazine/article/0,9171,1580438,00.html Accessed May 23, 2020.

Covey, S.R. (1989). *The 7 habits of highly effective people*. London, United Kingdom: Simon & Schuster.

Rogers, W.R. & Carter, J.H. (1991). *Never met a man I didn't like: The life and writings of Will Rogers*. New York, NY: William Morrow.

Brown, B. (2018). *Dare to lead: Brave work. Tough conversations. Whole hearts*. New York: NY: Random House.

Nautical Language. (n.d.). *See the Sea*. https://see-the-sea. org/nautical/naut-body.htm#:~:text=Now%20the%20 expression%20or%20its,positions%20and%20prepare%20 for%20action. Accessed November 17, 2020.

Bolton, R. & Bolton, D.G. (2018). *Listen up or lose out: How to avoid miscommunication, improve relationships, and get more done faster*. New York, NY: Amacom.

Senge, P. (2006). *The fifth discipline: The art & practice of the learning organization*. New York, NY: Doubleday.

Argyris, C. (1970). *Intervention theory and method: A behavioral science view*. Boston, MA: Addison-Wesley.

Thornberg, D. (2013). *From the campfire to the holodeck: Creating engaging and powerful 21st-century learning environments*. San Francisco, CA: Jossey-Bass.

Stein, J. (1964). *Fiddler on the roof.* New York, NY: Crown Publishers.

Lyubomirsky, S. (2008). *The how of happiness: A scientific approach to getting the life you want.* New York, NY: Penguin Press.

Cramer, K.D. & Wasiak, H. (2008). *Change the way you see yourself through asset-based thinking.* Philadelphia, PA: Running Press.

The happiness-health connection. (n.d.). *Heartbeat.* https://www.health.harvard.edu/healthbeat/ the-happiness-health-connection Accessed January 9, 2020.

Chapter 13

Churchill, W.S. (1932). *Amid these storms.* New York, NY: Charles Scribner.

Lyubomirsky, S., Sheldon, K. M, & Schkade, D. (2005). Pursuing happiness: The architecture of sustainable change. *Review of General Psychology, 9*(2), 111-131. Retrieved from https:// escholarship.org/uc/item/4v03h9gv

Pascual-L.A., Nguyet D, Cohen LG, Brasil-Neto JP, Cammarota A, Hallett M. (1995).

Modulation of muscle responses evoked by transcranial magnetic stimulation during the acquisition of new fine motor skills. *Journal of Neurophysiology,* 1995 Sep; 74(3):1037-45.

Franklin, B. (2020). *Autobiography of Benjamin Franklin.* CreateSpace Independent Publishing Platform.

Diener, E. & Seligman, M. E. P. (2002). Very happy people. *Psychological Science, 13*(1), 81–84. https://doi. org/10.1111/1467-9280.00415

Diener, E. & Seligman, M. E. P. (2004). Beyond money: Toward an economy of well-being. *Psychological Science in the Public Interest, 5*(1), 1–31. Pehttps://doi.org/10.1111/j.0963-7214.2004.00501001.x

Sanders, S. (2019). *10 life lessons learnt from meditating every day for 30 days.* Thrive Global. https://thriveglobal.com/stories/10-life-lessons-learnt-from-meditating-everyday-for-30-days/ Accessed December 30, 2019.

Rhoades, W. (1938). *The self you have to live with.* Philadelphia, PA: J.P. Lippincott Company.

Taylor, J.B. (2009). *My stroke of insight: A brain scientist's personal journey.* New York, NY: Penguin Books.

Seigel, D.J. (2015). *Brainstorm: The power and purpose of the teenage brain.* New York, NY: TarcherPerigee.

Siegel, D. (2018). *Aware: The science and practice of presence— The groundbreaking meditation practice.* New York, NY: TarcherPerigee.

Baldwin, E.B. (1896). The search for the North Pole. *Electrical Review.* p. 520.

Martinuzzi. B. (2010). *The 90-second pause.* American Express. https://www.americanexpress.com/en-us/business/trends-and-insights/articles/the-90-second-pause-1/ Accessed January 20, 2020.

Chapter 14

Snyder, M. (2019) *Strategy points from the Hoosier Tournament of Roses.* Inside Indiana Business. https://www.insideindianabusiness.com/story/41477031/strategy-points-from-the-hoosier-tournament-of-roses Accessed November 1, 2020.

Nyad, D. (2016). *Find a way: The inspiring story of one woman's pursuit of a lifelong dream.* New York, NY: Vintage Books.

Chapter 15

Hilton, W. (2010). *Technique of success.* Whitefish, MT: Kessinger Publishing.

Kethledge, R.M & Erwin, M.S. (2018). *Lead yourself first. Inspiring leadership through solitude.* Bloomsbury Publishing.

Thoreau, H.D. (2018). *Walden.* CreateSpace Independent Publishing Platform.

Memory improved 20% by nature walk. (n.d.). https://www.spring.org.uk/2009/01/memory-improved-20-by-nature-walk.php Accessed December 30, 2019.

Forest bathing is great for your health. Here's how to do it.(n.d.). *Time.* https://time.com/5259602/japanese-forest-bathing/ Accessed December 30, 2019.

Katherine Johnson: American Mathematician. (n.d.). *Brittanica.* https://www.britannica.com/biography/Katherine-Johnson-mathematician Accessed December 31, 2019.

Kethledge, R.M. & Erwin, M.S. (2018). *Lead yourself first: Inspiring leadership through solitude.* London, England: Bloomsbury Publishing.

Berman, M. G., Jonides, J. & Kaplan, S. (2008). The cognitive benefits of interacting with nature. *Psychological Science, 19*(12), 1207–1212. https://doi.org/10.1111/j.1467-9280.2008.02225.x

Thinking like a trim tab. (2014). *Buckminster Fuller Institute.* https://www.bfi.org/dymaxionforum/2014/09/thinking-trimtab Accessed January 9, 2020

Acknowledgments

The journey of writing this book was extremely rewarding and would not have been possible without the many inspiring, influential, positive leaders in my life.

In researching for this book, it became even more evident to me that the world is a better place thanks to the people who inspire, influence, and lead others in a *positive and effective* way. What makes it even better are the people who share their valuable time to *Listen Wholeheartedly* to understand others' *Inward* thoughts and feelings, and then *Outwardly* support them in any way they can. I've been fortunate to have so many people like this in my life that have *Propelled my PH2E*. Therefore, I want to thank the following people for inspiring me:

- My wife Ann, my children Amanda Rose, Emma Ann, and Eric Bartolo, who are my "Life Anchors."
- My "Life Leaders," Grandpa Vincent Famularo, Dad Bartolo Famularo, and Mom Rose Famularo.
- Vinny and Donna, Tony and Sue, Pete and Karen, George and Christi, and my nieces, nephews, and extended family, who I know are always there for me whether it's stormy or clear sailing.
- My Board leaders, Janet Goller, Jay Breakstone, Marion Blane, Brian Desmond, and MaryAnn Kelly who make sure all decisions are aligned to our Vision and Mission.

- Dr. Joanne Dacek, who is an inspiring principled centered Life Leader.

- The Leadership Team of Robin Lufrano, Joe Fiorino, Elise Cahill, Sally Curto, Patrice Matthews, Patti Castine, and Kerriann Sanpietro who are the epitome of synergy and are focused on a shared Vision and Mission.

- My administrative assistants Randy Yee and Mary Giorgio, who keep our organization and my *Life Ship* on course.

- The Star teachers and non-instructional staff inspiring our students to lead and learn every day.

- The Star parent leaders, who continually provide support for our staff and children.

- The Star students, who are rising, winning, and shining leaders.

- To the great inspiring family, friends, teachers, and spiritual leaders, who have positively affected my life— Monsignor Frank Caldwell, Dom Famularo, Pat Keegan, Gary McGuey, Ray O'Keefe, Hank Sessa, Dr. Reynolds Holt, Dr. Barry McNamara, Dr. George Cavuto, Dr. Robert Manley, Dr. William Johnson, and Joe Carbone.

- My nature team leaders, Brent Shaum and Tom Hakiel, who lead and promote the love and care of the *Outward* natural world every day.

- To the many other colleagues and friends who have sailed with me on my *Life Journey*.

- Kary Oberbrunner and the Author Academy Elite publishing staff for their constant research, knowledge, and support in safely steering this book to its final port.

- The inspiring principle-centered work of Dr. Stephen R. Covey.
- Amnon Tishler from Booklovers Paradise for finding and researching key material for this book.
- The Sea Crest/Main Street Diner staff, especially Diane, Jaunita, Marcella, Silvia, and Jenny for reserving my corner booth, letting me sit for hours, encouraging me, and keeping my coffee cup full as I wrote this book.

The voyage of writing this book contains a piece of each and every one of the *Life Leaders* named above. They make up my "*Life Map*" of the world. *I Wholeheartedly Thank You!*

Vincent Famularo
1895-1987

I O U

LIFE LEADERSHIP™

YOU OWE IT TO YOURSELF AND OTHERS!

www.iouliving.com

Download the *IOU Anchor Planning* pages

Free at www.iouanchors.com

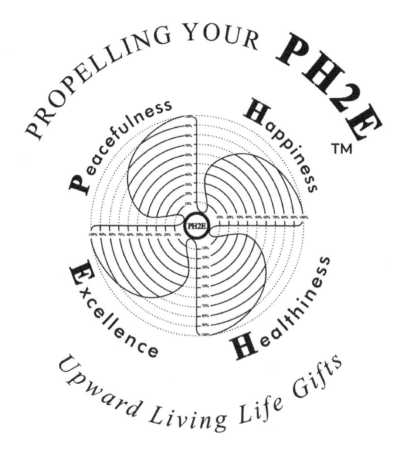

Take the PH2E Assessment

www.PH2E.com

Made in the USA
Coppell, TX
16 March 2021